# CHILD

# CHILDCARE

## The Guide for Busy Parents

KATE GOODHART

**crimson**

This edition first published in Great Britain 2008 by
**Crimson Publishing**, a division of Crimson Business Ltd
Westminster House
Kew Road
Richmond
Surrey
TW9 2ND

© Kate Goodhart, 2008

The right of Kate Goodhart to be identified as the author of this work has been asserted by her in accordance with the Copyright, Designs and Patents Act, 1988.

All rights reserved. No part of this publication may be reproduced, transmitted in any form or by any means, or stored in a retrieval system without either the prior written permission of the publisher, or in the case of reprographic reproduction a licence issued in accordance with the terms and licences issued by the CLA Ltd.

A catalogue record for this book is available from the British library.

ISBN 978 1 85458 408 3

Section 5 contributing author: Suzie Skipper
Research Editor: Lianne Slavin

Printed and bound by Mega Printing, Turkey

To our lovely children

# Contents

| | |
|---|---|
| Acknowledgements | xiii |
| Introduction | xv |

## SECTION ONE: The Different Types of Childcare — 1
    What is available? — 2

**1 Day Nurseries** — 5
- What is a day nursery? — 5
- What kind of care will a nursery provide? — 6
- What will children do at nursery all day? — 8
- How much will a nursery cost? — 10
- Time off — 10
- How long can a child stay in a nursery? — 10
- Staff qualifications — 11
- Staff ratios — 11

**2 Childminders** — 13
- What is a childminder? — 13
- What kind of care will a childminder provide? — 14
- The National Childminding Association — 15
- How much will a childminder cost? — 16
- Time Off — 17
- How long can a child stay with the same childminder? — 17
- Relationship between childminder and parent — 18
- Who is likely to be a childminder? — 19

**3 After-school Care: Clubs, Babysitters and After-school Nannies** — 21
- What is after-school care? — 21
- What is an after-school club? — 22
- What will an after-school club provide for your children? — 22

|   | What is the cost of an after-school club? | 25 |
|---|---|---|
|   | How long can your child use an after-school club? | 25 |
|   | What will an after-school babysitter or after-school nanny do? | 26 |
|   | How much will an after-school babysitter or nanny cost? | 27 |
|   | Time off | 27 |
|   | Who should you be looking for? | 28 |
|   | Who is likely to be applying for this role? | 28 |
|   | How long might this arrangement last? | 28 |
| **4** | **Nanny** | **29** |
|   | What is a nanny? | 29 |
|   | Types of nanny | 29 |
|   | What will a nanny do for you and your family? | 30 |
|   | What is the cost of a nanny? | 32 |
|   | Time off | 33 |
|   | How long are you likely to keep a nanny? | 33 |
|   | What kind of candidates should you be looking for? | 35 |
|   | What sort of person can you expect to hire as a nanny? | 36 |
|   | Job combining | 36 |
| **5** | **The Nanny Share** | **37** |
|   | What is a nanny share? | 37 |
|   | What can you expect to get from a nanny share? | 38 |
|   | Advantages and disadvantages of a nanny share | 38 |
|   | What is it likely to cost? | 39 |
|   | Time off | 40 |
|   | How long is this arrangement likely to last? | 40 |
|   | What kind of candidates should you be looking for? | 40 |
|   | Who are you likely to find? | 41 |
| **6** | **Mother's Help** | **43** |
|   | What is a mother's help? | 43 |
|   | What does a mother's help do? | 43 |
|   | What is a mother's help likely to cost? | 44 |
|   | Time off | 45 |

|   | How long will a mother's help stay? | 45 |
|---|---|---|
|   | What kind of candidates should you be looking for? | 45 |
|   | Who are you likely to find for this role? | 46 |
| **7** | **Au Pairs** | **49** |
|   | What is an au pair? | 49 |
|   | What will an au pair do for you and your family? | 49 |
|   | What will an au pair cost? | 53 |
|   | Time off | 54 |
|   | Who should you be looking for? | 55 |
|   | How long is an au pair arrangement likely to last? | 55 |
|   | Male au pairs | 56 |
| **8** | **Granny** | **57** |
|   | What can you ask granny to do? | 58 |
|   | Alternative family childcare arrangements | 58 |
|   | What is the cost of this kind of arrangement? | 60 |
|   | How long can you expect this arrangement to last? | 61 |
| **9** | **Maternity Nurses and Night Nannies** | **63** |
|   | What is a maternity nurse? | 63 |
|   | What will a maternity nurse do? | 64 |
|   | What is the cost of a maternity nurse? | 65 |
|   | How long will a maternity nurse stay? | 66 |
|   | Time off | 66 |
|   | What kind of candidates should you be looking for? | 66 |
|   | Who is likely to be applying for this role? | 67 |

| **SECTION TWO: What is Right for You** | **69** |
|---|---|
| Why do you need childcare? | 71 |
| What kind of help do you need now and in the future? | 72 |
| Nursery or nanny? | 73 |
| What is the effect of childcare on children? | 75 |

| **10** | **What Sort of Family Are You?** | **77** |
|---|---|---|
|   | Are you outgoing or reserved? | 77 |
|   | Family activities | 80 |

| | |
|---|---|
| Quiet or noisy? | 81 |
| Where do animals feature? | 81 |
| Tidy or messy? | 82 |
| Town, city or rural? | 83 |

## 11 What You Need the Help For — 87

| | |
|---|---|
| Working full time | 87 |
| Working part time | 89 |
| Working from home | 90 |
| In need of extra help at home | 91 |
| Help with young babies | 94 |
| Temporary help | 96 |
| Children with special needs | 101 |

## 12 Ages, Gaps, Boys and Girls — 105

| | |
|---|---|
| How many children do you have? | 105 |
| How old are your children? | 106 |
| What is the age range of your children? | 106 |
| How old is your nanny? | 110 |
| Boys, girls or both | 110 |

## 13 The Live-in or Live-out Debate — 115

| | |
|---|---|
| Live-in help | 116 |
| Live-out help | 121 |

## SECTION THREE: How to Go About Finding Your Childcare — 125

| | |
|---|---|
| Five lists to start off with | 126 |
| **Getting on with the search** | **127** |

## 14 Looking for Childcare — 129

| | |
|---|---|
| Word-of-mouth recommendations | 129 |
| Agencies | 131 |
| Using the internet | 138 |
| Print advertising | 143 |
| Noticeboards | 143 |
| Finding local nurseries, childminders or after-school clubs | 144 |
| How to find a babysitter | 147 |
| How to find a maternity nurse | 149 |

| | | |
|---|---|---:|
| **15** | **Choosing the Right Childcare Away From Home** | **151** |
| | A note on checking that providers are registered | 151 |
| | Childminders | 152 |
| | Nurseries | 161 |
| | After-school and holiday clubs | 179 |
| **16** | **Choosing the Right Childcare at Home** | **183** |
| | How to identify the best nanny, mother's help, au pair, babysitter or maternity nurse for you and your family | 183 |
| | The interview | 188 |
| | The follow up | 194 |
| | What to ask referees | 196 |
| | Second interviews | 197 |
| | Final stages | 197 |

## SECTION FOUR: Managing Your Childcare — 201

| | | |
|---|---|---:|
| | **Regular check-ups** | **202** |
| | **Keep hold of your common sense** | **202** |
| | **Trust** | **202** |
| **17** | **Managing Your Relationship with Your Childcare Provider** | **205** |
| | How to manage your relationship with …. | 205 |
| | … your nursery | 205 |
| | … your childminder | 208 |
| | … an after-school club | 210 |
| | … an after-school nanny or babysitter | 212 |
| | … your nanny | 214 |
| | … your mother's help | 224 |
| | … with your au pair | 227 |
| | … your granny | 233 |
| | …your maternity nurse | 238 |
| **18** | **Coping if Things Go Wrong** | **243** |
| | Reasons for childcare to go wrong | 243 |
| | Keep in touch with your children | 245 |

|  |  |  |
|---|---|---|
| | Your child's development | 246 |
| | Back-up plans | 247 |
| **19** | **The End of the Affair** | **249** |
| | All good things come to an end | 249 |
| | Bad things come to an end rather more quickly | 251 |
| | Learning from bad experiences | 253 |
| | The end of the relationship | 254 |
| | A final word | 254 |

## SECTION FIVE: Technical Questions — 255

| | | |
|---|---|---|
| | Cost of childcare | 255 |
| | Childcare Vouchers | 260 |
| | Tax | 264 |
| | Contracts and Letters of Employment | 269 |
| | Legal Obligations of employers and employees | 275 |
| | Insurance | 277 |
| | Health and safety issues | 278 |
| | Ofsted | 279 |
| | Children's Information Service | 280 |
| | Visas and work permits | 280 |
| | Government Guidelines for au pairs | 281 |
| | CRB checks | 283 |
| | Qualifications | 285 |
| | Childcare hours | 289 |
| | Childcare ratios | 289 |

## SECTION SIX: Listings — 291

| | | |
|---|---|---|
| | Agencies | 293 |
| | Children's Information Service | 325 |
| | Useful Websites | 333 |

## Index — 343

# Acknowledgements

Thank you to everyone who spoke so openly to us for our case studies, which have helped to bring the book to life.

Thank you to the team at Crimson – especially to David, Holly, Lianne and Sally.

I would like to thank my family and friends for all their support – especially to Will, Lizzie Charlotte, Sophie and my parents for all the extra help with our gang.

---

Contributing author, Suzie Skipper, would like to thank Åsa Nilsdotter and colleagues at Nannytax for their invaluable input on the tax, legal and insurance issues surrounding employing a nanny, Jerry Beere at Morton Michel for his help with the insurance section, Vikki Moyles at CWDC and Natalie Worpole at CACHE for guiding me on the complexities of qualifications, Lynne Keeble and Fay Bliss at Accor for their help with the childcare vouchers section, and Sandra Landau founder member of BAPPA for her advice on the au pairs section.

# Introduction

Whether you are planning to return to work, or just need to keep your head above water with a young family, finding the right childcare is a challenge.

In *Childcare* we aim to make the process easier. We will give you all the information you need to help you make your choices in one easy to read handbook. And, to make sure that our advice is practical, useful and up-to-date, we have talked to mothers and fathers, childminders, nursery staff, nannies, grannies and au pairs. These personal insights can be found throughout the book and provide invaluable first-hand advice about specific issues.

Childcare is likely to be needed by all families at some stage or another – even if it's just the odd bit of babysitting or finding someone to watch your children while you have a weekend away. At-home mothers or fathers can suddenly find themselves unable to be in two places at once (a magic trick often required!) and may need a bit of extra help a few times a week to cope with a growing family. Mothers who work full-time obviously need to consider help as soon as they are preparing to go back to work after the birth of a child. Then there are all the mothers in between – working part-time, freelance, or from time to time – who need to have flexible childcare arrangements at hand.

From fully qualified, full-time nannies to live-in au pairs; from a mother's help to a childminder or nursery, there are many childcare options. And there are as many different kinds of people who need help as those wishing to offer it. Finding the right fit can seem a daunting task. But there really is something to suit every family.

One size certainly doesn't fit all. Each family has different needs and expectations, and what is right for one family will be completely wrong for another. A nanny who delights one mother could be another's worst nightmare. We will clarify the choices to help you decide what is best for you and your family.

Of course, there are no guarantees. First of all, finding childcare can be hard work. Then, the person or place that you initially choose may turn out not to be right for you and your family, leaving you with the prospect of starting all over again. This book will help you in both areas – how to narrow down your initial search to make the task less daunting and how to manage if you make a mistake.

## INTRODUCTION

The book will begin by looking at the kinds of childcare available, and then we will move on to consider what is right for you, how to go about finding your dream childcare and, finally, how to manage your childcare once you have found it. Then we include a section detailing the technical information you will require, and an extensive listings section at the back. In all parts of the book we will bring you an personal accounts from parents and childcare professionals so that you can recognise the issues you face and see how others have dealt with them.

One thing is true of all parents we spoke to – we all agreed that none of us had any idea what we were doing or what to expect when we started out on the search for childcare. There is a large range of options and taking a step towards one form of childcare can feel like a leap of faith. The key is to try not to worry too much. This is easier said than done, but it is important to remember that children are resilient and that if you do make a mistake in your childcare choices, it can be put right. You will be able to move forward to a new childcare arrangement and put the experience behind you.

Finally, learn to trust the people that look after your children. While there are some dreadful stories out there (and a few in here), most people that choose to work in the area of childcare are trustworthy, kind and keen to work with children.

## 10 important points to remember during your childcare years

### 1 Know what you need

Be thorough in your planning. Lists detailing who you are, what and who you are looking for and the job you are looking to fill will help you to find your childcare match. Keep referring to these lists throughout the process, to make sure that they reflect the true picture.

## 2 Choices are unique to each individual

What suits one family won't suit another. We will make every effort in this book not to be prescriptive, but will help you ask yourself the right questions so that you can make the right choice for *your* family.

## 3 Manage your expectations

Control your expectations of your childcare and certainly don't ask for more from your child's carer than you are capable of achieving yourself. Your priority will of course always be the well-being of your child – any extra help is purely a bonus.

## 4 Show respect

All relationships are two-way. Polite behaviour will invite the same in return. Seeing you behave in a certain way will also encourage good manners from your children – they need to be respectful of their childcarer. Avoid undermining your childcarer – all sorts of problems lie ahead if your children think they have an alternative person to resort to when one adult has said no.

## 5 Communicate with your childcarer

Be constantly aware of your relationship with your childcarer and of any external factors that might affect its smooth running. Remember that a change of circumstances in your family, for example death or divorce, will affect your childcare situation. Just as a teacher should know of any major changes in a child's life, so should a nanny, childminder or nursery nurse. Even if it all feels very personal and close to home, it is important to your children's well-being that their carer is kept up to date. Talk about any problems that arise as soon as the appropriate moment presents itself. Equally, you need to recognise that circumstances can change for the worse for your carer too, which can impact their care for your children – make sure they know they can talk to you, if they would like to.

## 6 Be aware of your children's development

Children are constantly changing, growing and developing and you and your childcare provider need to keep up with those changes. Children outgrow activities and playgroups – make sure you all notice when this happens and avoid sticking with the old routines for nostalgia or convenience's sake. Childcarer and parents need to keep working together to monitor the development and progress of the children.

(Childcarers should monitor speech development, social interaction with peers and should ensure that children have an opportunity every day to be read to, to take physical exercise and to play in a creative way.)

## 7 Pass on your parental choices

Every parent has their own idea of what they would like their child to be doing. You will have your own list of dos and don'ts, things that you would like your children to be exposed to and things that you would rather they could avoid (possibly forever, if you had your way!). Share your views on television, outings, diet, treats and friends with your childcarer early on. Be sure to share your tips for routines, habits, likes and dislikes with your childcarer. Everyone will be happier if there is a good continuity of care and everyone is reading from the same page. If your child has a favourite lullaby, teach it to the babysitter!

## 8 Make your house rules known

Anyone coming into your home to look after your children needs to be aware of your house rules. This comes down to a matter of safety. If you never leave your children alone while they are eating, or while they are in the bath (principles that a good childcarer will adhere to regardless of your personal views) make sure the carer knows, understands and appreciates your reasons for asking them to behave in the same way.

## 9 Look out for outside interference

Be wary of others interfering with your relationship with your childcare. Guard your relationship fiercely and avoid gossiping about your helper. If you suspect your best friend or mother-in-law is trying to undermine your childcarer, keep them apart.

## 10 See the need for change

Recognise that when you find the perfect childcare (which is undoubtedly a cause for major celebration), it won't last forever. What is right for you and your family now probably won't be right in five years' time. As your family grows older, your needs will change and your childcare arrangements may need to change to reflect this.

Knowing you have the right childcare for your family can completely change your perspective on the work/life balance. The knowledge that your children are well cared for in your absence will allow you to get on with work or enjoy other aspects of your ife without constant worry. There might just be a moment when you realise it is all going well – seeing your child and carer play together, totally absorbed in a game when you come home. Heavily pregnant with twins, I came across our babysitter with our two-year-old, sitting in the middle of a sea of toys, with 'Doctor's Surgery Open' scrawled on the blackboard and teddies being asked in a very serious way about their health. Of course, we all wept when that particular babysitter left, thinking we would never find anyone as lovely again to help with our children. But our needs changed, our children grew older, and other good solutions have been found along the way.

The best childcare will be when you find the right childcare for you and your family, at the right time. Follow our guidelines, give yourself enough time and space to find the right care, and you'll succeed.

## Notes on the text

- Through the text we have used 'she' and 'he' and 'him' and 'her' interchangeably when referring to children. We also refer to 'child' or 'children' to mean either, as seemed appropriate in each instance.
- We have chosen to use 'she' when referencing childcarers, except when we have specifically been looking at male childcare providers. Of course, all childcare providers can be men as well as women. We decided to write it this way to keep things simple and to avoid constantly writing 'she or he'. There are more men in childcare than ever before and more and more families are choosing men for traditionally female childcare roles. Nurseries which employ men as nursery nurses are proud of this and will be keen to point them out.
- Nursery schools are not included in this guide, since they are 'preschool' and do not offer childcare in the same way that the other options we have considered do. In fact, choosing a nursery school is rather more like choosing a school than choosing childcare. Nursery schools operate on school term times, and children usually start at nursery sometime after their second birthday. In the state sector, nursery places are given after the child's third birthday. Nursery schools should offer free play in a structured environment, an opportunity for children to develop their social skills and learn to interact in a group. Children usually attend for a morning or an afternoon session. In private nurseries older children can often stay for lunch; at state nursery schools there will usually only be morning or afternoon sessions until the child starts full-time school in Reception.

## Every Child Matters

Every Child Matters is the government agenda which focuses on bringing together services to support children and families. It sets out five major outcomes for children:
- being healthy
- staying safe
- enjoying and achieving
- making a positive contribution
- economic well-being.

| Type of childcare | Cost/week |
| --- | --- |
| Day Nursery | £150-300 |
| Childminder | Varies |
| After-school club | £40 (average) |
| After-school nanny/babysitter | £100-200 |
| Babysitting | Varies |
| Holiday clubs | £80 (average) |
| Nanny living in | from £250 |
| Nanny living out | £350-500 |
| Mother's help living in | £200-250 |
| Mother's help living out | £250-300 |
| Au pair | £60-70 |
| Au pair plus | £80-90 |
| Maternity nurse | £500-900 |
| Night nanny | £375-650 |

# section ONE

# the different types of childcare

1 DAY NURSERIES
2 CHILDMINDERS
3 AFTER-SCHOOL CARE: CLUBS, BABYSITTERS AND AFTER-SCHOOL NANNIES
4 NANNY
5 THE NANNY SHARE
6 MOTHER'S HELP
7 AU PAIRS
8 GRANNY
9 MATERNITY NURSES AND NIGHT NANNIES

## What is available?

In this section we are going to examine the different kinds of childcare options available to you. There is an obvious dividing line – childcare at your home or outside your home. Within those two categories there are many more options. You may even decide on a combination of both, to offer your children a more varied experience – we will be taking a closer look at what is going to be right for you in Section Two. But first, we'll stick to what there is, and what you can expect from the various choices.

It would be wise not to rule any out to start with. It is important to try to remain open-minded at the very early stages of your search. An option which you might not have thought of previously may turn out to be the best solution for you and your family.

The grid shown in the introduction gives you an at-a-glance guide to the various childcare options, with an outline of how much they are likely to cost on a weekly basis. The detail, however, is in the text.

The case studies in this section come from the childcare providers. We'll hear from nannies, nursery nurses, childminders, grannies, au pairs and mother's helpers and maternity nurses. It's important to know what they think of their work and why they do the job they do. Their statements are honest and revealing. Later, we will feature case studies from parents who have both positive and negative stories to tell.

In this section we will look at each category of childcare and what the service will offer you as a parent. We will give an indication of cost, though this is always just a guide as childcare costs can vary significantly from area to area. We will look at how long the arrangement is likely or able to last (some daycare providers only cater for children up to the age of five, for example). In the cases of individuals offering childcare, we tell you who is likely to be available and discuss the kind of candidates you might be looking for.

At the end of this section you will have a pretty good idea of what your choices are, and be ready to think about what might suit you best, when reading Section Two.

## Childcare Act

The **Childcare Act** came into force in July 2006 and is the first ever act to be exclusively concerned with early years and childcare. The act guarantees accessible, high quality childcare and other services for children under five, and gives parents greater choice in balancing work and family. The government is working hard to provide good access for families, and has placed responsibility for this provision firmly with the local authorities, charging them with raising quality, improving delivery, and achieving better results. The act formalises the important role of local authorities through a set of new duties, which include a responsibility to:
- Improve the five Every Child Matters outcomes for all pre-school children and reduce inequalities in these outcomes
- Secure sufficient childcare for working parents
- Provide a better parental information service

The local councils are expected to make sure that parents' views are heard in the planning and delivery of new services, so that new childcare schemes and businesses in each area reflect the real needs of families.

The aims include ensuring that working parents have a good choice of regulated childcare that they are able to choose from with confidence, that services are 'joined up' and made easier to use by combining them where possible in Children's Centres (see Chapter One), and offering a high quality early learning and development framework for young children.

The act also provides for a new Ofsted Childcare Register. The government aims to bring the act's main provisions into effect in 2008.

# Day nurseries

## What is a day nursery?

Day nurseries are the first choice of childcare for many families. They are flexible, year-round providers, which suit many families' needs. They are an increasingly popular choice with over 675,000 nursery places available in around 14,500 nurseries across the UK.

Day nurseries offer full day care for children under the age of five, with an increasing proportion of places taken up by children under the age of three. Day nurseries are privately operated and must all (along with other forms of day care, including crèches and part-time nurseries) be registered with and inspected by Ofsted. All staff working at a registered nursery must be police checked and a proportion of staff must be qualified. There must always be a qualified manager on duty and a qualified member of staff in every room.

Day nurseries offer parents a safe environment in which to leave their child, on either a full-time or part-time basis. Nurseries will recommend, or even request, that a child attends at least two morning or afternoon sessions a week, to give the child the best chance of settling in and making the most of his surroundings. You may be able to subscribe to just the amount of care that you need, whether it is one, two, three or four days a week, or full-time, five days a week, though popular nurseries will be in a position to ask for more commitment.

Most nurseries are open 50 or 51 weeks of the year and are almost always closed over the Christmas period and on Bank Holidays. Nurseries generally operate from 8am to around 6pm, though this will of course vary from nursery to nursery. Some will be able to cater for longer hours, although you must expect to pay extra charges for this service. There will be a limit, too, to the amount of hours that can be offered – due to staffing and insurance issues, it is rare for a nursery to be able to provide care for children after 7pm.

The Children's Information Service (branches of which are being renamed Family Information Services (FIS) going forward) can provide you with information on day care nurseries in your area. These services will be able to advise you on which nurseries accept which childcare voucher schemes and how to apply for Working Tax Credits. You will find details of these in Section Five. In some parts of the country different schemes are available to help parents with the cost of day care. In the London boroughs, the Childcare Affordability Programme (which was operational through to 2008) offered childcare in a day care setting for no more than £175 per week for lower income families that are in receipt of the Child Tax Credit at a rate higher than the family element. Your local CIS or FIS will be able to offer advice on schemes in your local area. See Section Six for how to contact your local CIS or FIS.

All nurseries have to adhere to government guidelines on childcare and follow the Early Years Foundation principles set out by the government, as well as be inspected by Ofsted. Some nurseries may follow a particular philosophy, for example the Montessori method of teaching where children lead the way and choose the activities in which they wish to take part. When you are considering nurseries, remember to ask if there is a particular philosophy which dictates the way the nursery is run, to make sure that you are comfortable with the ethos of the place.

## What kind of care will a nursery provide?

Day care nurseries will provide full day care which caters to every child's needs. Each child will usually be assigned a key worker, who will become a familiar figure, monitoring the child's progress. The key worker will be available to the parents for meetings and should keep the parents updated with any news and events relating directly to their child. (We discuss the important role that key workers play in Section Three and how to manage your relationship with the nursery and key worker in Section Four.)

The care that is given will be specific to the age of the children. Babies are usually cared for in a separate area so that their specific needs can be looked after. Babies will be given lots of cuddles, eye contact and verbal communication. They will, at the appropriate age, be encouraged to move on to solid foods, feed themselves, crawl and walk, and may start to join in with 'messy play'. Babies will usually have their own changing area, separate meal times and a quiet sleeping room or area. The ratio of staff to children under the age of two is required by law to be no less than 1:3.

Children will usually move up to a different room within the nursery when they are confident walkers (space permitting), where they will be encouraged to start to mix more with other children and enjoy some different toys and activities. There should still be a quiet area for children of this age to take a nap, and ideally, an opportunity for outside play. The ratio for adults to children in the two to three years age group is legally required to be no less than 1:4.

The government sets guidelines for Early Years Development and nurseries will work towards those goals. Usually children from the age of three to five are looked after in another separate area, where they will be encouraged to share, support each other, enjoy games, toys and messy play, and gently start on some early number work and reading skills. For the three-to-five year age group, the staff to children ratio must be at least 1:8.

Ideally, there will be some fluidity between rooms – it is good for siblings to be able to see each other during the day, for example. However, it is important for each age group to have its own space, to cater for their specific needs. This will create the best environment for learning and development, and also decrease the chances of clashes between older and younger children. Research has shown that while younger children can benefit in some ways developmentally by being with older children, they can also find it quite stressful.

## Carol is a nursery nurse working in Nottingham

I have been a nursery nurse for a long time. I love working with children – this isn't a job you could do if you didn't! You need the patience of a saint and a good imagination.

My favourite part of the day is probably story time. We all sit together in a group and it's a chance for us all, children and adults, to share our experiences.

We interact and involve ourselves fully with the children from when they arrive at 7.30 in the morning until they go home at night. A lot of the

THE DIFFERENT TYPES OF CHILDCARE

children at my nursery are 'early birds' as many parents work in the city and have to travel to work, so we start the day with breakfast. For the rest of the day the activities will depend on the room — the pre-schoolers follow quite a structured routine, whereas the babies' day will just flow.

We work very closely with our parents. The management and staff are all very approachable and parents can call whenever they want. The parents of the younger children are given a sheet each day, telling them what their child has done during the day, when they've slept, when they've had their nappy changed and how much milk they've had to drink.

> We work very closely with our parents

We promote positive independence to get the children ready for school. I think it's great for children to have the social interaction that a day nursery offers.

---

### 10 good signs at a nursery
- Space • Light • Tidiness • Cleanliness • Smiles • Busy children
- Paintings on the wall • Singing • Chatter • Interested staff

---

## What will children do at nursery all day?

A day nursery will usually follow quite formal routines, while trying to accommodate each child's particular needs and requests from parents. Babies will be nurtured, toddlers encouraged to try lots of new things, and older children will be encouraged to start learning and will be prepared for school. There will be messy play, outside time (space allowing), adventurous games, meal times to share, tidy up time and rest time built into each day. Registered nurseries will be working to government guidelines and activities will be structured around the Early Years Goals.

All three-and four-year-old children are entitled to six terms of free, part-time early education from the start of the term following their third birthday. All settings in receipt of Government funding to deliver free early years education are required to deliver the Foundation Stage curriculum. Practitioners delivering the Foundation Stage curriculum support children's learning through planned play and by extending and developing children's spontaneous play.

The Foundation Stage Curriculum is organised into the following six areas of learning, which also form the basis of the Early Years Goals:

- Personal, social and emotional development
- Communication, language and literacy
- Mathematical development
- The development of knowledge and understanding of the world
- Physical development
- Creative development

Birth to Three Matters is a framework to support children in their earliest years. All registered day care providers will be working towards achieving these goals within this age group:

- A STRONG CHILD – developing a sense of self, feeling acknowledged and affirmed, developing self assurance, having a sense of belonging.
- A SKILLFUL COMMUNICATOR – enjoying being together with others, finding a voice, listening and responding, making meaning.
- A COMPETENT LEARNER – making connections, being imaginative, being creative, representing.
- A HEALTHY CHILD – emotional well being, growing and developing, keeping safe and making healthy choices.

## How much will a nursery cost?

Costs of day care nurseries will vary from area to area, but in central London can reach £300 per week. Discounts are usually offered for siblings. For more than one child, a nursery becomes an expensive option for childcare.

Financial assistance is available through childcare voucher schemes, as well as tax credits. Details of these can be found in Section Five.

When you sign up to a nursery you are vulnerable to the nursery's ability to increase the price. Of course you have the right to take your child away (most contracts will require one month's written notice) if the costs goes up unexpectedly. Usually nurseries will undertake to give parents at least six weeks' notice of any price rises.

Nurseries will often include nappies (and all the necessary extra kit that goes with them, including wipes, creams and disposable bags), milk and all meals in the cost of the day care. Be sure to ask for a complete list of what is included in the cost as this will obviously help you in your comparisons between nurseries. Provision of these essential items can also make a nursery more attractive to parents simply because it takes away another thing to remember in the morning when leaving home in a rush. It will count for a lot if meals are included – saving you the effort of preparing meals for the children to take with them at breakfast time.

You will be asked to sign a contract (and usually a direct debit mandate for payment) with a nursery when your child starts. This should set out costs, notice periods, requirements from both parties, the nursery's policy on illness and what to do in case any complaints arise. We include a sample contract in Section Five.

## Time off

Day care nurseries usually close for Christmas and Bank Holidays – the nursery should make sure that all parents are well aware of these dates. The cost of these days is built into their monthly charges, so you won't usually pay less if you are getting one day less in a month. If you choose to take your child out of nursery for a holiday, you will be asked to pay for that time regardless of the fact your child is not there. This is because the nursery still maintains a place for your child's return, which they cannot fill with another child in the short term.

## How long can a child stay in a nursery?

Each nursery will have fixed numbers of children of different ages that it can provide care for. If the nursery caters for children up to school age and all goes well, your children could stay at the nursery that they started in as babies until they go to school. Ideally the nursery will be large enough to give the children a chance to progress through different rooms and environments, where they will be exposed to different routines, activities and learning opportunities as they grow older.

Some families may feel that their children should be exposed to a different environment before starting school, but this is really a matter of personal choice. In many ways a nursery is a good preparation for school – your child will be with lots of other children, mixing with children of other ages and with other adults, in a setting outside the home.

## Staff qualifications

Fifty per cent of staff in a registered nursery must hold an official childcare qualification, for example NVQ Childcare Level 2, or equivalent. See Section Five for a full list of childcare qualifications.

At least one member of staff on duty at all times should hold an up-to-date first-aid certificate. Supervisors at nurseries must hold a higher qualification, for example NVQ Childcare Level 3, or equivalent. There must also be a qualified nursery manager available at all times.

## Staff ratios

To summarise, the number of children that can be in a nursery is strictly controlled by government guidelines. There are ratios for adults to children of different ages:

   1:3 for children under the age of two
   1:4 for children of two-three years
   1:8 for children of three-five years.

THE DIFFERENT TYPES OF CHILDCARE

## Children's Centres

Children's Centres are a new initiative under the Sure Start Scheme. Children's Centres are designed to offer full family support, including childcare facilities or help with finding childcare, advice on health, job searches and benefits and community drop-in groups. The idea is that by September 2010 there will be a Children's Centre in every community providing early education integrated with health and family support services and childcare from 8am-6pm. The combination of services that centres provide for young children and families contributes to the Every Child Matters outcomes by:

- Improving health outcomes for children and families
- Reducing crime rates
- Reducing child poverty
- Enabling parents to study and work
- Helping lone parents to access work and training opportunities

# Childminders

## What is a childminder?

A childminder is a person who is paid to look after other people's children in her own home. Children who are looked after by a childminder have the advantage of being cared for in a home-style setting, often with the opportunity to socialise with other children of a similar age.

Anyone who looks after other people's children in their own home for more than two hours a day for payment (or other reward) must, by law, be registered as a childminder, and inspected by: Ofsted in England; their local authority in Wales; and by the Care Commission in Scotland.

Registered childminders must also hold other documentation to keep their registration up to date. Childminders must have a Criminal Records Bureau (CRB) check, public liability insurance, have undertaken a first-aid course and have a certificate to prove it, and have undertaken a food hygiene course. Every two years they should also take part in a Child Protection course. The regular, three-yearly inspections will make sure that all these courses and certificates are up to date. Other adults (the childminder's partner for example, or children over the age of 16 living in the childminder's house) must also undergo a police check. If Ofsted or the registering authority finds any of these certificates missing, they will give the childminder a certain time frame within which they must be up to date, or risk being struck off the register.

Childminders are restricted by law to the number of children that they may look after at any one time. One childminder at home may look after six children under the age of eight. Of these six, no more than three may be under five years of age.

Of these three youngest children, no more than one child may be under the age of one. These numbers must include the childminder's own children. Exceptions can be made, for example for multiple births, or for the younger siblings of children who are already being cared for. Children who are four, but attending full-time school, may be classed as age five for these ratios. Children over the age of eight are treated separately – the childminder may care for over eights without them counting towards their ratio.

## What kind of care will a childminder provide?

A childminder looks after children in a home environment, and activities will reflect this. Childminders can be spontaneous in the care that they are providing, and are able to follow a quiet, relaxed routine at 'home' where the children can flourish in a secure environment.

Each childminder is free to organise her own day, and will usually have to take the needs of several children of different ages into account. There will usually be some form of routine, including taking and collecting older children to and from school or nursery, trips to the park, play time, outdoor play and rest time. Meals will be provided by the childminder during the day; most childminders will be able to accommodate a particular child's dietary requirements. The hours that a child can be looked after by a childminder can vary, so this is something to discuss early on if you have unusual requirements. However, a usual day would be from around 8am to 6pm for pre-schoolers and before and after school hours for older children.

Parents will be encouraged to share information about their child's routine with the childminder and the childminder will usually try to accommodate this, as much as is possible, while being realistic about catering to the needs of the other children in her care. If a child is with a childminder for at least two full days a week, it will probably not matter too much if the routine is different to the child's routine at home. Children will be able to understand that things work differently in the two different settings.

It is reasonable to expect that a childminder will be undertaking some of her own household chores while she is caring for the children. While there are stories of children being taken around the supermarket for the big weekly shop, this is rare – most childminders would avoid this at all costs! – but a trip to the market or post office can be turned into a fun outing, while being useful to the childminder, too.

## The National Childminding Association

While all childminders are required to be registered and inspected regularly by Ofsted, many also choose to become members of the National Childminding Association (NCMA) or the Scottish Childminding Association in Scotland. Details for the NCMA and the SCMA are found in Section Six. The Childminding Associations offer guidance for members about pricing, insurance and contracts. Specialist materials are made available (for example painting smocks, progress charts for open communication between childminder and parents) at preferable rates to members. Members also sign up to a number of quality standards, which offers a great deal of assurance for parents that the person they are leaving their children with takes their role seriously. Other home-based childcarers, including nannies, are also welcome to join the associations, although uptake is lower among this group.

## The 10 NCMA Quality Standards

- NCMA members undertake to pursue a professional approach to their work, keeping up to date with skills and theory, legislation, regulations, registration and insurance requirements.
- Members commit to a positive approach to managing children's behaviour, giving praise and discipline appropriate to the child's behaviour and age.
- They agree to promote equality of opportunity – to treat every child equally and ensure that each child has the opportunity to learn and develop while under their care, and promote understanding about a child's own culture as well as that of others.
- An NCMA member will undertake to respect the confidentiality of the families that they are involved with, unless working in the interests of protecting a child.
- Members will promote learning and development of each child and will support learning that the child is doing elsewhere – at home, nursery or school.
- Members commit to working in a partnership with parents. This includes recognising that parents know their child best,

> respecting parents' beliefs and the way parents wish their children to be cared for, keeping lines of communication open, being up to date about what to do in an emergency and reviewing contracts at least once a year.
> - Members undertake to keep the children safe. They will pay attention to safety and hygiene, know what to do in an emergency and who to contact, and guarantee a smoke-free environment while caring for children.
> - Members will understand nutrition and will discuss dietary needs with parents, and provide a healthy diet for the children in their care.
> - Members will have good business practise – keep good records of attendance, personal details, development and details of any accidents, as well as detailed financial records.
> - Members will seek help from other professionals where necessary and often will be part of a local childminding group, where they can share experiences with other childminders and look for support

Of course, childminders who are not registered with the childminding associations will mostly follow the same guidelines, and just because a childminder is not part of a scheme doesn't mean that she or he would not subscribe to the same policy and ethos. However, the associations are recognised bodies, which offer advantages of membership for both childminders and parents.

## How much will a childminder cost?

Childminders are self-employed and can set their own fees. An average charge is between £4 and £7 per hour, depending on where you live, the number of hours' care you are looking for and the childminder in question. For a full-time place, you might expect to pay between £150-£250 for the week. The National Childminding Association can give some guidance on hourly rates and other pay-related issues. See Section Six for contact details.

You will normally be asked to sign a contract with your childminder – if you are not, you should ask for one. Under the contract you are likely to be obliged to pay your childminder (often in advance) even for the time when your child is not with her, either due to holidays or illness. You are expecting the childminder to keep your child's place open during these times, so this is reasonable. You will not usually have to pay when your childminder is away on holiday. It is a good idea to iron out these issues in a contract between you and the childminder when you start. The National Childminding Association can also provide sample childminding contracts, and will advise on common practice with regards to fees, contracts, holiday and sick pay.

Childcare Vouchers can be used to pay registered childminders (see Section Five for details).

## Time off

Your child's childminder is obliged to give you notice of when she is going to be unavailable to look after the children that are usually in her care. Childminders might have a quarterly newsletter to keep parents informed about future plans. It is common for a childminder to book up to four weeks off in each calendar year. Parents are not normally obliged to pay for the weeks when the childminder is unavailable. However parents are often obliged to pay for the weeks that they choose for their child to be elsewhere – this is because the childminder still maintains a place for your child's return, which they cannot fill with another child in the short term.

## How long can a child stay with the same childminder?

In successful childminding situations, a child may stay with a childminder from babyhood to school age, and perhaps even longer if the childminder is able to offer a school collection service. Child and childminder can form a strong bond in a successful relationship. A childminding situation can change however; for example if the childminder starts to look after more children in a different age group to your own child. This could change the dynamic of the group as a whole. If, however, you continue to be happy with the situation, and your child is confident and settled, there can be no need to change the arrangement. Keep an eye on the other children who are being looked after and how your child reacts to them, to ensure that a happy arrangement stays that way.

Placing your child with an established childminder brings many advantages. She will have experience with lots of different children and could be helpful in raising your child, rather than just watching him during the day. A childminder with experience will very likely have a good eye for spotting illnesses and know when to call the parents. She will be quick to recognise any issues among the children in her care, and know how to deal with them. A childminder with experience is also likely to offer a chance of continuity of care – rather than a nanny, for example, who is more likely at some point to want to move on. Don't go to one with a 'For Sale' board outside her house!

Remember that a childminder's experience could have been gained in ways other than childminding – some go from being a social worker or a nanny to a childminder when they start their own family, for example. Parents might like to look for a breadth of experience when looking for a childminder.

A childminder can offer a good balance between a nursery and a nanny in terms of socialising children – your child or children are offered the chance to mix with other children in a cosy, homely setting. The children are likely to form a strong bond with their caregiver, while also practising skills for school, of being in a group and sharing. Children are also likely to be able to be with the same group of children at a childminder's house, allowing them to form friendships in a secure environment from an early age.

## Relationship between childminder and parent

A childminding situation is different to other forms of childcare, in that it is care in a home which isn't your own. When you go to a nursery, you subscribe to their rules; when you invite a nanny or other caregiver into your home, you expect them to follow your rules. A childminder sits somewhere in the middle. You are asking for the childminder's services and, in the same way as a nursery operates, the childminder is in charge of how she would like to offer them. While you can inform a childminder of your rules and routines, it is unlikely that she will be able to follow them to the letter – after all, it is more than likely that she will have other families to cater for, too. It would be impossible for a childminder to follow lots of different sets of rules and routines in one setting. Childminders will try to follow your routines, but it is a good idea for everyone to be realistic about this from the outset.

A similar childcare ethos ought to set you on the way to a good relationship with your childminder. It is vitally important that the childminder and the parents can form a good relationship with each other. This is a very personal relationship and shared values will help you to form a close bond with your childminder.

An important part of the childminder's role is to keep up good and open communication with the parents of the children in her care. An NCMA childminder undertakes to do this, and will keep records of activities, accidents and events in each child's diary.

## Who is likely to be a childminder?

Childminders are usually women, occasionally men, whose own children may be at school or even older. Sometimes a childminder might have similar aged children to the children she is minding – providing herself with an income and a playmate for her own child. Childminders are usually experienced in childcare, most often having gained that experience in a hands-on way with their own families. Sometimes childminders will have had careers in childcare or social work, prior to deciding to work from home. It is important to feel a rapport with your potential childminder. As with all kinds of childcare, it is a good idea to look around and meet a few childminders to get a feel of what you are looking for in a childminder. You will need to feel confident that you can freely discuss any issues that may arise, and that you could even become friends. This can be a personal, close relationship.

## Doris is a childminder in Cheshire

I've been a childminder for 18 years. What I like most about my work is the children, of course, that and the fact that the days are so varied.

I've had some children for as long as ten years and some come to me as young as five months, so there is usually quite an age range.

Parents and I interview each other. I begin by explaining how I do things. I have a list of all the things I cover. I emphasise that I don't discipline the children — I love them and that way they don't seem to need disciplining. I'm happy to follow the parents' routine — they are welcome to bring their own food and so on. I think it's best if a new parent can observe me with some of the other children — see me at work.

There's not really a structured routine to the day because I let the child tell me what they want to do. They'll say to me, 'Can we bake?' or 'Can we play such a thing?' and I say, 'Of course you can,' because that way they're happy in what they're doing. It's not regimented in any way. Then we all have lunch together, and we'll drop some of the older ones at nursery in the afternoon. Sometimes we go on nature walks and collect conkers and beech nuts, or go to the park and play on the swings. When the Commonwealth Games were on we had our own version in the back garden — the children all raced and stood on chairs like podiums.

I like being able to offer childcare in a home setting. I once took on a little boy who shouted all the time, even when I was sitting right by him. I realised that he had previously been looked after in a nursery and was shouting because he thought he needed to get somebody to notice him. It took me weeks to quieten him down.

The main thing is to keep the children happy. Sometimes the children don't want to go home, especially if they're in the middle of something. It's great that they are not in a hurry to fly out of the door.

Most childminders I know are older people who have had children. Kindness is key.

> The main thing is to keep the children happy

# After-school care: clubs, babysitters and after-school nannies

## What is after-school care?

If your children are of school age, you may be able to arrange childcare for your children just for the hours that you need it – after school in term times, and for the school holidays. Your children could in this case either attend an after-school club (a registered after-school childcare provision for children of primary school age), or be collected from school and looked after until the end of the day by an after-school babysitter or nanny. During the holidays, there are also a few options to consider. After-school clubs often become holiday clubs; an after-school babysitter or nanny may be available for longer hours during the holidays, or the holidays could be the time that you call on family for help.

If you are an at-home mother, you may be juggling a busy school run and need an extra pair of legs to go and help with collections at the end of the school day, and an extra pair of eyes, ears and hands to help out with homework, listening to reading, music practise, tea, bath and bedtime for children of different ages. An after-school babysitter or nanny could be the perfect answer.

Some families with working parents will prefer to continue to employ a nanny full-time, regardless of the fact that the children are at school. There will inevitably be days when a child is sick and can't go to school, and, as anyone with school-age children will know, there are many school events, activities, meetings and outings which require a parent or carer to be present for the child. Alternatively, you may be able to find a nanny/housekeeper, who is happy to run your house for you during the school day in term time, and who is a suitable person to fulfil a nanny role in the afternoon and school holidays.

## What is an after-school club?

After-school clubs are run by local councils. They are usually either run at a primary school, or at another central location to which children are brought at the end of the school day after collection from local primary school. The children are looked after at the club until around 6pm (collection times will vary from centre to centre). After-school clubs usually cater for children between the ages of four and twelve. Some after-school clubs will also operate during school holidays, as holiday clubs, to cater further for working parents. Holiday clubs usually run for a whole day and children can be looked after for either a full day or part of a day.

After-school clubs are staffed by a manager, deputy manager and play workers. All staff are trained to level 2/3 NVQ or hold CACHE qualifications. Staff are also regularly trained in child protection, health and safety, behaviour management and food hygiene. The number of staff will obviously depend on the number of children at a centre – they will operate to strict ratios. There must be one qualified staff member for every eight children under the age of eight. There must be enough other staff to ensure that the number of older children at the facility does not have a negative impact on the younger children. After-school clubs run by councils will be registered and inspected by Ofsted. All staff working at an after-school club are required to be police checked.

## What will an after-school club provide for you and your children?

- A collection service (a walking bus if the centre is in a city centre and this is practical) from certain schools to the club during term time.

- A point of contact for the family and the school, where the centre is used daily for childcare after school.
- A light and healthy tea.
- Planned activities, including plenty of arts and crafts activities, painting, drawing, model-making, and possibly cooking and gardening.
- A quiet place to do homework, with some assistance if required.
- Ideally, IT facilities and an outside games/play area.
- A comfortable, homely place for the children to feel cosy and supported. This is after-school time, when children might otherwise be at home, so the centre will try to replicate this.

The activities on offer at an after-school club will vary from centre to centre, and depend on the ages of the children, the centre's resources and the staff team.

Children will be split into age groups and activity groups. Each child will be assigned a key worker. The groups are not usually rigid, but provide a framework for the children.

Some centres will give children an opportunity to take part in the decision making. For example there might be a Children's Council, where representative children will be given a voice in the planning for the centre, including the purchase of equipment and planning the weekly activities. They can even meet with other Children's Councils to share ideas. This can all help to build children's confidence, something that the after-school clubs take seriously as part of their role.

Children should be allowed time and opportunity to just play and relax at an after-school club, as well as to take part in more structured activity. Remember that this is after-school time, and is not intended as an extension of school, nor are clubs usually manned by qualified teachers. However, after-school clubs will usually support children's learning and their school activities.

Activities and resources might include sports, indoor and outdoor games, arts and crafts, painting, music and dance, computers (including literacy and numeracy programmes as well as games) and cooking activities. There may be inter-centre events, depending on the area and the density of clubs.

If the after-school club also operates as a holiday club, the timetable will be different for the holiday periods. There may be trips out to local attractions, or perhaps the cinema for certain age groups. There are strict guidelines for outings, including minimum staff ratios, fixed criteria for travel arrangements, and risk assessments to be carried out prior to the trips. Holiday clubs will usually run a full-day programme, to help working parents manage their childcare needs during the long school holidays.

After-school clubs are sometimes run at primary schools, after the end of the school day. If you are interested in this kind of childcare, try to find out early which schools in your local area offer after-school care, and what your chances are of your child being offered a place at the school. Full Service Extended Schools are being trialled in some areas of the UK (see below). Some private prep schools also offer after-school care for their pupils.

## The future of Full Service Extended Schools

FSES is a project that has been trialled successfully in some parts of the country since 2004, where schools provide access to a range of support services, including 8am-6pm childcare in primary schools, as well as study support, health services, adult learning and support for parents. Wraparound care, from 8am to 6pm, could provide parents with a good childcare solution – although this kind of care could be exhausting for young children. In 2007 the government envisioned that all schools will be able to offer access to a core set of extended activities by 2010 (though not necessarily wraparound childcare). Subsidy schemes will also be put in place so that these facilities and services which are charged for outside the school day will be accessible to all.

Research from the Universities of Manchester and Newcastle study into FSES has found that this kind of service had a positive impact on the attainment of pupils and on engagement with learning, family stability and enhanced life chances and generated positive outcomes for families and local people.

These services, if rolled out successfully across the country, will support working parents enormously during term time – making the short school day, usually from 9am to 3pm, into a day much more like a working day, from 8am to 6pm. Parents will obviously still be left with the holidays to worry about –

as well as concerns about whether it really is a good idea for children to be at school for such a long day, particularly the younger children. However, if schools are able to provide age-appropriate activities, then this could be a successful model.

## What is the cost of an after-school club?

Costs will vary depending on the council and the centre, but in central London for example, you can expect to pay around £8 per day for after-school care, including collection from school, tea and all activities. Full days during the holidays will cost around £20 per day. There is often a sibling discount.

## How long can your child use an after-school club?

Most clubs cater for children of primary school age, from four to twelve years. You are able to book your child in for as many days a week as you wish, and will need to renew at the appropriate time for each new school term. It is likely that a child will be happy to stay in the same after-school club – the familiarity of the surroundings and the staff will make for good continuity of care for your family. If a child shows signs of tiring of the after-school care centre, it might be a good idea to see if you are able to make alternative arrangements for one or two afternoons a week, or encourage your child to take a more grown-up role at the centre, for example sitting on the Children's Council, if appropriate.

## We talked to Ian, a facilitator at an after-school club in Kidlington

There is a great need for out-of-school care — before school, after school and during holidays. Parents who work outside of school hours — which is just about everyone — are our prime users, but we also cater for parents returning to study.

Most of the children who come to the club are aged between five and eleven — primary school age. We have a few younger ones and some children with special needs who are older. Our staff undergo extra training to look after these children.

Our after-school clubs offer a wide range of activities and play opportunities. A pool of staff means that parents won't ever get a phone call to say the club is closed because someone is ill. Our clubs cater for all ages and personalities. They are a great environment for children to improve their social skills. If the after school club is being used by more than one primary school it can pay dividends when the children go to 'big' school as they will already know lots of the other children.

> A pool of staff means that parents won't ever get a phone call to say the club is closed

The children are collected from school by our staff and because it's a universal truth that children come out of school starving, we give them a healthy snack right away. It might be hot soup, bread or curry on a cold day or something like salad-filled pitta bread and melon when it's hot. We stay in and do some indoor activities on cold afternoons, or get the bouncy castle out and set up field games if it's sunny.

I would advise parents to visit the clubs they are thinking of using before they sign up. Look to see whether the children are happy and the staff are interested. Always ask about staff training. Talk to the children about their club — they will give you an honest view!

## What will an after-school babysitter or after-school nanny do?

An after-school babysitter or nanny will collect your children from school, ferry children to and from after-school activities, supervise homework and music practise, prepare their evening meal and clear up afterwards. It would not be appropriate to expect an after-school babysitter or nanny to do any housework if she is only spending time at your home with your children, supervising and organising all these other activities. Don't expect more than you could reasonably take on yourself. You could use an after-school babysitter or nanny if you are at work, or if you just need support at this busy time of day.

## How much will an after-school babysitter or nanny cost?

This will depend on how much experience she has, where you live, how many children you have, what duties you are expecting her to perform, and how many hours' work each week you can regularly offer. Ideally, you should be able to offer at least three hours a day, five days a week, on a regular basis. In most areas, you can expect to pay between £7 and £9 per hour for this kind of arrangement. You will be saving on the very much larger cost of a full-time nanny, though do bear in mind that you will need to pay for holiday cover if you are working full-time and don't have willing grandparents or other family members nearby. You may also have to pay more for emergency back-up, if a child needs to stay home from school and you aren't able to stay at home and provide that care yourself.

Depending on the help you need, you could employ your after-school babysitter or nanny during the school holidays on a full-time basis – this is a great solution for working parents. Building up this relationship has advantages for everyone – a continuity of care for the children, a reliable income for the babysitter and, of course, it is brilliant for the parents to have the continuity, too, thereby avoiding having to find new help at the start of each new term, as well as constantly showing the ropes to a new babysitter or nanny. Even if you don't need your after-school helper in the holidays, it can be worth paying a retainer, to encourage the same person to be available for the next school term.

## Time off

As this is far from a full-time job, you will need to decide how generous you want to be about paid time off. You may wish to pay a retainer during holiday times, if you don't need your after-school care to help you manage during school holidays. A retainer could be around 50–70% of her usual weekly income. It is reasonable with this kind of arrangement to stipulate that the babysitter or nanny should be available for all the term times – it is specifically her role to either collect children from school or support a mother after school during term times. Any paid holiday should be taken outside of term times. Of course, you have to make allowances for emergencies.

## Who should you be looking for?

Parents with this kind of childcare requirement will be looking for a candidate who is mature and able to learn quickly. This kind of role requires someone who can cope by herself, and who is responsible enough to be caring for children while getting around on public transport, or who is experienced enough to be driving children, if this is necessary and part of your school-run arrangements. Good spoken English is important, as the babysitter or nanny is likely to be in sole charge of young children – on the way home from school, if not for the rest of the afternoon. Be sure to ask for police checks and references.

## Who is likely to be applying for this role?

Candidates for after-school babysitters or nannies are likely to be young students, possibly studying for a teaching qualification, either from this country or abroad, who are looking to earn some money while studying. These candidates will appreciate fixed hours and a steady supply of work. Limited hours each day will fit in well with studying, as do school term times. Alternatively you might find an ex-au pair, looking to build up her experience while continuing her English studies. Nursery school teachers who finish their working day early would be very suitable – if they have the energy to come to a family after a busy day with very young children.

Be careful to find the right person for this role. Avoid hiring someone who is desperate for work – they are likely to continue looking for a full-time job and when something with more hours comes up, they will move on quickly. It is worth searching hard for the right candidate – there are people out there who want this job as much as you want to hire someone for the role.

## How long might this arrangement last?

This kind of arrangement is likely to be quite short-term, particularly if you choose not to pay a retainer when you disappear for long school holidays. However, there are great success stories where families and after-school helpers click, and stay together for three years or more. If a relationship goes well, an after-school babysitter or nanny may well stay with a family while she completes her studies – it can be a great arrangement for everyone involved.

# Nanny

## What is a nanny?

We all have wonderful pre-conceived ideas about nannies – mostly based around Mary Poppins, or old images of Norland-trained, uniformed nannies pushing Silver Cross prams around London's finest parks. Nannies are now generally less traditional than in the past, and not everyone who asks for the title of 'nanny' will actually hold a qualification. And as for Mary Poppins, well, you might get lucky.

A nanny is either a qualified childcarer, or a person with sufficient experience and maturity to be capable of taking sole charge of children at any age. A nanny will nurture and entertain your children in your absence, or support you in raising your children if you are looking for support at home in a shared care role.

Nannies need to be registered and inspected to qualify for part-payment with childcare vouchers. This is something which is being encouraged, but is still far from the norm. There are member associations that nannies are able to join, such as the NCMA, though again, this is far from usual.

## Types of nanny

Here we will be looking at full-time nannies and part-time nannies, as well as the live-in and live-out options as well as sole change and shared-care roles.

A nanny may be employed in either a shared-care role, or have sole charge of your children. In a shared-care role, the mother (or father, depending on who is at home) will take the lead, but will need to give a degree of responsibility to the nanny. The nanny will take the children on outings, and will be able to be left in charge of the children for a day. A nanny in this role needs to be diplomatic, happy to learn from the parent and be willing to occasionally take a back seat. A shared-care nanny needs to feel she is in a different role to that of a mother's help (see Chapter Six). This is a more responsible position, as reflected in the pay, but also in the tasks that she will be asked to perform. Mothers with a shared-care nanny sometimes fall into the trap of doing all the housework while the nanny plays with the children all day – probably not what the mother was originally hoping for.

A nanny has sole charge when both parents are at work for all or most of the day (even if the work is taking place upstairs at home). A sole charge nanny will usually have at least two years' experience and may hold relevant qualifications. (For details on the latest qualifications suitable to a nanny role, see Section Five.) It is a huge responsibility, to look after another's children, and most people agree that there are great advantages to be gained from learning on the job in a shared-care role before assuming full responsibility. When you are employing a sole charge nanny, it is important for the parents to stay in touch and be interested in what the nanny and children have been up to all day, while making sure that the nanny is allowed to get on with the job by herself. As a parent you will need to learn to trust the nanny, or the relationship will be off to a bad start. A sole charge nanny is almost more likely than a shared-care nanny to take on some extra roles, for example running errands with the children, or being involved in school runs and events – purely because she is the adult in the house for the day and, therefore, assuming more of a parent's role.

Male nannies are becoming more common these days and some families, often those with lots of boys, swear by 'mannies'. This may well be appropriate to your family (see Section Two), but when taking on a male nanny, make sure they are willing and able to undertake all the roles of a traditional female nanny, if this is what you require.

A live-out nanny will come to work each day and work for set hours. She will come and go, and be independent of the family. While she is likely to be able to babysit, she will need to be paid for this on top of her salary. A live-in nanny will usually work slightly longer hours and often has some babysitting written into her employment contract. A live-in nanny should have her own bedroom and may have a separate entrance to the family home. Sometimes live-in nannies are even offered private accommodation in a separate flat or annex.

## What will a nanny do for you and your family?

A nanny's role is specifically to look after your children at your home. A nanny will usually be flexible over working hours and will agree hours to suit the family. A nanny will either live in with a family, or live out and come to work on a daily basis, but either way will expect to work fixed hours. Nannies usually work a five-day week and between ten and twelve hours a day. A nanny would expect to be able to have some rest time during the day – it wouldn't really be fair to leave a huge pile of ironing for her to get on with while the children are taking a nap, for example. She will be better able to look after the children when they wake up if she is able to sit down with a coffee and a magazine for half an hour.

As the children are a nanny's responsibility, a nanny will also take on responsibility for keeping the children's bedrooms clean and tidy, changing their sheets, and taking care of their laundry. She can also be expected to clear up after cooking and children's meal times.

A nanny will not undertake any other household tasks, though she may be prepared to run errands while out with the children; if this is important to you this should be discussed at interview stage.

A nanny can be expected to stand in for a parent in all aspects of a child's life, so will be involved with school if the children are school age, and can be expected to arrange play dates and other social activities for your children. She will be capable of going out and about with the children, either using public transport, or driving.

It can be good for children who are cared for at home to have an opportunity to socialise with other children. Your nanny could be expected to take her charges to music classes, swimming classes, regular drop-in toddler groups or a local playgroup to mix with other children of the same age. Here your child will have a chance to mix with her peers, in different, yet familiar settings.

## Judith, 39, works as a full-time nanny

I worked as a mother's help for a couple of years and graduated to being a nanny. I haven't had any formal training, I have just gained lots and lots of experience and excellent references. I have only used an agency twice as I usually find work by word of mouth.

I have been working for my present family for four years, looking after two girls. I prefer to stay with a family for a longer period of time rather than short, sharp bursts, as I think it's good for everyone to have some continuity.

I felt comfortable with my present family as soon as I met them. I usually go with my gut feeling, though sometimes of course you can get it wrong. That is why a three-month trial period is a must. I keep in touch with the parents every day about what I am planning to do with the girls, how they are and if there's anything to report. I also think a review every few months is a really good idea, just to see how you all feel about everything.

I always make sure we discuss discipline and time-keeping at interview. Discipline is a priority — nanny and parents must share views. And with time-keeping, obviously you have to be flexible as the nanny, but I think it is reasonable to ask to be kept informed if parents are running late at the end of the day. It is important for everyone to be courteous in this relationship.

My favourite thing about being a nanny is seeing the children grow and mature. I find that so rewarding. I like hearing the children repeat something I have taught them, passing their newly acquired knowledge on to a younger sibling.

> I keep in touch with the parents every day

## What is the cost of a nanny?

The cost of a nanny will vary depending on where you live and the level of experience of the applicant. A sole charge, live-out nanny in a city can cost between £350–£500 per week. This is net, and, as the nanny's employer, you are responsible for your nanny's NI contributions and tax. Don't forget to work out the gross amount when you are figuring out your costs.

For a live-in nanny, you must expect to pay from £250 per week, net, plus all board and lodging expenses.

In-demand nannies can also command the most wonderful array of perks – these can range from use of the family car in the evenings and at the weekend (or even their own car) to self-contained accommodation. Self-contained accommodation might actually suit everyone rather well – it is an obvious way to give everyone some privacy, though of course isn't always feasible. We will be looking much more closely at live-in and live-out help in Section Two, What is Right for You.

## Time off

A nanny usually works a five-day week, with the weekends free. If you want her to work weekends, you will probably have to give her a day off in lieu (or pay extra for the overtime she has undertaken).

A sole charge nanny will be able to organise her own day with the children, and would expect to be able to rest for an hour or so while the children are sleeping, if appropriate. A mother with a shared care nanny would ideally allow a little time off in the middle of the day.

A nanny who is a full-time employee is entitled to four weeks paid holiday a year. You cannot insist that she takes this holiday at a set time, though you can hope that both sides will try to accommodate the other's needs.

## How long are you likely to keep a nanny?

It is reasonable to ask for a commitment of a year (or a school year if this suits you better) when you take on a nanny. This is a serious job and it will inevitably work best if you are able to build up a long-standing relationship between parents, children and nanny.

The days of the nanny who stays with a family and helps to raise all the children are largely gone, although there are still occasional cases. There are even a few wonderful stories of a nanny coming back to help out the next generation. Of course, if everyone gets on well, having someone stay with you for a long time is a fantastic solution, but today, with more travel and mobility, it is rare to find a nanny staying with a family for more than five years.

Some families actually relish the change that a new nanny brings. Every new nanny will have different interests, enthusiasms and skills that they can share with the children in their care.

## Natalie has been nanny to Isabella and Freddy for seven years. She lives in with their family in London.

When I started this job we were all hopeful that it would be for the long term. My employers had a two-year-old daughter and a baby on the way, and both parents work full time. They were looking for stability for their children. Until this job, my longest stint with a family had been 18 months; families' childcare needs change as their children grow older, so as a nanny you are often moving on to a new position. I never imagined that seven years later I would still be looking after Isabella and her younger brother Freddy, but it still suits us all perfectly.

The job has, of course, evolved over the years. For the first eight months I was just looking after Isabella, sole charge. Then Freddy came along. Isabella went to nursery school part-time and in turn so did Freddy; then Isabella started full-time school. This then allowed me to have (like many mothers) a little breathing space to get other things done during the day. Now they are both at full-time school and I can still fulfil the role the family requires as their nanny, while having some time for my own interests. I have done a few short courses and spend lots of time outdoors (which I love) trying to exhaust the family's Labrador!

I am very fortunate to have the employers I do. They have never asked me to take on major chores. I have always done my best to keep the house running as smoothly as possible, but they appreciate that is not always easy with two small children in tow! Their priority is always the children, which is in contrast to some other jobs I have had. Their expectations are extremely realistic and they know I would do anything for them, though they never take me for granted.

*Earlier this year I was lucky enough to take a three-month holiday. It was a wonderful break and a good amount of time to refresh and revitalise myself. The family employed a temporary nanny to 'hold the fort', but at the end of my trip I was welcomed back with open arms by both children and parents.*

*The security and stability of having me stay so long is wonderful for us all, especially for the children. We all know each other so well and understand how we all operate (most of the time!). Many people comment that I have become like a member of the family, and I suppose I have. We have all been very fortunate that the whole situation has worked so well. I do consider I have a special bond with Isabella and Freddy and have never felt as if their parents resent our relationship, as I know fellow nanny friends have sometimes felt. They are a unique family and I doubt after all this time another family would come close to treating me as they do. It will be a sad day when we do all finally part company.*

> I have become like a member of the family

## What kind of candidates should you be looking for?

Energy, enthusiasm and experience could be your watchwords when looking for a nanny. Many parents would add qualifications to this list, particularly if they are looking for a nanny for a sole charge position. Some families will insist on qualifications; others will decide that experience counts for as much. Agencies will usually not refer a candidate for a sole charge nanny position without at least two years' experience, regardless of whether they hold qualifications.

Ideally, you will meet a nanny who matches your wishes in terms of experience and/or qualifications, and who you think you can have a good working relationship with. You will see more or less of your nanny depending on how much you go out to work, but either way, your children will be exposed to your nanny for long hours each day. It is important to find a candidate who shares your childcare ethos and with whom you think you will be able to communicate well, someone who will treat your children as you would treat them yourself.

Nannies are privately employed by families – be sure to ask for police checks and references, even when you hire through an agency.

## What sort of person can you expect to hire as a nanny?

There are various reasons why people choose to be nannies. There are those for whom it is a vocation, who have taken courses to gain qualifications, and who want to make a career out of being a nanny. Others will use nannying as a means to an end – to save up for a trip, or to fill in time between courses, or to gain experience for a different career path, for example teaching. The different motivations will lead to a different perspective on the role – try to find one whose goals fit with your family.

## Job combining

Once children are at school, families often reassess their childcare needs. Some will still employ a full-time nanny, so that there is someone available for school holidays and in case of one of the children is ill. Other families may take the opportunity to cut childcare costs, manage with an after-school babysitter or nanny, or an after-school club, and deal with the constant juggling that this will inevitably involve. Others will try to find a candidate who will be suitable for more than one role in the household.

A parent running a business from home might look for a candidate who could provide some administrative support during the day and look after the children after school – a PA/nanny. Families with two working parents might look for a candidate who can look after the house during the day, and then fulfil the role of nanny after school and during the holidays. Suitable candidates must be very flexible; and the job description must be very clear.

Sometimes a full-time nanny might use the opportunity of her charges going to school full-time to take on an extra role away from the family. Nannies with experience often fit very well into nursery schools, where they can work for the morning, and still be free to collect 'their' children from school in the afternoon, and take care of them during the holidays.

# The nanny share

## What is a nanny share?

Would you like to hire a nanny to care for your children, but find that the cost puts it out of reach? Or perhaps you would choose a nanny to look after your child but you are only going back to work three days a week. A nanny share could be the answer. A nanny share *is* a different experience to having your own nanny – but can make a nanny an affordable option for childcare in your home, as well as offering other advantages.

A nanny share describes a situation where a nanny looks after children from two families. The share is normally arranged between the families, who should work out between them out how to share the nanny's time effectively. The nanny may work for one family on some days and the other family on others, or for both families at the same time. If she is caring for children from both families on all days, the families need to work out where is the best place for her to do that – always at one house or the other, or one house some days, the other house on other days.

It can all get rather complicated. The trick is to figure out how to share a nanny evenly between two families, so both families feel they are getting a good deal. In practice, one family often feels that they are being slightly hard done by, even if this really isn't the case. Things aren't going well if both sides of the share feel hard done by.

## What you can expect to get from a nanny share

A 'shared nanny' will undertake all the same duties and fulfil the same role as a nanny for one family – but for two families at the same time. A shared nanny is more likely to be a sole charge nanny, where all the mothers (and fathers) involved are going out to work. You would expect the nanny to offer a high level of care for the children and to undertake the traditional role of the nanny – taking care of all the needs of the children, including cooking their meals, looking after the laundry, keeping the children's bedrooms tidy, making beds and changing sheets. Obviously some of these tasks can only be carried out at the home in which she is working on a particular day.

One family may be the dominant partner if this is agreed. The shared nanny might live in with one of the families and agree to undertake some extra duties for that family, including running errands and picking up shopping. The child or children from the second family may be dropped off with the nanny in the mornings to complete the nanny share. This may suit the host family as it offers a way to alleviate the cost of a full-time nanny, and also gives their child a built-in social life.

Alternatively, the nanny may live out and go to look after the children at one house some days and at the other house on other days. The nanny would then be expected to fulfil the role of a nanny for both children, with any extra benefits going to the family whose house she is in on that particular day.

## Advantages and disadvantages of a nanny share

There are great advantages to a nanny share. If you want to work part-time, would like a nanny, but do not want to pay for one for the whole week, this could be for you. A nanny could be hired to look after your children two days a week and to look after the children of a friend of yours on the other three days. In many cases this makes a nanny affordable and easier to find than a part-time nanny. If the nanny is looking after your child or children together with the children from another family on the same days, the cost saving is even greater, and the children have the added advantage of built-in playmates.

It can also be beneficial to have another mother and family to share the nanny relationship with. Any relationship with a nanny can be intense, and while it might cause tension for the nanny to have a relationship with two sets of parents, particularly if a problem arises, it can be very useful to share the relationship when all is going well.

However, a nanny share can lead to problems if one family forms a better relationship with the nanny than the other, or if one family feels the nanny favours the other. It is healthy for the parents to talk among themselves and to come to an agreement over any awkward decisions before facing the nanny. We will be looking further at the potential pitfalls of a nanny share in Section Four, Managing Your Childcare.

There are many pros and cons to this situation, and it is for each individual family to think hard about whether the advantages outweigh the disadvantages. As well as being equally sure about the nanny you hire together, both families need to be confident that they will be able to have an open and honest relationship with the other family.

## What is it likely to cost?

Nannies in a nanny share situation can usually earn above the going rate for a nanny in their area. This is because it is a harder and more complicated job than just looking after the children of one family and so the pay should reflect that. Of course, the pay will be split between the families, which makes this a much more affordable option for most parents.

The nanny's pay will usually be split between families along time lines, not to do with how many children each family has. If the nanny is living-in with one of the families, this should either be taken into account when working out how much of the nanny's pay each family contributes, or the other family could reimburse the host family separately for costs involved in hosting the nanny and children each day. The family who have the nanny living in will be bearing all the costs that that involves; such as food, heating, water, phone and internet use, as well as the nanny taking up space in their house, space that could alternatively be kept for the family or even rented out for an income. The host family may balance the equation by taking the inclusive nights' babysitting. If the nanny lives out, but always cares for the children at one family's home, there are costs involved there too – again, heat, light and food bills – which can either be reflected in the division of the nanny's pay between families, or accepted by both sides as an advantage to the host family (more laundry and errand-running will take place for example) which makes their slightly raised costs reasonable.

The families will also need to split the nanny's NI contributions and tax. The agencies that look after nanny tax will be able to arrange this.

## Time off

As a full-time nanny, a shared nanny is entitled to four weeks' annual holiday. A nanny will usually be expected to try to accommodate the family over holiday times (and vice versa) and this is obviously much more complicated when it comes to trying to accommodate two families. This arrangement calls for a great deal of flexibility from all parties. It helps if the families in the share have a similar schedule, for example if the schools the children go to have the same holiday dates.

A shared nanny will work the same hours as a nanny working for one family – five days a week with two days off, or days off in lieu. Shared nannies will work around ten hours a day, possibly more if they live in with one of the families.

## How long is this arrangement likely to last?

Families should ask for a commitment of a year from the nanny at the outset, if that suits everyone. As with any new nanny, it is advisable to have a trial period at the outset, to ensure all parties are happy with the arrangement. If all goes well, and the families and the nanny settle down well together and find a happy balance, everyone should try to prolong the arrangement for as long as possible. This is a hard one to get right – when it goes well, hang on to it.

Problems may arise when more children are added to the mix. As the families grow, it could become difficult for the nanny to cope in a home environment with, for example, four children. This may be the moment that the families decide to go their separate ways. If the nanny involved in the share has been a great success, there may be a tussle ahead over who gets to keep her on.

## What kind of candidates should you be looking for?

Flexibility on the part of the nanny is hugely important for this kind of arrangement. A shared nanny needs to be mature enough to cater for the needs of two families and, very importantly, she needs to be a great communicator. You would be fortunate if you could find a nanny who has undertaken a nanny share before, who has experience of the pitfalls and how to overcome them. Ideally she will have a great deal of experience in childcare, be confident about looking after more than one child, and competent enough to cater to two families' wishes and needs.

It would be a good idea to look for a more mature person for this role. You will really be looking for an independent, capable nanny who can cope with a busy schedule and take things in her stride.

## Who are you likely to find?

Experienced nannies will often be interested in a nanny share position, unless they have had a bad experience with this kind of arrangement previously. Some nannies will prefer to work just for one family, so will rule out this kind of job; others, however, will enjoy the variety and challenges (and extra pay) that a nanny share role provides.

### Jenny, 60, lives in London and works for two families in a nanny share

I was hired by one family and we were all keen for there to be a share; I would earn a little more money and it would cost the original family less. The mother I was already working for came up with the share. I had worked in a nanny share before, so was able to advise both families about how it would work. Essentially, everyone has got to agree about everything.

It can be tricky working in a nanny share situation. I find it so hard trying to work out everyone's holidays. We've all agreed that, where possible, we'll go at the same time, but there are inevitably hiccups. It is a challenge to try and keep two sets of parents happy. The other thing to watch out for in a share is timekeeping. If the mum whose house the share is taking place in is home at six and the other mother doesn't arrive until later to collect her child, I can be hanging around waiting, when the host mother would probably rather I was out of the house.

I find nanny shares a good experience though. It works especially well for parents with one child — it is all equal and it is lovely for each child to have a friend. The children bring each other on, copy each other and can get into a good routine when they spend time with another child.

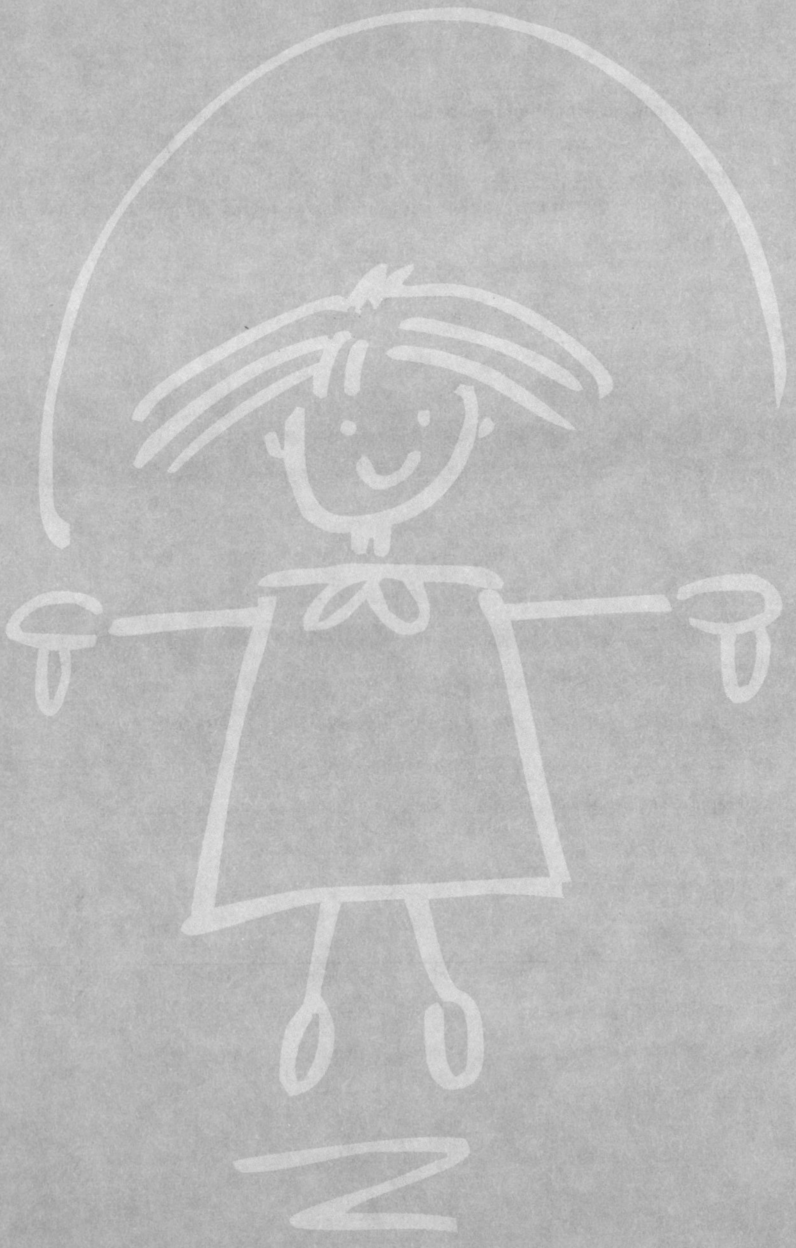

# Mother's help

## What is a mother's help?

For at-home mothers wondering how to collect children from school while the baby takes a nap and wanting to have a little time with each of her children individually, while disappearing under a pile of laundry and ironing, a mother's help can provide the answer.

A mother's help is a shared care role and usually full-time. Someone in this role will either live in with a family, or come to the family's home each day to be an extra pair of hands for parents and help with the children and light household tasks.

A mother's help may have experience with young children – perhaps she has younger siblings, or has done some babysitting as a teenager. She may hold some childcare qualifications and be keen to work as a mother's help for a year before embarking on a nanny role. Most agencies will not recommend a candidate for a sole charge nanny job until they have some experience in a shared care role under their belt.

You might be lucky and find someone who has already been a mother's help, and wants to broaden her experience with another family. Possibly she is saving up for travelling, has no aspirations to be a nanny and enjoys the company that a shared care role offers.

## What does a mother's help do?

A mother's help will usually work for ten hours a day. If she is living-in she will also babysit for two nights each week. A live-out mother's help will usually babysit too, at mutually convenient times, for extra pay.

A mother's help will help with all tasks that a mother (or father) would undertake whilst running the family home and looking after the children, but will probably prefer to lean more towards childcare than housework. She will, however, be expected to undertake more household chores than you could ask or expect from a nanny.

### Helping with the children could include:
- Assisting the children with getting dressed in the morning (depending on arrival time).
- Helping to prepare breakfast, lunch and tea for the children.
- Walking older children to and from school and nursery.
- Reading stories.
- Playing with the children – including encouraging everyone to tidy up afterwards.
- Taking the children on trips to the park.
- Accompanying the children to music groups or playgroups.
- Bathing the children at the end of the day and getting them ready for bed.

### Helping in the house could include:
- Running errands to the shops, post office, dry cleaner's and so on.
- Washing the dishes including loading and unloading the dishwasher.
- Helping with the family's laundry – including ironing when not looking after children.
- Vacuuming and dusting.

## What is a mother's help likely to cost?

How much you pay a mother's help will depend on where you live and on the level of experience of the mother's help. Most families can expect to pay from £250-£300 per week for a live-out mother's help. Live-in rates are usually around £50 less per week. These are figures for a net salary and if the mother's help is employed by just your family, you will be responsible for the NI contributions and tax. See Section Five for details on how to do this and on finding an agency who will arrange it all for you.

## Time off

A mother's help will usually work for around ten hours a day, five days a week. She should have two full days off each week. If the family requires help at the weekend, the mother's help should be given time off in lieu during the week, or paid for the extra hours. Be clear about weekend work at the early interview stages.

A mother's help should have a formal contract and should be given four weeks' paid annual holiday, to be taken at mutually convenient times. It is not reasonable to insist that she takes holiday when you do, but if there are particular times of the year when you know you need help, you can stipulate this – it is best to raise this at interview with a candidate you are interested in.

## How long will a mother's help stay?

It is a good idea to ask for an initial stay of a year – if this suits you. This will allow everyone to benefit from the arrangement. Your children will have a chance to bond well with the mother's help and you will be able to teach your mother's help how to do things your way, then reap the benefits. The mother's help will benefit by having a good stint on her CV.

It's a good idea to have a trial period at the beginning of the arrangement. Families should also make allowances for things to go wrong and write a notice period into the contract.

A mother's help tends to be less likely than a nanny to stay in one job for more than a year. She may be saving up for travelling (Kiwis, Australians and South Africans are popular mother's helps) or may be building up a CV in order to be ready to take on a sole charge job. Good childcarers with ambition will want to move on to a sole charge job to test out their own abilities and instincts, rather than be happy following another's instructions for long.

## What kind of candidates should you be looking for?

Ideally you will find someone who is keen and willing to learn. It is important that you get along well – think hard at interview about whether you could spend large amounts of time with this person.

Would you like someone with ambition, who wants to learn to think for herself and use her initiative, or someone who is willing to just do what you ask? If you go for the former, it is more likely that you will be looking for childcare again in a year's time, as your dynamic mother's help moves on to greater things. Find the balance – not many of us want to spend our time with someone with no dreams or aspirations.

Mother's helps recommended by agencies should have finished school and are usually under the age of 30. They should be reference and police checked, and interviewed face-to-face before being put forward for a family. If a family finds a mother's help without the help of an agency, it will be down to them to enquire about police checks and to follow up references.

## Who are you likely to find for this role?

Families are likely to find young(ish) girls who want to broaden their childcare experience in a shared care role. Candidates may be keen to have some practical experience before or after undertaking a childcare qualification. A mother's help may be keen to move to a city and living in with a family is a good way to achieve that in a secure environment. Look for the candidate's motivation when you interview – it is good to find out why someone is keen to take on this role, and what they are hoping to do afterwards.

Occasionally a newly-qualified nanny might take on a mother's help role in her first year of working, to build up her experience and CV. You are also likely to come across girls who are travelling and are prepared to stay in one place long enough to earn some money before continuing on their way.

The mother's help role also appeals to girls from abroad who have been living in the UK for a while, perhaps as an au pair. This role is definitely a step up from that of an au pair, and is a step closer to becoming a nanny, without qualifications, perhaps, but with plenty of experience.

## Rachel, 23, is a student and part-time mother's help in Surrey

I have been a part-time mother's help while I have been studying. I have been able to fit work around my courses and have worked more during the holidays and at weekends. A mother's help is an extra set of hands. I'm not responsible for the children full-time — I'm just there to help the mother with whatever she needs, so it covers a vast range of things. You have to be willing to pitch in. I could be picking the children up from nursery, preparing a meal for the family, vacuuming or going off to the supermarket with a shopping list. I love a varied job where you can be doing all sorts of different tasks. With this arrangement I feel I get to know the whole family, rather than just the child.

> You have to be willing to pitch in

The relationship between you and the parent is vital. If the parent sees you more as a friend and a support throughout the day that's great, but if she just sees you as someone who is there to get all the jobs done, it won't be such a happy relationship. Also, communication is so important. I feel that I have become friends with the mothers I have worked with. We'll have coffee and chat about life.

I find I do all sorts of things. Sometimes I need to be creative to entertain the children. I'm not being paid to switch on the television. I usually help during the afternoons, as the children are at nursery during the morning. I go to help with teatime, bathtime and bedtime. I might be asked for some extra hours if the mother has to go to a doctor's appointment, or if she needs an extra pair of hands to cope with extra children coming over to play. If I'm not at college, I'll always try to help her out.

The first few weeks are interesting. You're both getting to know each other and learning to work alongside each other. That's when I think it either works or it doesn't.

Discipline can be an awkward area. As a mother's help you have to have boundaries and be able to instil some discipline, but at the same time you need to make sure your methods coincide with the mother's. It can be hard when two adults are around for the child to know who is in charge.

I think that when parents are thinking of hiring a mother's help, they need to be very specific about the help that they need. Of course needs change, but if this is as clear as it can be at the outset, there should be fewer problems ahead. It is important that neither side takes advantage of the other. The interview is important, as the mother's help and the mother really need to get along well together for this to work. You also need to have a similar approach to children and childcare.

I had never realised how hard having two young children is — sometimes when I arrive the mother goes to have a bath! The children can't be left on their own in a room; when one is awake the other is asleep and vice versa — sometimes it is just lovely for the mother to have a minute to herself.

# Au pairs

## What is an au pair?

An au pair is an extra pair of hands, who comes with a degree of responsibility for the host family. An au pair is not an employee, but is suitable for some childcare arrangements. Au pairs always live in with their host family and will work 25 hours a week, spread over five days, with two nights' babysitting each week on top. An au pair plus will work 35 hours a week, over five days, with two nights' babysitting. Au pairs are usually young women (sometimes young men) who wish to come to the UK to improve their English (there is a list of countries that au pairs may come to the UK from in Section Five). They may have some experience with children, but this is not always the case.

Au pairs should not be treated as an employee, but rather as a long-term guest in your home. This unusual guest will offer childcare and help with light housework, in return for pocket money, board and lodging. In practice, families and au pairs usually work out a way to live symbiotically, making allowances for their own wants and needs and for each other's privacy.

## What will an au pair do for you and your family?

An au pair will help with, entertain and look after children for limited periods of time, and help with some light housework and other chores around the home.

THE DIFFERENT TYPES OF CHILDCARE

### Helping with the children can include:
- Helping the children to get dressed in the morning.
- Preparing breakfast, lunch and tea for the children.
- Walking older children to and from school and nursery.
- Reading stories.
- Playing with the children – including encouraging everyone to tidy up afterwards.
- Taking the children on trips to the park.
- Accompanying the children to music groups or playgroups.
- Bathing the children at the end of the day and getting them ready for bed.

These tasks could be performed alone once the au pair has gained some experience, or in conjunction with a parent to offer extra support.

### Light housework includes:
- Making children's beds and changing their sheets.
- Washing dishes, including loading and unloading the dishwasher.
- Keeping the kitchen clean and tidy, including cleaning the floor and sweeping up after meals (and as anyone, with babies and young children knows, this is a job for after every meal!).
- Taking care of the laundry – this can be the whole family's laundry if there is time in the day, otherwise just the children's laundry, including loading and unloading the washing machine, drying, ironing where necessary and putting the clothes away again.
- Vacuuming and dusting. (It would be ideal, if possible, to have a separate arrangement for weekly cleaning of the house and let your au pair keep on top of things during the in-between times.)

An au pair would also be expected to keep her own bedroom clean and tidy and to clean the bathroom that she either has to herself or shares with the children.

### Other duties for an au pair can include:
- Shopping for the household – not the big weekly shop, but popping to the local shops with a short list.

- Running errands, for example to the post office and dry cleaner.
- Walking and feeding pets.
- Taking out the rubbish and emptying rubbish bins in the house.

## Unacceptable household tasks for au pairs (as suggested by the British Au Pair Agencies Association) include:

- Gardening (unless this is a personal enthusiasm).
- Window cleaning.
- Spring cleaning.
- Cleaning the oven.
- Washing the carpets or the car.
- Clearing up after untrained pets or cleaning out hutches and cages, or undertaking pet training.

An au pair may wish to cook occasionally for the family – and then could reasonably expect to take part in the meal that she has prepared.

All guidelines suggest that au pairs are not suitable as sole charge carers of children under the age of two, though they may, of course, help out with children of this age. Sole charge means being the only responsible adult with the children for a whole working day – taking care of children while both parents are out at work. Young au pairs with limited experience cannot be expected to undertake such a large degree of responsibility.

Don't expect your au pair to be Superwoman. It is unlikely that she will be able to do everything (even everything on the lists above), and it is important that you choose the tasks that you would like her to take on carefully. Be realistic about what is possible in her day and within her allotted time. Don't expect miracles, or for her to be able to do more than (or even as much as) you could.

As the duties expected of an au pair are so extensive and varied, it is important to be very clear about your expectations before an au pair joins your household. This will avoid unrealistic expectations on both sides and set a good precedent for communication. A welcome letter, setting out your house rules and expected tasks is a good idea – we include a sample welcome letter in Section Five and tips for managing your au pair in Section Four.

## Mirabela, 25, from Romania is an au pair living in Bedford

I decided to come to England as an au pair as I like children and I wanted to improve my English. The local paper in Romania carried an advertisement from an agency in the UK — I got in touch and found myself with a family in Northamptonshire soon afterwards.

My first experience wasn't great. The family had an 18-month-old boy and a five-year-old girl. My contract said that I would be looking after the girl, but in practice I was looking after the boy, too. It was a hopeless situation for me — I don't have experience with babies and I wasn't improving my English at all. The communication between me and the parents was terrible too. I felt like I was a housekeeper — they expected me to do a lot of cleaning and ironing. The mother wasn't very patient, which was a problem as I was having trouble understanding her instructions. They also didn't want me to go out in the evenings — it was as if they didn't trust me.

My next position was much better. I looked after two children, 10 and 12 years old. They were an American family and my English improved quickly. The family were very welcoming. When they had little parties they invited me; the mother was very talkative and kind. She even bought me flowers; when I asked why, she replied, 'You have been very good with the kids this week'. We had a good relationship.

> Make time to talk to your au pair

I think an au pair is like a big brother or sister for the children. I can look after and entertain the children as well as help the parents.

My advice to parents is to make time to talk to your au pair. We often arrive without many friends in a new area. We need to have a good relationship with our host family.

## What will an au pair cost?

An au pair is paid 'pocket money' and given her board and lodging in return for 25 hours' work each week and two nights' babysitting. The minimum pocket money for an au pair is £60. An au pair plus should be given a minimum of £70-£80 pocket money each week in return for 35 hours a week, plus two nights' babysitting. If either an au pair or an au pair plus occasionally works more than their regular hours, she should be paid an hourly rate for the extra hours worked.

Don't forget, as with all live-in childcare, to take into account the cost of having an extra person living in your home. An au pair arrangement includes full board and lodging. You must give the au pair her own room, and furnish it to a standard equivalent to the rest of your home. She should also be given space to study – either in her room, or elsewhere in the house. The family will provide an au pair with her own linen and towels. An au pair can share a bathroom with other family members (though this will ideally be with just with the children).

An extra person in the house will use extra light, heating and hot water. You will also be providing all her meals. While the amount that an au pair will eat will vary wildly from one to another, you must be prepared to buy her food that she specifically requests (within reason) and accept that you will inevitably go to the fridge to start cooking the children's supper, to find that what you were planning to cook has disappeared. It would be awful to restrict an au pair over what she can eat – there are dreadful stories of au pairs being limited to rice and pasta, or, 'Not those yogurts, they are just for the children', which only makes for an unhappy relationship. It is far better to be generous and do some extra shopping. Just don't forget to add this in when you are looking at your costs even though additional costs are likely to be pretty minimal.

You may decide to be generous and pay for the au pair's language school (see below). This is becoming more common, and is also a good way to encourage an au pair to go to school, which has obvious benefits for the host family. She will improve her spoken English, and have an opportunity to meet other language students (quite likely au pairs) who will probably be living locally. A social life is a great thing for an au pair – as long as they quickly develop skills at creeping into the house late at night – and it is great for everyone if they have the opportunity to socialise with friends outside of the host family.

If an au pair has recently arrived in the country, you may wish to give her a mobile phone, perhaps on a pay-as-you-go basis. It will benefit you if your au pair has a phone, and you can explain that you will top it up every now and again. You will want to be able to reach her, particularly when she has your children in the park, for example, or when you might be running late, or just want to check in with her. By giving her a phone, you will appear to be generous and thoughtful. You will also probably save yourself money in the long run, if she is using your landline less. While on technical things, it would also be generous to make your internet access available to your au pair, for her to use when she is off duty, as long as it is convenient.

As well as the financial cost, there is also the emotional cost to consider. You are inviting a young and often fairly inexperienced person into your home, and probably expecting a lot of her. Be prepared to be the grown up in the relationship. Your au pair may from time to time need some emotional support. She may feel lonely, or homesick, or find it hard to be in a big city (or away from one in the countryside), possibly for the first time. You will be her mother figure, however much you want to avoid it. This won't happen all the time, but is part of your responsibility if the situation requires it.

## Time off

All au pairs must be allowed time to go to a language school during the day. There are language courses widely available for free for students from EU member states, and ideally an au pair will be able to find a place locally. The family should try hard to be flexible over lesson times to accommodate everyone's needs.

All au pairs should have two free days a week, and if their regular hours include weekends, they should be given one free weekend a month.

Au pairs earn one week's paid holiday for every six months that they stay with a family, two weeks in a year. This does not have to be taken at the same time as the family's holidays. You may want to invite your au pair to join you on your family holiday, but do remember that if an au pair joins you, she should still only be working twenty-five hours a week, ideally spread over five days, with two days off. It is hard to get the balance right on holiday. You must allow free time, but depending on where you are, the au pair may be isolated without transport and without her network of friends and will be a presence for more than her allotted helping time. It is more important than ever that she is included as part of the family. Don't expect her to be on duty for all the hours of the day and night.

## Who should you be looking for?

The perfect au pair is flexible, hardworking, discreet and enthusiastic, with a clear purpose and motivation to be in the role. Their main priorities will ideally be to experience life in another country and learn to speak perfect English.

You are likely to find someone who is young (the recommended age for au pairs is 17 to 27) and therefore likely to be relatively inexperienced, all of which makes the above attributes more important. Ideally, you will find an au pair who has some experience with babysitting, or looking after younger siblings. Au pairs should have completed their schooling and may be taking a break, or improving their language skills before work or further study. They should have a working knowledge of English, though the family should be prepared for English to be basic if an au pair arrives directly from her home country.

It is ideal to find an au pair who already has some contacts in your local area – he or she may be following a friend or family member to a particular town or region. An immediate support network is likely to make for a happier transition to a new country and role.

An au pair post is not suitable for someone whose main focus is to make money.

An agency will police check their au pairs and follow up references. Families are always advised to check references, too, for their own peace of mind. If hiring an au pair independently, it is wise to ask for checks and references.

## How long is an au pair arrangement likely to last?

Au pair agencies suggest that arrangements should last for six to nine months, but it is usually preferable for the family if a placement can last longer. The shorter time frame is likely to fit with students coming to learn English over their summer holidays, or those spending some time travelling between school and college.

Many au pairs, however, are prepared to stay much longer. Working as an au pair is often a first step on the childcare ladder – our first au pair stayed with us for almost two years and is still in the UK four years later, working as a nanny with another family. The au pair role is a great starting point for a young person coming to the UK and provides an opportunity to live and work in a new environment, without having to worry about board, lodging, or money. They will be able to learn the language and build up a network of friends and acquaintances, before heading off to be more independent.

## Male au pairs

Male au pairs, along with male nannies, are becoming more common. Some families with all boys absolutely swear by male au pairs, finding lots of reasons to hire a boy rather than a girl; others rule it out without even considering it as an option. (Fathers have been known to be a little sensitive on this subject!) You will find much more about this in Section Two, What is Right for You.

# Granny

We can't really have a heading, as in other chapters, 'What is a Granny?'! It's an old saying that 'Granny knows best' and, in the end, most parents have to admit that she probably does. For many families, childcare provided by grandparents, or indeed, other family members, can turn out to be a real blessing, in more ways than one.

Formal childcare arrangements are not for everyone. Many parents like to and try to get around their childcare situation without looking for help beyond that on offer from their extended family. This may either be for financial reasons, or just because it is generally a great childcare solution and there are family members nearby, willing and able to help. When grandparents, or other family members, care for the younger generation in their own family, parents are usually completely reassured that their children's carers have their best interests at heart. Many parents wonder what better form of childcare there could possibly be.

There are different solutions to managing childcare from within your family group, if you have enough family members living close to home. Grandparents in particular take on a huge amount of childcare and are often responsible for looking after their grandchildren for extended periods while both parents are out at work. Don't ignore other alternatives from within the family group, including support from siblings and the option of parents sharing the care of their children between them, while both also managing to work.

Some parents are so sold on the idea of an older, more experienced carer for their children that they will advertise for a 'granny nanny' or an older babysitter. Many parents like the experience that an older person will bring to a childcare role, especially if their children either don't have grandparents, or aren't able to spend much time with their own grandparents.

## What can you ask granny to do?

If one of the grannies is going to take on a childcare role, think hard about what you will be able to ask her to do for you and your family. In an ideal world, you would ask everything that you would ask of another person in the childcaring role. In the real world, you are less likely to ask a granny looking after your children to take on any more than the essentials of the task. Older people are bound to find children tiring, and unless you have particularly young grandparents, they will be physically more exhausted by this task than a younger nanny.

Parents are unlikely to be able to ask for too much in terms of errand running or picking up a few items from the shops on the way home. When a grandparent offers to look after your children for you, she is unlikely to think she is also offering to take on all these tasks, too. You won't have had an interview stage with a family member, so won't have been able to make all aspects of the role clear, if you are expecting anything extra. Also, even if you are paying granny, you are likely to feel more beholden to her than you would an employee, and you will quickly feel as if you are taking advantage if you ask too much (and your relative will undoubtedly feel this, too).

Some grandparents might share the childcare with another family member, or might look after the children a couple of days a week, while the family finds the resources for a day nursery or childminder for the other days of the week. Grandparents are often asked for help with after-school care, and will often look after their grandchildren at the end of the day during term-time and perhaps all day during the holidays.

## Alternative family childcare arrangements

- Parents split childcare by working different days each week. Great for children as they always have a parent around, and great for both parents' relationship with their children. Possibly less good for the parents' relationship with each other, as they may end up never seeing one another, as they pass at the front door. Parents who manage their childcare needs this way are also likely to end up taking holidays at different times to cover the childcare.
- Siblings or good friends who live close by may be able to help each other out by taking it in turns to look after each other's children.

## Sarah, 63, has two grandsons and lives in Kent

When my eldest grandson was ten months, my daughter went back to work for three days a week. I work four days a week but was thrilled when she asked me to look after him on my free day. The other granny would cover the other days.

My daughter emphasised that she would like me to look after him in their own home, to avoid him being moved around. In fact it worked very well. Everything was set up for him at his own house and it was very reassuring for my grandson to be in his familiar surroundings while his mummy was at work.

Of course, I had fallen out of practise with nappies and so on, but it soon all came back! It did all get rather harder when the second baby came along and I was trying to take the older one out along with the baby. We used to go to Jumble Jots, which was great fun. It was a big effort, but I didn't want him to miss out because of the baby.

I approached my role as giving one day a week over to the boys. We would play, have lunch at home and then go out to the park or a pet centre, unless it was bucketing down with rain. I'd make a point of doing special things with the children, activities that they could not have taken part in with a childminder or if they had been at a nursery. I was able to give them a very high degree of attention. I have always enjoyed books and would read to the boys from an early age. I have a collection of books at my home and I would take five or six with me each week when I went to look after the boys. They were always very excited when I arrived and would rush to my bag to see which books I had with me that day, which was lovely.

I don't think there are any downsides to using family childcare. I was always very careful to respect my daughter's wishes with regard to the

> I was always very careful to respect my daughter's wishes behaviour, well-being and upbringing of her boys, irrespective of my own views. I feel that is very important. Luckily we tended to agree on discipline — I was quite strict with the boys about things like holding hands when we were out by the river. They knew that if they didn't, we would all be getting back in the car. My daughter would back me up on discipline issues and I would always draw her attention to any problems that had arisen during the day.
>
> I enjoyed the experience and am very grateful to my daughter for giving me the opportunity to share in my grandsons' early years. I'm sure it has helped us all build a closer relationship. My daughter's family has now moved away, so we will have much less contact. I will miss them terribly.

## What is the cost of this kind of arrangement?

Families often use this form of informal childcare arrangement when they find the cost of formal childcare too high. It is impossible to put a figure on this one as individual families will obviously come to their own arrangements over paying family members for childcare.

Grandparents may have given up their own paid work to take care of their grandchildren, and might either expect or need to be renumerated in some way for their time. Others may be willing and financially able to give their time for free, perhaps with expenses covered by the parents.

Don't shy away from talking about money and payment for family members – you will need to feel you can discuss everything with your family if they are going to be this heavily involved in raising your children. Over the course of time, you will need to address other awkward subjects with them, too. Discipline, the way things are done, diet, television and treats are all potential areas of conflict with family childcarers. It is so easy to take these things personally and your mother is likely to be put out if you criticise her methods of childrearing. Woe betide you if you comment on your mother-in-law's methods!

Members of your family caring for your children in your home cannot be paid by voucher schemes, even if they are registered as a childcarer. If you are coming to a financial arrangement, make sure you have accounted for tax and National Insurance payments in the usual way.

## How long can you expect this arrangement to last?

The age and health of the grandparents will be of primary importance here. If your children are lucky enough to have young, healthy and fit grandparents, this kind of arrangement could see you through the early years and even on into the period when your children are at school and need collecting at the end of the day and looking after during the holidays – assuming, of course, that they live close by and are still willing and able to help.

It is physically and mentally exhausting looking after babies and young children full time – even if full time means for the larger part of the day, with evenings and nights off. Try to make sure that you can make arrangements for your parents to have time off every now and then if they are helping you with your childcare. Check in regularly to make sure that your family members are still feeling up to the task. It will be tricky for them to volunteer that they are finding it difficult, since they will not want to let you down.

You will have to stay on extremely good terms for this to last, and trust your family members completely to care for and discipline your children in the way that you would yourself. Be honest in all conversations regarding the childcare that they are offering, and keep communication open all the time.

## Ruth, 70, lives in London and has looked after her two granddaughters for the last seven years

I was more than happy to take on the care of my grandchildren when my daughter-in-law wanted to go back to work. I've been looking after the girls for most of their lives. I used to live close by, and would go round early in the morning. I'd wait until the baby woke up, get her dressed and bring them back to mine. I find it so much easier in my own home. There's no reason why I couldn't have spent the day in their house, but in your own home you can do your own thing.

When they started nursery I would take them and pick them up; now I collect the girls from school. My son and daughter-in-law are now divorced but I still have the children. When my daughter-in-law has to get to work early she will still call me and ask me to drop the girls at school.

I had already raised three boys so felt confident about helping out with the girls, even though I was that much older. I changed nappies, fed them, gave them baths. I used to take them to the baby gym and swimming classes. I had the pleasure of the first tooth, first steps and first words all over again. As they grew older, I got to go to all the pantomimes and Christmas parties. I thoroughly enjoyed it!

Nowadays we do lots of arty things. I have a houseful of cardboard boxes and bottle tops and books. They make cakes and they like helping with cooking, preparing the vegetables, things like that. The girls are very comfortable here — they have their own bedrooms and lots of toys. I think our relationship is quite special — we have been a big part of each other's lives. Sometimes my other grandchildren, who I don't see as much, can feel a bit put out.

Grandparents do spoil their grandchildren — it's natural. When you haven't seen your grandchildren, you tend to buy them things or let them have sweets, but it is different when you see each other all the time. Discipline can be tricky. If there's a problem I'll speak to their father about it. I might tell them off if they've done something wrong but if it's anything serious I don't do it, it goes back to their parents. At the end of the day it's the parents' responsibility.

I am not paid for looking after the children. It is part and parcel of living, of being a family. Every so often my daughter-in-law will send me a beautiful bunch of flowers, or she'll take me out for a meal. A treat like that shows me that they appreciate the support I give them.

# Maternity nurses and night nannies

## What is a maternity nurse?

A maternity nurse can be the answer to a new mother's (and father's) prayers. Like a knight in shining armour, a maternity nurse can save the day. She is usually hired in the short term, to help parents immediately after the birth of their baby. New parents can often arrive home from hospital with their brand new baby and face the realisation that they don't have a clue about what to do next. This is an intensive form of childcare, in partnership with the parents, to settle the baby or babies into a routine and to help the mother recover from the birth.

This type of childcare might also be sought by parents who are having a baby for the second or third time and, knowing what lies ahead, decide they want to hire a maternity nurse to help them weather the storm.

A maternity nurse might also be able to help a mother who is suffering from postnatal depression and help to give her the confidence to cope with her baby by herself.

While some families might find the presence of a maternity nurse overwhelming, other families love the reassurance that she offers. Maternity nurses certainly are a presence – they are usually on duty 24 hours a day, six days a week.

Maternity nurses are self-employed and are often booked up to nine months in advance. They can be recommended from mother to mother, booked by families for the second, third and fourth time when a relationship goes well, or referred through an agency.

If you are looking for a maternity nurse for the first time and don't have any personal recommendations to follow up, you will need to contact an agency early in your pregnancy. It is a good idea to interview more than one maternity nurse to give yourself a choice and, if possible, interview widely for this role – it really matters that you get on with your maternity nurse, even though the help they provide will usually be in the short term. Meeting your maternity nurse in advance has other advantages, too – she might be willing to give advice on what you should buy in preparation for the new baby and you will be able to find out her own personal likes and dislikes in advance of coming home from the hospital, exhausted.

Successful maternity nurse relationships are treasured. A maternity nurse can even be the first person a mother calls with news of her second pregnancy.

## What will a maternity nurse do?

The role of a maternity nurse is primarily to help the new mother bond with her baby. This is done by:

- Allowing the mother the time to recover from the birth, by assisting in the baby's care and perhaps preparing nutritious meals for the mother.
- Helping to establish breastfeeding or assisting with bottle feeding.
- Helping the mother to establish a routine.
- Teaching the new mother how to care for a newborn day-to-day.
- Practical help, including taking care of the baby's laundry and sterilising bottles, if appropriate.

Guidance from an experienced pair of hands can be an enormous support in the early weeks.

The maternity nurse will usually sleep with the baby, and bring the baby to the new mother in the night for feeding, if breastfeeding is the preferred option. Alternatively, the maternity nurse will feed the baby with bottles during the night, allowing the new mother a chance to sleep through (older children permitting!). Even if the mother is woken to feed in the night, she will still be able to catch much more sleep than if she were without the maternity nurse, who will take care of any nappy changes, winding and settling, which can all take much longer than the feed itself.

Maternity nurses will, of course, have their own style and approach, making it very important to meet beforehand. Some will be very old school, keen to instil a routine and take the baby away from the mother at every opportunity to ensure the mother recovers from the birth. Others will be more relaxed and modern in their approach, encouraging on-demand breastfeeding and lots of cuddles. Maternity nurses are also likely to have varying opinions on letting babies cry. Be sure to find out a potential maternity nurse's views on all these issues around a baby's first few weeks of life at interview. If this is your second or third baby, you will know what kind of approach you prefer. If this is your first baby, try to imagine how you will feel by talking to your parents and friends about their experiences.

Some maternity nurses will be willing to share in the running of the household, and be prepared to help out occasionally with other children. Most, however, will prefer to stick to the rules and just apply their help to the mother and newborn.

## What is the cost of a maternity nurse?

The cost of a maternity nurse will vary but starts at around £500 per week. For an experienced maternity nurse to help with twins, expect to pay around £800 per week. Care of triplets will earn a maternity nurse £900 plus per week. Maternity nurses with formidable reputations and bags of experience can earn even more.

You will, of course, also be offering full room and board to the maternity nurse. She will usually expect meals to be provided for her, and to eat with the parents, baby and routines allowing.

Maternity nurses are self-employed so will look after their own tax and National Insurance.

Knowing when to book your maternity nurse is a tricky question. You might choose to have the nurse a couple of weeks after your due date, so that you have some time together first as a family, before the cavalry arrive to help you all out. However, if you would like the security of someone there when you get home from hospital, you will be taking a gamble on your due date. If the baby hasn't arrived by the time your maternity nurse is due to start work, you will be obliged to pay half-pay for the first week, and full-pay if you go into a second week. Of course, as maternity nurses tend to be booked up, there is no guarantee that you will be able to extend your booking at the other end.

The cost of a maternity nurse may sometimes be claimed from private health insurance providers if the maternity nurse is a registered midwife and there have been birth complications, or if the baby has been delivered by caesarean section.

## How long will a maternity nurse stay?

As the cost of this kind of help is so great, it is usual for maternity nurse bookings to be brief. A week can be helpful, even if just to allow the new mother to get some sleep. Maternity nurses prefer bookings between two and six weeks, to have time to allow the mother to recover and settle the baby into a good routine. Very occasionally, a maternity nurse will be asked to stay on to help with the mother's return to work. This is obviously an extremely expensive childcare option for the long term.

It is part of the maternity nurse's job to give the parents, particularly the new mother, the confidence to manage without her. Strangely, a successful placement will be one when parents are happy to say goodbye at the end of the booking – the maternity nurse has done her job and the parents are ready and looking forward to managing alone.

## Time off

A maternity nurse is on duty for 24 hours a day. Of course she will need to rest during this period – if you have family visiting during the day, that might offer a good opportunity for your maternity nurse to slip away for a couple of hours. Every seven days a maternity nurse is entitled to one full day (and night) off. Some maternity nurses may prefer to save this up and take one weekend off in a fortnight. You will usually not face holiday complications as placements tend to be short.

## What kind of candidates should you be looking for?

You must look for a candidate that you feel you can develop a good rapport and trust with. She will be with your family at such a precious time that any distractions really won't be welcome. If there are other children already in the family, it is a good idea to check that the maternity nurse you are considering hiring is child-friendly, as some will may not want to be involved with other children at all, other than in relation to the baby. This can cause friction, so it is good to check at interview what your potential maternity nurse's feelings are about this.

## MATERNITY NURSES AND NIGHT NANNIES

## Who is likely to be applying for this role?

'Nurse' is a bit of a misnomer, as maternity nurses are not always qualified. They are most often extremely experienced nannies, who have developed special skills or had particular experience with newborns.

Some maternity nurses are registered nurses or ex-midwives. If you are hoping to claim the cost of your maternity nurse on your health insurance, make sure your maternity nurse qualifies by being a registered midwife.

As with all childcare, be careful to check references. Most maternity nurses will arrive with a stack of letters from happy parents. Pick a few out of the pile and make a call – a phone conversation can throw a lot of light on what it will be like to share those first few intense days and weeks with this person. Responsibility for checking references and police checks lies with the family that is employing the maternity nurse.

## Paulette has years of experience as a maternity nurse. She usually works in London and the surrounding areas

I was working as a nanny when I had a call from my agency looking for an emergency maternity nurse. I said I would give it a go and I loved it straightaway.

My job is to give the mother confidence to manage by herself when I leave. Some mothers are so keen to learn — it is great working with them. Often new mothers have not had contact with a baby and don't know anything about their care. I have had my own children and love to guide new mothers. I help them with bathing, feeding, breast or bottle, whichever they prefer, and settling the baby.

As a maternity nurse you need broad shoulders and a thick skin. The new mothers can be very emotional so you need to be a confident person to cope with anything that comes at you. I always make sure I discuss everything I am going to do with the baby with the mother. I know a few maternity nurses that might bottle-feed babies in the night without telling the mother — I

## THE DIFFERENT TYPES OF CHILDCARE

think that is dangerous territory. I know from having my own children that as a new mother you want to be in charge of everything.

Sometimes families expect a maternity nurse to be housekeeper, chauffeur and nanny. A maternity nurse's role is really to take care of the mother — keeping an eye on her diet, health, helping her back on her feet after the birth — and the baby.

> A maternity nurse's role is really to take care of the mother and the baby

My calendar is booked about six months in advance though I am occasionally called at the last minute. The longest I have stayed with a family is eight months — we got along very well.

I always meet the family before taking on a new job. Our personalities have to match, and I'm not afraid to turn a family down if I think we won't get along.

I always remember that a new baby in a family is such a special time. I feel very lucky to share that time with my families.

### Night nannies

A night nanny will care for your baby (or young child) throughout the night, meaning that you can sleep through without having to wake for a feed, a nappy change, or to settle the baby. Night nannies will also prepare bottles and dress the baby in the morning. Nannies will also offer advice on breastfeeding and on encouraging the baby to settle into a good sleep routine. Night nannies offer an alternative to maternity nurses and, because they are only with you half the time, cost quite a considerable amount less. Usually parents will pay a fee to an agency and an overnight rate directly to the nanny. An overnight nanny will usually arrive at 9pm and stay until 7am the next morning, leaving you fresh (or fresher) for the day ahead.

There are details of agencies which offer this service in Section Six.

# section TWO
# what is right for you

10 WHAT SORT OF FAMILY ARE YOU?
11 WHAT YOU NEED THE HELP FOR
12 AGES, GAPS, BOYS AND GIRLS
13 THE LIVE-IN OR LIVE-OUT DEBATE

## WHAT IS RIGHT FOR YOU

Now that you know all the options, it's time to examine exactly who you are, what you need, and what you want. It is best to be clear about what childcare you are looking for before you start to look for it. There are vast differences between the different types of childcare on offer and it will help to narrow down your search before you begin looking for help.

Although finding your childcare match may seem daunting at first, it is possible, with careful planning and sufficient thought, to find the right person or place for you and your family. By thinking hard about what is going to be right for you early on, you will make the process easier for yourself and your family and will be better able to avoid some of the most common mistakes we have all made. Take heart from the experiences of those who have been through it all before you.

> ### Victoria, 26, lives in Leeds and has used different types of childcare
>
> I went back to work when my daughter, Rebecca, was nearly three and I opted for a childminder initially. I thought that because my daughter had been with me all the time up until that point, a childminder would suit her better than a nursery. With hindsight, I wish I'd put her in a nursery earlier because she's absolutely blossomed.
>
> *I wish I'd put her in a nursery earlier because she's absolutely blossomed*
>
> The nursery has suited her so well. She goes in, chucks her coat at me and legs it. She's got a couple of really good friends there and she rushes off to see them and completely forgets to say goodbye to me. I have to call her back to get a kiss before I leave for work.
>
> Our childminder gave us three months' notice when she decided to stop childminding. There was a mad scramble at first, as I thought I wanted to find another childminder. But then we went to see the nursery and we all liked it straight away. We like the fact that it is small and all the children are looked after together and the ages are mixed.

*The nursery is good at telling me what my daughter has done; if she has misbehaved, why she has misbehaved, and what they've done about it. This is good because if I ask her what she has done at nursery, she says, 'Nothing'; she is practicing for school already!*

*I recently split up with Rebecca's dad, but I found it very easy to talk to the nursery and let them know what was going on. Rebecca was behaving badly for a while, but the nursery understood our situation at home and they coped fantastically well with it all, and provided a lot of support. They are consistent in their discipline, and the boundaries are clearer than they were with the childminder.*

*Rebecca starts school in September so we've found a local childminder who will be able to collect her from school and look after her until I get back from work. The childminder specialises in this kind of arrangement, so there will be other children there too, which will suit her well.*

*My tip would be to take your child with you when you go to look around a nursery. You should be able to spend some time and see how your child responds to the environment.*

## Why do you need childcare?

There are as many different reasons why families need childcare as there are types of childcare available. Consider carefully why you need childcare, and this will help you decide what childcare you need.

For many families, two incomes are a financial necessity and the idea of one parent staying at home is just not a practical reality. Both incomes are needed to keep up with the cost of living, particularly as the family expands. The cost of childcare will have to be taken into account to assess whether it is really worth both parents working. There are ways to make childcare more affordable, including voucher schemes and Working Tax Credits. There is also a government subsidy available to make it possible for every child over three to have two-and-a-half hours of nursery provision, five days a week, for 38 weeks of the year.

Families finding it hard to meet childcare costs but needing two incomes may want to explore other childcare options, such as relying on the help of family to look after their children.

Staying at home is an option which suits many parents and avoids the complications of childcare to some degree. However many at-home mothers still need extra help at crunch times of the day. Managing two school runs and a baby, for example, can pull a mother in too many directions at once. An extra pair of hands can be not only a huge advantage in this situation, but sometimes a necessity.

Finally, staying at home to look after your children, even if it is a possibility, is not for everyone. Some mothers strongly prefer to continue with work after the birth of their children. This can be for many different reasons, including wanting to maintain a sense of their own identity. Mothers may have worked for a number of years prior to having children and feel reluctant to give up on their career altogether. Working through the early years can preserve a career in the long-term. These mothers may love their work and find it professionally, emotionally and financially rewarding.

## What kind of help do you need now and in the future?

The kind of help you need will change a great deal from when you have babies and very young children, to when your children are older and at school. Parents who work full time, whose children need full-time care, will have to make sure that the kind of care they decide upon will be suitable for the changing needs of their children. Mothers at home are also likely to find that the times of day they will most benefit from help will change as their children grow older. It may suit at-home mothers with babies to have full-day care for a couple of days a week to give them a break from, or help at the beginning and end of, the day may be more appropriate. For mothers with older, school-age children, help is most likely to be appreciated during the after-school hours.

It is also important to consider carefully how long you want the arrangement you are putting in place now to last. While nothing is ever certain, you probably have some idea of if and when you might hope to have another child, which is quite likely to change the way you will arrange your childcare. Keep in the back of your mind the idea that you are probably not looking for the childcare that will suit you forever. Look for a solution for the immediate future – time frames you can be reasonably certain about. If you are pretty confident that you are looking for an arrangement that could last for five years, bear that in mind when you are interviewing or searching for your childcare match.

Don't forget to consider your finances carefully when you are looking at the options. Some childcare options may not be as out of reach as you think, but overstretching obviously leads to more stress for everyone involved. The grid in the Introduction will give you an at-a-glance impression of the costs of different kinds of childcare. There is more detail on the cost of childcare in Section Five.

Also bear in mind whether there are any important cultural issues to take into account. Perhaps you live in a multilingual household and if so, you might want your childcare to support this. You might choose to look for someone who can speak to your children in another language, or who can help you provide your children with a better understanding of their own culture and heritage.

You will undoubtedly learn along the way – of course we don't all make the perfect choice the first time round, or the second, third and fourth time round for that matter. But we do become a little less green as we go and as you learn from experience, you are more likely to be better equipped to make good choices for the future.

## Nursery or nanny?

The charity What about the Children? strongly favours one-on-one childcare in the home environment, over nursery care for young children. In this kind of environment, they argue, children can be given the individual support, love and attention that they need in order to develop well in all areas and on all levels.

However, there are many arguments for and against nursery care. Here are some points which tend to be agreed upon:

- It can be beneficial for toddlers to mix with older children, although educational development may come at the cost of emotional security. Younger children will be more challenged among older children, which can help their educational development, but they can also feel less emotionally secure with the older, physically bigger children close by, which could lead to behavioural problems.
- It is commonly observed that children who spend time in centre-based childcare can be confident and sociable compared with children who have a one-on-one childcare relationship at home.

However, it is thought by some that long hours spent at day care may have a negative effect. It is claimed that more than 30 hours a week can lead to anti-social behaviour, more than 35 hours a week can lead to children harbouring worry. Children who are cared for in a one-to-one setting either at home or with a childminder could benefit from spending some regular time at a drop-in centre, playgroup or other toddler group to improve their social skills.

- A nursery with a high proportion of trained staff can be beneficial to your child. Qualified staff at a nursery makes a positive impact on the outcomes for the children.
- Nursery-based care can be improved by the quality of the environment, including space, light, furnishings and suitable equipment. If all of these are to a high level, this will have an effect on the children's experience of and behaviour within the nursery.

## Paula, 24, is a nursery nurse in London and believes 'childcare combination' is best

I came over from South Africa when I was 16. I started working in a crèche in London while I was studying for my childcare qualifications. I absolutely love my job. I work with children between six months and 12–15 months — they move on to another room in the nursery when they can walk. It's exciting, because every day they do something new.

The children will be in my care for between six and nine months. I would prefer to stay with the same children for longer — we are all bonded and then they move up. But it is beneficial for the children to be in an age-appropriate room. It is also good for the children to be used to different adults. We can still see each other, as the two rooms are linked.

> It is also good for the children to be used to different adults

The parents are great. I make sure that I communicate with them on a daily basis. It can be daunting for new parents, leaving their child for the first time. We encourage parents to call us whenever they like and we are happy to call them during our lunch break to let them know everything is going well. We just like to reassure new parents — they can take more settling in than the babies! Some parents will even pop in during their lunch break if they are near by. We are always happy to see them.

My feeling would be that if both parents had to work full-time, an ideal situation might be to have the children looked after half the time in a nursery and half the time by a nanny. That way they could have the social interaction that a nursery offers and a one-to-one relationship with a nanny — the best of both worlds.

## What is the effect of childcare on children?

There is always something being written in the press about the effects of childcare on children. It can sometimes seem that this is designed to add to parents' concerns and stoke the fires of the great debate over whether it is better to have a parent at home with the children in the early years. The arguments over working parents and the effects of childcare on young babies and children rumble on and on. Research is constantly being undertaken, published, talked and argued about in the childcare arena, and studies continue to give out contradictory results. Some say that there is potential harm to be done to children, others that there is a great potential for good that can come out of children going to a day care setting and spending time with a variety of other children and adults.

It is very easy to read a piece of research, or another scaremongering report in a newspaper and make a snap judgement. It is important to try and avoid doing this at all costs. As we have learnt, childcare is an intensely personal issue – for the parents, the children and the family as a whole.

Studies constantly contradict each other and sometimes, even the same study can be interpreted in different ways. One of the problems with the research in this area, acknowledged by the people that carry out the studies, is that there are so many variables to be taken into account that it is hard to measure children and their experiences against each other. The number of hours per week the child spends in the childcare situation, family wealth and background, parental income and education, genetics and the amount of time that parents are able to spend with their children at home are all variables that need to be considered; variables which make it extremely difficult to draw fair comparisons.

Research tends to be able to (almost) agree on a couple of things however – that high quality childcare can be beneficial for children in the long term, and, unsurprisingly, that poor quality childcare can be detrimental for children's well-being. It is also generally accepted that children need strong connections with the people looking after them. If children are in a childcare setting where the staff are constantly changing, or there is no provision for them to have a particular relationship with one carer, the children may not feel sufficiently supported emotionally to be able to develop at their natural rate.

So, finding good childcare is of the utmost importance. But just as the perfect childcare situation for one family will not suit another, good childcare for one child will not necessarily be 'good' for another. You know your child better than anyone and we hope that with the help of this book, you will find you have a head start on deciding which will be the best route to follow for both you and your child.

# What sort of family are you?

In this chapter we will give you some of the questions you should try to answer about yourself and your family to help you find the right childcare fit. We will encourage you to examine closely your likes and dislikes, habits and personalities. Good childcare is like completing an equilateral triangle: you need to get the balance right so that all sides of the childcare triangle – parents, child and childcare provider – are balanced and in accord with each other. Examining yourself and your child will give you a head start on finding the right third side of the triangle for your family.

By thinking about your family and lifestyle, you may find that childcare choices are easier to make.

## Are you outgoing or reserved?

Do you thrive on being surrounded by friends and other families? Are you at your happiest when catering for large numbers at the last minute? If you operate best when in the middle of a busy group, or if you are happy with people coming and going, you are more likely to enjoy having someone else around. If you are happy when friends or family just drop in, rather than when you invite them, or can cope well when friends come for lunch and stay for the weekend, then you are more likely be able to reap the benefits that live-in help can offer.

## Sophie, 37, lives in London and has employed live-in nannies to look after her two boys

My husband and I are both investment bankers. A live-in nanny gives us the flexibility that we need. If we are running late in the evening it is not the end of the world. We also chose a nanny for our childcare because I wanted my children to be looked after in their home environment. I've set up loads of classes for the boys to go to so that they can socialise regularly with other children. Being looked after at home means they are able to nap in their own beds and eat the meals I choose for them.

We have a big room at the top of our house which we are able to give the nanny. We never eat meals with our live-in nanny. I put the boys to bed while she goes and has her supper in the kitchen. We have always been up-front about this at interview — it is important to me and my husband to have some time together each day.

I think it's important to lay out the ground rules with a live-in nanny right from the word go. You also mustn't be afraid to talk about anything with your nanny. Make sure you have a regular dialogue — even a review process if you like that formality. I regularly ask, 'Is there anything you want to talk about? Are you happy with the way everything is going? Is there anything about our arrangement you would like to change?' If things get bottled up it does no good to anyone.

I think it's very hard to employ a nanny for the first time. You have to hand over responsibility and control. You have to take a bit of a backseat because you have got to allow the nanny the authority with the children. Sometimes I'm dying to step in, but have to stop myself. I always try and make sure I have a couple of days off when a new nanny starts. It's good for the children to see you both together and to be able to really show a new person the ropes.

We think there are lots of benefits to having live-in help. Fewer sick days, never late for work in the morning — and a babysitter on hand. It's fun to have an extra person around for the children, too.

> It's fun to have an extra person around for the children

If you prefer to keep different elements of your life separate, if you like to compartmentalise, then care away from the home is a better idea. This doesn't mean that you are admitting to being unfriendly, but if you like your privacy and like to be left to get on with things on your own as a family you are unlikely to enjoy having someone else in your home on a permanent or even semi-permanent basis.

A childcarer coming into your home each day will have an impact on how you and your family work as a group. Childcare outside the home, either at a nursery or from a childminder, will be more separate from your family unit and life. If you and your family are a close-knit group and like to shut the doors on the world and curl up together and love the intimacy that that brings, don't invite a childcarer to share it with you. It could be an unhappy experience for everyone.

## Amanda started with live-in help and swapped to live-out when the time was right

We decided to switch from live-in help to live-out when our youngest turned two. Live-in help was fantastic when we really needed a lot of hands on deck, coping with three children close in age.

The trouble was, as soon as we didn't need the help as much, I found it irritating to have people around — and so did my husband.

Live-out help is obviously more expensive but definitely worth it when you don't need as many hours.

> *The only downside is that we don't have the flexibility we were used to with live-in help. But the best thing about live-out help is we know that when we shut the door at the end of the day, our home is our own.*

## Family activities

Consider the kinds of activities you enjoy as a family. Perhaps you and your family are particularly sporty. You might spend weekends chanting at football matches, or getting covered in mud playing football in the park. Cycling might be your activity of choice, as you lead your family on bike rides at the weekend. Or you might choose a family run, swim or tennis game.

If you are fanatical about sports, it would make sense to find a helper who can understand your passion, even if they don't necessarily share it. There is a much greater chance that you will get along if you have something in common. A sporty family who spend Saturday morning standing on freezing rugby touchlines followed by a family cycle ride will find it hard to understand an au pair who wants to spend all her free time in bed. It isn't that you would expect your au pair to join you on the touchlines and cycle routes; far from it. It's more that you are likely to get along so much better if you share some common pursuits and attitudes towards life.

If you would like your childcarer to take play sports with your children, or encourage your children in their sporting pursuits, make sure that they are sporty themselves before hiring. When you ask a candidate back for a session with the children, following a successful interview, send them all outside with a ball and see what happens. If you like your children to go swimming during the week with their carer, make sure that she will be happy to get wet and that she is a competent swimmer herself.

Some families are more musical than others. When we struggle to fit in piano practice, friends can't understand what else we would be doing with our time. Again, this is another interest you might want to share with your childcarer. Music can shape a personality and a shared passion will get you a long way in a childcare situation. If you are keen to introduce your children to music, it will of course help to find a childcarer who shares your enthusiasm. Your childcarer will be much more keen to take the children to baby music classes and instrumental lessons and encourage your children to practise their instruments, if she shares an enjoyment for music.

If you are opting for care outside of the home, look for an environment where music is played – you might be lucky enough to find a childminder who you can share this enthusiasm with. She may be happy to play music in the background during the day, and talk about what the music is and how it makes the children feel. Nurturing this kind of enthusiasm must, of course, come from the parents, but it is helpful if it is reinforced by the person that is looking after the children during the day.

## Quiet or noisy?

Think about what you enjoy doing with your down time at home, and what you would like your children to be encouraged to do. Perhaps instilling a love of reading is top of your list of priorities, or perhaps you enjoy spending time as a family playing board games. How do you feel about television, movies and time spent at a computer, either playing games or online? It is a good idea to bear in mind your own preferences when you are looking for childcare and to share your thoughts with your eventual childcarer. It will be confusing for children to be allowed to do one thing with their parents, and a different one with their carer – unless you consciously look for this to give your children a very balanced upbringing. You might prefer the time your children spend with their carer to reflect the activities and interests you share as a family, or use that time to provide a contrast for your children. Some families actively look for a childcarer who will offer a counterbalance to the activities they enjoy with their children.

Do you want someone who will read to your children for hours on end? Our twins loved sitting curled up on the sofa with a pile of books with our au pair – it was a happy, peaceful time for everyone. You might prefer your childcarer to spend lots of time running around in the park, rain or shine.

## Where do animals feature?

Not to be too simplistic – but if you are dog lovers, check with prospective candidates that they are happy with this before they come for an interview. Daily or live-in childcare will need to have a relationship with your pets as well as with your children. Check for allergies, which could rule out a candidate before interview stage.

Even if you don't have pets now, but are planning to add to your family in this way in the near future, check with your prospective childcarer that she will be comfortable with this new arrangement, especially if you will be expecting her to look after the pets as well as the children during her working day.

If you have a menagerie at home and you are out at work, you might want to look for a childcarer to look after the children and the animals. Be clear about this extra role at interview.

## Josh, 33, lives in Somerset and explains why he wanted a nanny who would be comfortable around dogs

We are in the countryside and always look for someone who likes rural life. We have two chocolate Labradors and we're surrounded by farmland. We agreed there was no point taking on a girl who had come from a city and who would feel isolated and nervous going down the lanes and with the dogs. The girl we took grew up on a farm not far from here. She looks after the dogs and will take them out walking with the children.

## Tidy or messy?

If you have an immaculate home, like everything to be in exactly the right place, and have achieved the near-impossible by continuing to live like this as your family has grown, then this will affect the kind of childcare that will suit you best. If you fall into this category and are out at work all day, you may prefer to take your children out of the house for the day for their childcare, so that your pristine home remains so.

Care in the home will undoubtedly involve mess. It is good for children from a certain age to be allowed to paint, model play dough (which will inevitably get onto the floor and into the carpet) and enjoy messy play with water. If you can't bear for this to go on around you at home, a nursery or childminder could be a great option for you – be sure to look for a nursery or childminder with lots of messy play opportunities.

If, on the other hand, you don't mind being surrounded by total chaos and the last time you had a proper clear out was when you nested prior to the arrival of your first child (join the club), you could save yourself the trip to the nursery or childminder and have your childcare take place at home. Following this to extremes, you might ideally find a nanny share with a mother who can't bear the idea of it all happening in her home, thereby sharing the cost, gathering all the brownie points from the other family, having the nanny share take place in your house and enjoy all the advantages that has to offer (laundry, errands, deliveries) and still not mind a messy house at the end of the day. Perfect.

## Town, city or rural?

If you live in a city you will probably have more childcare options available to you. There will be a higher density of nurseries, more childminders in your local area, a greater chance of another family nearby keen to set up a nanny share. It is also likely to be easier to find a childcarer to live in with you (assuming you have the space), especially if you are near the centre of a city or town, or near good transport links.

The location of your home will also affect the kind of candidate you are likely to see for interview. Some nannies, mother's helps and au pairs, particularly if coming from abroad, will be tempted by a job in a big city. It might make your post easier to fill, but be aware of the flip side – you are much more likely to have your live-in help coming back to your home late after a night out. There are lots of tales of au pairs asleep when they are supposed to be helping at breakfast, after a night out on the town. If you are a family who likes to be tucked up early, whether you live a city life or a country life, be careful about whom you hire. A party animal will not suit you well and you may be better off with childcare provided outside the home, or at least live-out help.

If you are a family living in a remote, rural area, you may be tempted to have a live-in helper to avoid a long commute to a nursery or a childminder. Be sure you have fully thought through all the implications this will have for you as country dwellers. Make sure a potential live-in helper has fully understood your location, be clear about transport links and whether she would be able to reach the nearest town independently. Most of all, be prepared to spend more time with your help as a live-in childcare provider is much more likely to be dependent on you for her social life if your home is far from a town centre, where she is likely to be able to find friends.

So, have a good long think about yourself, your partner and your family. You could make lists of what you like to do to help you clarify your thoughts. Be honest about your feelings about untidiness, extra people and noise. How do you think where you live will affect your needs and the kind of candidate you are likely to attract? You may be easily able to see after this process that you are better suited to one kind of childcare over another and be well on the way to solving your childcare conundrum.

## Heather, 51, is a mother of three, and lives in rural Devon

We've had about eight au pairs over the years. Working with an au pair has always been a team effort. To begin with, I guide and help them. As they become more confident, I leave them to get on with things and stop always peering over their shoulder.

I always enjoyed doing art and craft with my children and was always looking for someone who was creative. We also love cooking. Lots of pastry-making, tarts, cookies, you name it. I wanted the children to learn to cook and it was also good for the au pairs — they could practise English by reading recipes and they were improving their life-skills too — some of them arrived unable to cook a thing!

You need to find an au pair with the same sort of outlook as you. We live in the country, on a farm, a couple of miles from the nearest town. We needed au pairs suited to our lifestyle, not someone expecting shopping and nightlife — it's just not here!

> *Find an au pair with the same sort of outlook as you*

The majority of the time we had successful partnerships. We have had some hiccups, and some didn't suit, but on the whole we've been very lucky. I'm a nurse and was having to work shifts; my husband is out on the farm, and although he pops in and out during the day I couldn't depend on him for childcare. Live-in help suited us well because of the flexibility that it offers.

We found our au pairs through an agency, who would interview the au pairs and match them with us. The agency would provide us with some information and then we could contact each other by phone.

I started with a 17-year-old. She was the eldest of six children and was used to being at home, cooking and helping her mum to occupy the five younger children. I was a little bit concerned to begin with because I thought she was very young, but it worked out very well. We are still in touch — she's married now, with three children of her own. We used to have tears when the au pairs left. You can make a friend for life. We've just been to Turkey for an old au pair's wedding; she was with us for three years and left nearly five years ago now. The more you put in to a relationship with an au pair, the better it will be. We've always encouraged our children to make welcome cards, and try to help our au pairs meet up with others in the area.

We've had two unsuccessful au pairs over the years. It was very difficult and I didn't like asking them to leave, but it's better to do it quickly if you realise that the au pair has a different agenda and isn't really prepared to help you in the way that you need.

Our children have usually bonded well with our au pairs — my fourteen-year-old daughter chats to our au pair about make-up and fashion. We have learnt that when a new au pair first arrives, you have to make plenty of allowances for the language barrier and be flexible about how you want things to be done.

> Try and match an au pair's profile to your family and your way of life

My advice would be to try and match an au pair's profile to your family and your way of life. If you can offer an au pair something in return, something of interest to her, she is likely to be happy, which will get you all off to a good start.

# What you need the help for

Try to examine this closely and be clear about what exactly you want. If you are returning to work, be as definite as you can be about your working schedule. If you are staying at home and looking for back up, avoid hiring a nanny if you actually need more help around the house – everyone will be disappointed. If you are working from home you may be choosing between having your child or children out of the house for the day at a nursery or childminder, and having someone look after them at home so that you are able to have more contact during the day. Whatever you need the help for, for however many hours and for however many days of the week – welcome to the world of juggling.

## Working full time

If you are returning to work full-time, you will need to consider the full care options. If you have pre-school age children, these will range from nursery to childminder to nanny, either shared with another family or your own. Mother's helps and au pairs are not suitable for parents of young children who work full-time. If your children are of school age, you may be able to drop them off yourself in the mornings and manage with an after-school nanny or babysitter who can collect the children from school in the afternoons and look after them until you come home. Alternatively, an after-school club can provide care at this time of day. After-school nannies, babysitters and clubs may be able to provide childcare during the holidays, or you might be able to call on grandparents or other family or friends to help out during the school holidays.

When looking at nurseries, you need to be very sure that the opening hours will be long enough to suit your working hours. You could be the first to drop off every morning, but you will not be popular if you are the last to collect, after the official hours, every day. Be realistic about when you will be able to collect your children. If you are regularly late, you may even be given notice that you will have to leave the nursery and look elsewhere for childcare. The same will be true with a childminder, though there is likely to be a little more flexibility in that childcare scenario.

When considering employing a nanny to look after your children at home, be honest about your working schedule. If you and your partner are often required to work late at short notice, you might be better off with a live-in nanny, rather than one who expects to be leaving at a fixed time each day. A live-in nanny, of course, needs to know her regular working hours and will need to be paid on top for every extra hour that she works. Give as much notice as you are able to if you are going to be late back. Always running a little late is unacceptable for your childcarer – remember that she has had a long day at work, too. Constant lateness, relying on her good nature or pushing of boundaries will put pressure on the relationship and quickly lead to unnecessary tension.

If you work full-time, you may want to consider a nanny over a nursery, budget allowing. It will help the smooth running of your household to have an adult present for some or all of the day to accept deliveries, answer calls, be in for the washing-machine engineer and keep an eye on pets. Discuss all this at interview stage if you are hoping that your childcarer will take on these extra roles, to avoid disappointment further down the line.

Young children find home a settling and reassuring place to be. When both parents are working long hours, you may find that the children's hours away from home start to become excessive. Children enjoy being in a familiar setting, in their own home, with their own things. On the other hand, it can also be beneficial for children to have a different experience, away from home – by going to a nursery or childminder they have a chance to experience another environment, broaden their horizons and try out some new things.

## Susie, 28, works full-time and lives in the West Midlands. She sent her daughter to a day nursery until the age of five.

The nursery was great when our daughter was young. It offered us everything we were looking for. We wanted her to interact with other children as she is an only child. The nursery also offered us guaranteed childcare — I was worried that with a childminder I would have had to cope with potential sick days and so on. I think nursery also prepared her really well for school. She learnt her shapes and numbers at nursery and wasn't at all afraid to start school.

It was so hard leaving her when she was four months old. But she was so happy and content that I had to get over my own insecurity issues. I had looked at several nurseries and I just got a good feeling with the one we chose. It had a family feel to it — there were even members of the same family working there. I had to make one complaint about their opening hours — I had a long commute to work and they were meant to open at 7.15am but they kept turning up late, which then made me late. My complaint was dealt with well and the issue was resolved.

I think nursery was brilliant for my daughter. She is a confident young girl who is happy talking to other children, teenagers or adults.

> I had to get over my own insecurity issues

## Working part time

If you work a set number of days a week you will probably be looking at either hiring a nanny, either for yourself on the days that you need the help, or as part of a share, or exploring the nursery and childminder options.

You may want a nanny at home, who can organise things for the household in your absence. This way your children will stay in their familiar environment, doing all the things they would do with you on your at-home days. They will be able to go to the same park, have meals at home and go on trips to the local shops – just with a different carer.

Spending a day at a nursery or with a childminder is of course a total contrast to being at home but offers social time, a chance to interact with a group and can be particularly good for older or only children, giving them a chance to learn to interact and share. Nursery may suit a mother who works part-time – it can be simpler to have the childcare outside the home, leaving the mother able to run her home the way she likes it to be on her days off with her children. Children may really enjoy the contrast that a couple of days at nursery or with a childminder will provide to their days at home and can really benefit from being in this kind of setting for a number of hours each week.

Some parents with the budget to allow it will hire childcare to cover an extra day over their working days each week. Parents, especially those of young children, can find it extremely useful to have an extra day to get things straight or to do some of the family chores unencumbered by babies and toddlers. Others will want to gather their children round them at every opportunity they have.

## Sophie, 37, lives in London and employs her nanny for more days than she works

I employ my nanny for five days a week and I work for three days a week. This gives me the flexibility I need for work — sometimes I have to go in to the office on my days off. I really enjoy being able to have a bit of time to myself — I love playing tennis. This arrangement also sometimes allows me to spend time with just one of the boys, which is great fun.

## Working from home

This is tricky. You need to do a full day's work, but you are at home, and will inevitably have some breaks. Would you like to see your child in those breaks, and is it practical to your working day for you to do so? In their ideal world, some parents might choose to have a nanny at home so that they can see their children during the day – all have lunch together, perhaps. This gives parents an idea of the comings and goings of the day, contact with their child, as well as an ability to keep a close eye on the nanny – especially useful when there is a new nanny with the family.

There is, however, a downside to this scenario. In a situation where parents are working in one part of the house and children are being looked after in another, parents are incredibly likely to become involved at moments they would rather be left alone. You may find it impossible to get on with work while all the fun is going on without you downstairs, or you may find that you become involved at times when the nanny needs to be disciplining the children. You may simply decide it is too difficult for your children to grasp that you need to be left alone. A nanny share may be the perfect solution in this set up, especially if the share can take place at the other family's house half the time – that way you really might get the best of both worlds.

The other options to consider here are taking your children out to a nursery or a childminder, giving them a change of scene and you a chance to return to a quiet house to get on with your work.

## In need of extra help at home

You may be at home with your children full-time, not trying to balance work and home life, but trying to keep your head above water. In this situation, many parents still find themselves in need of an extra pair of hands. Reasons for needing extra help can range from having children close in age who all need lots of attention, or children spread over a wide age range with different needs and interests. You may have a child or children with special needs and want the support that an extra adult can give. If you, the parent, are going to be around most of the time, you will be looking for help in a shared care situation. A mother's help, a young and inexperienced nanny wanting to gain experience, or an au pair can all be perfect for shared care roles.

When you are in a shared care situation, it is particularly important to be sure about what kind of help you are looking for. If you hire an au pair or mother's help, you can expect some help around the house, but you must be prepared to hand over the children to your helper's care from time to time. Your mother's help or au pair will quickly tire of being your live-in cleaner, if she was (quite reasonably) expecting something different (see Section One, outlining duties). Be careful to allow some fun tasks and time playing with your children during each working day.

Extra help for an at-home mother can be required at surprising times. Just when you think you have survived the crazy days of babies and toddlers and find your children going off to school, it is not uncommon to realise you suddenly need more help, not less. The busy schedule of after-school activities, homework and playdates can prove impossible for one parent to manage on their own.

You will have experienced stressful points in the day with babies and young children – first thing in the morning, last thing at night, or perhaps a toddler's collection time from nursery when the baby is desperate for a sleep. Then all the children's routines will change (again) and you will be faced with a new set of challenges. There are times and ages that work well together and are easier to manage – we found one at school and two (the same age) at home in the year before they too started school was a good patch! But just when you think it will all be so much easier, is when so many at-home mothers find all the routines change for the five-hundredth time and they need some extra back-up again.

If you are at home with your children but need extra help, think hard about the role you want that help to play. When you are leaving your children in the care of others all day, it is clear that you need your childcare provider to be able to dispense care and discipline in the right balance. If you are at home with your helper, do you need someone fun to be around or someone to give some discipline? Don't hire a young, fun person and then expect her to play bad cop to your good cop. It is worth examining yourself quite closely here and the way you want to be with your children and the way you hope others would behave towards them.

If a parent is going to be at home as well as the helper, think about the skills that you need that helper to have. Does she need to be able to drive, or will she be able to collect children on the bus? Do you want someone to help with homework and music practice, or are you planning to look after that side of things, while your helper gets on with cooking supper in the background? Do you need the help to be practical or intellectual?

Examine closely whether you have the time or patience to help your helper – either with learning the ropes when you hire someone with little or no experience, or with language, when you hire someone with little or no spoken English. It is likely that an au pair, for example, will be here to improve her language skills. Finding yourself listening to your au pair read after you have listened to two children read aloud is not for everyone. Do you have the time and energy that this relationship can require?

## Elizabeth, 42, has four children and has experience with au pairs. She lives in Derbyshire

My au pair really helps me out — with four children I'm always popping out to take a child to Cubs or collect from a swimming lesson, and with an au pair I don't have to take all the children with me all the time. My au pair offers me back up, too. I know she is there to collect from school if I am delayed by caring for my mum, for example.

The way that I see it is that the relationship has to be beneficial to both parties and because I am at home, we've got to get along. But I'm not looking for another friend, and we've been lucky because our au pairs have been fairly independent. What I say to my new au pair girls is: 'If I'm not happy with something I will tell you and if you're not happy with something you must tell me. Don't brood about things; its better to get them out in the open.'

> We've got to get along. But I'm not looking for another friend

We chose an au pair because of the flexibility. I wanted someone to help out, not to take charge of my children for me. Our au pair has two days off a week. At the beginning, I'll say, 'This is what I want from you on a regular basis, but it might change. I'll be flexible if you are, and we'll work it out between us.' When a new girl arrives, I spend the first week showing her around. That way she can find out exactly how things work in our family. The second week I'll give her tasks to do. I do all the cooking and shopping, but then I might expect her to do the tidying up after we've eaten. She might do the bath time and I'll do story time. You need to lay down your house

> I wanted someone to help out, not to take charge of my children for me

rules early on — things like visitors coming over and where she can watch television in the evening.

I've used the same agency each time because I've been happy with every single person they have sent me — apart from the first one! They've always said, 'Never take somebody unless you feel 100% confident.' The agency might send me loads of details, but I always try to go with my gut instinct.

It helps if an au pair's introductory letter says they love children. The letter should give you an idea of their interests — if a girl says she likes walking and cycling, we are off to a good start, as it's great round here for those activities.

I like to talk to an au pair at least twice on the phone before we agree for her to come to us. The first call to say, 'Are you interested in us? Do you know enough about our family? Do you have any questions?'; the second time to say, 'Are there any questions you forgot to ask last time?' because girls can be very nervous the first time you speak on the phone. I wasn't that keen initially on the au pair I have now — we struggled to understand each other on the phone during our first call. I emailed her a list of questions and she called me back with answers which she had obviously spent a lot of time researching. She had showed me she was committed to trying to make it work and it has turned out fantastically well. She has been with us ten months and has just asked to stay another year.

## Help with young babies

Do you need some help with looking after little babies? Experience helps enormously here. Some families will hire a maternity nurse to help in the early days. We have looked at the very specific role of maternity nurses in Chapter Eight. You might consider hiring a maternity nurse if you are looking for help with settling your baby into a routine, when you are hoping for some help at night so that you can sleep well and recover from the birth, or perhaps to give you a little space in the day away from the new baby, to give you time with your other children. Having someone in the house whose sole responsibility is the baby can clearly be liberating for everyone else in that household.

## Shirin, 40, has employed a maternity nurse to help her with a premature baby

I already had help at home with my two boys when I fell pregnant with my third son. I thought that my mother's help would be enough support with the new baby, but I realised about halfway through my pregnancy that my baby was going to be premature. My blood pressure went up and I generally wasn't very well. It was a very stressful and emotional pregnancy, with lots of complications. I delivered Henry at 34 weeks. When I was still feeling awful after the delivery, I was encouraged by my family to hire a maternity nurse.

When the maternity nurse came for interview, I was immediately impressed, because she said, 'My job isn't just to look after the baby, it's to look after you, too.' She was fantastic. Her confidence around babies allowed me to relax and give her the responsibility for the baby. All the stress melted away. In two days my blood pressure went back to normal. We booked the maternity nurse for three weeks and then extended to six as she was making such a difference. Then the only reason we let her go was because she had to go to her next job.

> My job isn't just to look after the baby, it's to look after you, too.

We found our maternity nurse through an agency which was recommended to us. They were very efficient. They sent us the maternity nurse to interview the day after my call, and I decided to go with my gut feeling that she would work out well, rather than spending time going to lots more agencies.

The maternity nurse completely took over when it came to the baby. She was rather a good cook and would make me lunch each day because she

> knew I wasn't well. The maternity nurse also trained up my mother's help to take over after she'd left. She showed her how to bath the baby, how to change nappies and prepare milk. She was generous in sharing her knowledge.
>
> Our maternity nurse helped settle our third baby into a routine. My older two sons were awful sleepers but my last child sleeps beautifully. It could have been a coincidence but I think that the experience of the maternity nurse really made a difference.

If you are planning to go back to work early on and leave a young baby at home with a nanny, be sure to only interview candidates with lots of experience with babies. Not all nannies have this – experience with newborns can be hard to come by, as so many mothers wait a few months before returning to work. Check references carefully. Babies under six months need specific care and attention – obviously not more than at any other age, but definitely a little different. Some families persuade their maternity nurse to stay on, but this is an extremely costly way of hiring a nanny and is also often impossible, even if you fall in love with the idea, as maternity nurses are often booked up months in advance. Don't set your heart on it.

## Temporary help

You may find you suddenly need some extra help to get you and your family through a difficult patch of one kind or another, or to cover while your regular help is away on holiday. Perhaps you are the primary carer and you are taken ill. Perhaps your regular nanny is taken ill, or breaks her leg. You may be able to call on family and friends in the short term.

> ### Sophie, 37, from Wandsworth, has fallen back on help from grandparents in between nannies
> We asked grandparents to help out in between nannies. It turned up trumps. It is wonderful because the boys have been able to spend loads more time than

usual with their grandparents and you know, deep down, that there is no one better to look after them.

The negative side is that you can't be too particular about how you want things done because you don't want to tread on their toes. For us this is just short-term, so I'm happy to let a few things slide. I also find that I have to plan for the children a lot more — with a nanny I can delegate more responsibility. The grandparents will take on the children, but I'll still be planning food and taking care of all the washing and ironing and other chores that a nanny might take on. From the grandparents' point of view, they can find it exhausting — I think they forget how tiring children are for a whole day!

However, if you need extra help for an extended period, you may have to resort to some form of paid childcare. The simplest option here, if you can see light at the end of the tunnel, is to hire a temporary nanny or mother's help.

A temporary role will require no long-term commitment from either side. The most popular way to find this kind of help is through an agency. Agencies are experienced in placing temporary nannies and mother's helps with families in a time of crisis, or with families needing some extra support in the short term.

## Natasha, 44, lives and works in Clapham. She has hired temporary nannies to look after her two children

I work full-time and we have a live-in nanny. We have hired temporary nannies to cover holiday periods. I wouldn't want to use temporary nannies often because they appear to come out of the blue to the children. I'm a great believer in consistency as far as children are concerned. Whenever we've had a nanny change I've always had the new nanny coming in for at least one, possibly for two weeks, to do an overlap with the existing nanny. If you're having a temporary nanny because your usual nanny is on holiday for two weeks, obviously it doesn't really make sense to have a week's overlap. Often a temporary nanny won't be available for that long anyway. We try to have a two-day overlap, which in the past has worked well.

I went to our regular agencies when I needed a temporary nanny. There are three agencies that we have hired through successfully in the past. They all know enough about me to be able to send me suitable candidates.

The first time round, we found a wonderful temporary nanny. She had been a temporary nanny for three years when she came to us. She enjoyed being able to be flexible and to choose when she worked. She was absolutely fantastic. We had another temp last year who was between jobs. She'd worked in a nursery as well as with a family and she was great too. I did find that our temporary nannies were a bit more lax on the discipline side than our permanent nannies. As it's only for two weeks to cover a holiday period, I'm not too fussed about it.

If parents are thinking of using a temporary nanny to cover a holiday, my advice would be to plan ahead as much as possible. A handover period is brilliant because it really helps facilitate the transition. Try to have a stock of agencies you trust up your sleeve, which will be able to find you somebody at the drop of a hat.

> *A handover period is brilliant because it really helps facilitate the transition*

The nannies that agencies send out as temps are usually very experienced and will be able to hit the ground running. They will have particularly asked for this kind of work and will most likely have chosen it as they relish change and a challenge, as well as probably enjoying the flexibility that it offers. A temporary nanny will be able to come in to your home, quickly pick up the pieces, take the reins and cotton on to all your requirements and routines. They will be used to establishing a bond with new children quickly. When there is pressure on a family to cope with a sudden emergency or change in situation, it will help enormously to know that there is a capable person looking after their children and taking care of everything at home.

## Sarah works as a temporary nanny

I arrived in England while travelling around the world and I didn't know how long I was going to stay over here. I felt it would be inappropriate for me to take on a permanent position as a nanny.

I'm registered with a great agency. They know me well and won't put me forward for a job without consulting me first, which is nice. They really look after their nannies. We keep in touch and they can call me at the last minute. It's important to take on as much work as possible when doing temporary work, as there can sometimes be a bit of a lull.

When I came over here I had just left a family I'd been working with for two and a half years. I had become quite close to them — it was hard to leave. I was looking for temp work because I had been with that family so long that I wanted to get back into working with lots of different families. It's a bit like a relationship — you don't want to jump in to another one right away! You develop habits and routines with children and can become so used to one child and what they want and need. By working with different families you can get a fresh perspective. I also liked the freedom that temporary work offers —

> *Working with different families you can get a fresh perspective*

especially in terms of travel. I've worked all over the place and seen lots of different places that I probably would never have seen. I think I have learnt a lot more from being a temporary nanny than I did working with one family, because I have been through so many different experiences and seen things from different points of view.

It is very different working as a temp, to working as a full-time nanny. When you're temping, quite often you're just thrown into a situation, with very little preparation. You usually meet the family the week before, so that the kids can see you and then you'll just rock up Monday morning. I might have five minutes with the mother while she quickly points things out and leaves a list of things the children have to do and maps of how to get there — things like that. My first temp job was a bit daunting, but the more you do it the more you get used to being thrown in at the deep end.

Some families will hire a temporary nanny when they are in between nannies. I think it can be quite hard for the children. They may well have gone through a couple of nannies and a couple of temp nannies before I arrive. When I go in I try and make it as easy on the kids as possible, because it can be quite confusing for the younger ones. I try to make sure that I don't change the children's routine too much — we will stick to what the parents want us to do and their usual plans.

I think families tend to treat their temporary nannies in the same way that they would treat their full-time nanny — my relationship with the mother varies with each job. When you are working with a family as a temp the parents are often busy trying to find a full-time nanny and you're really there to keep the children busy in the meantime. However, in my last job the mother was absolutely lovely, we got along really well and she still calls me to make sure I'm doing well. I worked with another family for a week and hardly spoke to the mother, but that was just the way she was with her nannies.

I would advise parents to make sure the temporary nanny spends at least a couple of hours, or even a day, with the current nanny, if at all possible. Nannies and parents do things differently and I think it's more helpful for a temporary nanny to learn the ropes with the full-time nanny — a 'nanny handover' can help things to run smoothly.

## Children with special needs

A family may find they need extra help if one of their children develops special needs. This could be a long- or short-term issue. If a child is taken ill and you have other children to look after, you may find that you need extra help to get you through. Relatives can step in if they live close by and are able to give the time and commitment, though research shows that parents of children with special needs are less likely than parents of children without special needs to call on help from grandparents. If family support is not possible, parents may go down the temporary care route, outlined above for short-term needs or solutions.

Research in this field also highlights the fact that parents of children with special needs, particularly parents of children whose special needs are statemented (recognised and then provided for through a formal procedure), tend to experience more difficulty in finding childcare, especially at short notice, than parents of children without special needs.

In the case of children with long-term special needs, the childcare requirements will need to be reassessed altogether. You may need to enable a child to get to a centre each day where his needs can be catered for. If the child with special needs can still be well integrated into the family life, but there are particular demands that have to be met to cope with that child, you may need a specially trained childcarer to help your family manage. You may be looking for specific skills when looking for childcare – for example a nanny who knows sign language for a deaf child, who might also be able to help to teach the other children in the family to sign.

## Kate, 37, from Holland Park, has employed nannies to help with her busy family. One of her children has special needs

My son was under one when I found out I was expecting twins. I knew I wouldn't be going back to work and would need an extra pair of hands. We hired a nanny to come and help out and get used to us all before the birth.

At the beginning it was all rather informal. Our first nanny was about 25 and had quite a lot of experience. We're still in touch and I adore her. I was literally looking for another me. I wasn't looking for a disciplinarian or someone who could instil routine, I wanted someone who could play with my son, bond with him, get dirty with him in the park. I was just looking for someone I could rumble along with during the day.

Of course we all knew twins were on the way, so life would become pretty full on. None of us could have predicted quite how full on. Our girls were born three months' premature — our lives and my nanny's job changed overnight. The girls were in intensive care for three months. Our nanny was suddenly in charge of shopping, running the house and my son's day-to-day care, because I had to spend an enormous amount of time in the hospital. When they came out of hospital they were both taking enormous amounts of drugs so my nanny then was incredibly helpful with preparing syringes and helping me bath the babies.

When Imogen was diagnosed as being profoundly deaf, I came back from the hospital in pieces. By an extraordinary coincidence, our nanny's previous family had a deaf child, too, so she was amazing. I think it was fate that we had hired her — she knew what we had to do straight away.

I have never been particularly impressed by qualifications. I think personality is so important. I can teach someone what I want them to do. Some candidates aren't interested in our job — it is hard work with three children, sixteen months apart, one of whom is profoundly deaf. There are other jobs down the road with two children, one at school all day, for the same money. I am looking for the nanny who says, 'Great, what a challenge, I can learn so much in this role.' I'm looking for a nanny who isn't afraid of our set up, who is keen to broaden her experience and learn.

> I am looking for the nanny who says, 'Great, what a challenge, I can learn so much in this role.'

We had one awful experience. Day two with a new nanny was the girls' second birthday and Tom was singing happy birthday to them — again and again and again. The nanny was making sandwiches and shouted, 'Can you just shut up, you're doing my head in!' She was fired on the spot. We stuck with another nanny because she was so good with Immy. With hindsight, we should have parted ways earlier. She was always leaving the key in the front door, the cars unlocked, telling me where I was going wrong. It's hard making sure you have the balance right between someone being great with the children and easy to be around in a shared-care role.

I actually quite enjoy the interview process. Most nannies will interview very well and will tell you what you want to hear. I always ask whether they have ever been fired. It puts them on the spot. I think parents have the right to ask probing questions — if the nanny doesn't want to answer, that is their choice. I ask who they live with and I always ask about their family. I always ask a nanny to come for a trial day before she starts with us. It gives us a chance to see what she is really like with the children. I also try to ask some unusual questions.

People say a nanny will either last two weeks or two years. I think if you know pretty quickly it's not going to work out, you shouldn't be afraid to say so. Having a nanny gives me flexibility. The only bad thing is that sometimes I feel that there are just too many people around — it can be hard not to tread on each other's toes.

> People say a nanny will either last two weeks or two years

---

Childcare places for children with special needs or disabilities can be hard to come by – provision of places is much lower than for children without these extra needs to be fulfilled. Resources are less available, because so many extra facilities are required to cope with children with disabilities. Childcare for these children also tends to be more expensive – a report for DfES in 2005 suggested that parents of disabled children face three times the cost of childcare as parents of children without special needs. The DfES report refers to another report by the Joseph Rowntree Foundation that suggests that 95% of children with disabilities are looked after at home – the reasons for this statistic are likely to include lack of availability and cost, as well as parents often wanting, or needing, to provide this care themselves.

# Ages, gaps, boys and girls

When thinking about the kind of childcare that will suit you best, you will need to take into account the ages, age range and sex of your children. Your childcare needs will change over time – it is unusual to find a childcare situation that will see you through, or, realistically, that will suit everyone equally if you have more than a couple of children. As we said in Section One, the days of a nanny who stays with a family to raise all the children are all but gone – now we are much more likely to chop and change, adapting our childcare solutions to our changing needs as a family.

## How many children do you have?

Have a quick head count! All options are open to you, of course, with any number of children, but there are different factors, including cost and logistics, which you will want to take into account.

With one child, you will probably find that you are able to drop off at a nursery or with a childminder fairly easily on the way to work in the morning. Two, and things get a little more complicated. Three, and you have a major operation on your hands to get out of the house first thing in the morning.

For two or more children, the cost of a nursery place or a childminder and a nanny who will look after two children start to look a little closer. Paying for three children at a private nursery will cost the same, if not more, as the cost of a nanny, in most cases.

The more children you have, the greater your age range is likely to be (see below), unless you are one of the families we occasionally hear about with two sets of twins or even twins and triplets under the age of four...

## How old are your children?

Childcare, like schools, will be an issue for parents to think about whether their children are babies or teenagers. You will need to start off planning for babies – but remember that your baby is growing every day. It is unrealistic to be trying to plan for the far-off future from the outset, but it is important to recognise that if you need childcare, it is something that is likely to stay with you for a long time to come.

Babies, toddlers and pre-schoolers all require slightly different kinds of childcare. Their schedules will be different and you will want them to do different things at different ages. It's not all over when your children start school, either. The school day is much shorter than a regular working day, and there are holidays to plan for approximately every two months. If you are planning to be working full-time, you will need to plan for someone to collect your children from school and take care of them during the holidays.

Parents of babies and pre-schoolers will need experienced, perhaps qualified, childcare when they are planning to go back to work – the choice here is likely to be between nurseries, childminders and nannies. If you are at home, needing extra help with children of this age, you could look at options including mother's helps and au pairs, or a shared-care nanny if you think you need your childcarer to be more independent.

With older children, an au pair could be suitable for collecting from school and looking after the children until the end of the working day. Perhaps your children could go to friends or grandparents during the holidays, or you could look into an arrangement such as the one offered by after-school nannies.

## What is the age range of your children?

A competent nanny will be able to cope with children in one family ranging in age from babies to children at primary school and even older. You will also be making the most of your nanny – a good excuse for a larger family! Some families decide to keep employing a full-time nanny, even when the youngest has gone to school. If you can make this work financially, this makes great sense from every point of view.

It will be a fantastic asset to a family to be able to employ a childcarer who knows your family and your children, can look after the children after school and during the holidays, walk the dog during the daytime and to be at home on the occasional day that one of the children might be too poorly to go to school (but not so poorly that they need their mummy).

## Alison is a lawyer and mother of four children, who are all school-age and older. She lives in Chiswick and employs a full-time nanny.

We have four children. When the youngest began full-time school at the age of four, the others were aged ten, thirteen and sixteen. At that stage all of them were at different day schools in west/central London.

We did not really make a formal decision to continue with the day care being provided by a full-time nanny. We already had someone in the post, who had come to us when our youngest daughter was just starting nursery school a year before. She was used to us and we to her, and the arrangement was working reasonably well. She could drive well in London traffic, which was essential since our youngest's school was some way from our house, and she was also fond of our labrador dog, who needed to be taken for walks during the day.

It was also important to us (and still is) to have the reliability of someone in or around the house during the day — whether for errands or deliveries or to cover in holidays or during periods of illness — and for the necessary tidying, shopping and food preparation to be done. In addition we wanted the person providing the care in our absence to have English as her first language and for there to be continuity and a good relationship, so that she and the children felt comfortable.

Over the years (my youngest daughter is now nine), inevitably the job has changed. In particular the relationship between the nanny and our two eldest children, both of whom have left school (perhaps even with the third as well), is much more 'big sister' than nanny.

When we last recruited — about a year ago — I advertised for a 'nanny / housekeeper' and stressed that the job did involve all sorts of household tasks (including a lot of tidying; we were, at that stage, one of the untidiest houses in London, I suspect, and there was just never enough time to sort stuff out).

When I was interviewing, I described the job as 'doing all the things which I would do if I were here'. Of course it cannot be exactly that, because it is not fair to expect someone else to make those executive decisions about which of your child's beloved first dresses you keep and which you give away, but it does involve taking the car in for servicing, picking up the dry cleaning, monitoring the library books, ringing the local council for planning permission forms and so on and so on.

It is an expensive option, but if you can afford it and get the right person, I think it can be worth it.

My husband has a job which can keep him at work for long hours and, although I do not go to the office on Fridays and make a point of getting back reasonably early each evening, I could not keep my job going without quite a lot of help at home, because, with emails and blackberries and mobile phones, the demands of the clients are always pressing. Plus it is important for the children to have someone to whom they can turn fairly immediately — if they have forgotten something, or want to invite a friend over, or want to discuss something.

As with many things, how well it works is very much dependent on the character of the people involved — us and them — and on good

> I described the job as 'doing all the things which I would do if I were here'

> It is an expensive option, but if you can afford it and get the right person, I think it can be worth it.

communication. It can be quite a lonely life for the nanny / housekeeper during term time, with quite a lot of time on their hands. Certainly here, it is very important for them to take the initiative and organise their time during the school day (once we have together worked out roughly what needs to be done, priorities etc.).

We have talked with previous nannies about the possibility of their combining working with us with doing training courses, during the time when the children are at school, if they wanted that, but none so far has done so. Our present one loves walking the dog (she has owned a dog before, but cannot keep one in her flat) and cooking, so the dog is having a great time and the children are eating well! I think that she values the independence (as compared, say, with shop or office work) which the job gives her, plus I hope she likes being with us — at least most of the time.

If you are looking for childcare with a young baby or a toddler and are hoping for and planning more children in the near future, it might be a good idea to share this information with your potential childcarer. A nanny might like to know what she is getting into; a childminder might be able to look ahead and plan to make a space for your newborn when the time comes. A nursery can sell itself to you by pointing out any sibling discount and showing off their baby room to encourage you to send your children to their centre.

Try to think ahead when looking for the right childcare solution. You are highly unlikely to be able to solve your childcare conundrum for ever, but you could solve it in the short term by looking ahead a little. If you are pregnant, or hoping to have another baby soon, you may want to plan to keep your childcare in place even when your are on maternity leave. A child who goes to nursery full-time while you work, for example, could drop to going a couple of days a week while you are on maternity leave. That way, the older sibling still has continuity of care and will probably even enjoy going out to her own activity because she is such a big girl, while giving you a chance to spend time quietly, without distraction, with your new baby.

You may like to mix and match your childcare – perhaps a nursery for the baby and an after-school club and a holiday club for your older children. This will all take a little more organising and will rely on you being home from work on time to manage a round of collections, but it could be the way to provide the care that each of your children requires.

Managing the needs of your youngest and oldest children can pose a real challenge in a childcare situation. Collecting your oldest from football practice will inevitably coincide with your baby's tea time. Going home time at school is always somehow in the middle of the baby's afternoon nap. If you are looking for a carer at home to cope with all your children's various needs, she will need to be flexible, able and imaginative, to think of a way around all these different situations. Encouraging your nanny or helper to build up a network of other nannies and helpers is a good idea – this way they will be able to help each other out to cover these awkward moments. One nanny collecting extra children from school can be repaid by her charges being given tea at the other children's house – this can work in just the way that at-home mothers often help each other out. Make sure that you know about these arrangements and that you are comfortable with them.

## How old is your nanny?

How old is your nanny, mother's help, or au pair? How old are the nursery nurses at the nursery you are considering and how old is the childminder you like the best? It is worth thinking about the age of your children related to the age of their potential carer.

We once hired a nineteen-year-old au pair, who the children adored. She was fun, energetic, and wore really cool clothes. Of course, she was closer in age to the children than she was to me. She was like a fantastic big sister, who let the girls into her room to try on her new shoes and make-up. The flip side is obvious – a younger person may be more fun but will also carry less authority, especially with children over the age of around eight, who can appreciate that the age gap between them and a nineteen-year-old isn't very great. If you are looking for an extra pair of hands, a younger person can be a perfect solution. If you are looking to fill a sole charge position, think carefully about the care that you will expect and need.

## Boys, girls or both

You will know that if you have all girls, you are sinking in a sea of pink, and that if you have all boys, you are likely find Lego all over the sofa every time you go to sit down. However much we all try to avoid the stereotypes, it just happens, time and time again. So, does having a single sex family alter your childcare needs?

When the children are all young, the sex of your children is unlikely to affect your childcare needs greatly. You will be making your choices about nursery, childminder or at-home care based on other criteria, including practicalities, cosiness, personalities, settings and how it will all fit in around your work schedule. When the children are older, whether you are looking for care for boys or girls may make a bit more of an impact on your choices.

All children need space to run around, particularly at the end of the school day, but boys tend to need this even more than girls. When looking at after-school clubs for boys, make sure that there is plenty of outdoor space as well as the opportunity to use it. When interviewing after-school nannies for boys, be sure they will be happy to stop at the park on the way home, come rain or shine. Of course girls need space and fresh air, too. If you've got both to cater for, make sure the centre or babysitter is willing to take everyone's wishes into account, in terms of after-school activities.

Some families with all boys consider a male nanny, sometimes known as a 'manny', or a male au pair. Many families love the mood that this introduces to their home. Especially if the mother is around, either at home or working part-time, she may feel that her boys have enough of a female influence, and want her children's carer to do something different with them. Forgive the sweeping clichés, but we know there is always a grain of truth in there somewhere.

## Zoltan, 25, is a male au pair in London

Au pairing has been a good life experience for me. I'm a 25-year-old man, I have a degree — I didn't think I would be doing this job! But I have improved my English.

Some families like the idea of a male au pair; others still find it strange. I have just been working with a family where the two boys live with their mother and see their father every other weekend. My own mum is divorced and brought me up, and I think that in this situation a male au pair is a good idea. I think the boys see me as a friend and enjoy the male company.

> I picked the boys up from school and we would go to the park to play football. I looked after them while their mum was at work and helped out on the other days. Sometimes we would spend weekends together and I've even been on holiday with the family.
>
> My first family was a disaster. There was just a 15-year-old boy. I think his parents wanted me to keep an eye on him — he was always getting into trouble with the police. I found the job on the internet — I think I didn't know enough about the family before I started work. The communication between us was terrible and they treated me really badly. I was only allowed to eat from one part of the fridge! After that experience I only took placements through an agency.
>
> I would advise families to be patient and friendly with a new au pair to help him, or her, settle in.

A great phrase was coined in the press a couple of years ago – SMOGs, or Smug Mothers of Girls. With all girls in your family, your childcare needs may appear more straightforward, even if your world ends up being pink. You may not need to worry about muddy football boots, or the bits of Lego and can instead concern yourselves with dressing up and ballet lessons. We are being simplistic here, but you can generally fear less for your house and your carpet when your girls are young, but will probably fear more for their safety and well-being as they grow older. When looking for childcare at home for just girls, make sure that the babysitter or nanny you hire will be interested in taking time with the girls' interests – there will probably be more time making necklaces and a bit less rough and tumble. Of course, you will want to make sure that your girls aren't encouraged to be too stereotypical and that they are offered plenty of other opportunities too.

AGES, GAPS, BOYS AND GIRLS

## Holly is a qualified nanny with plenty of experience. She sees a difference between caring for girls and boys

I'm looking after a boy now; my previous job was taking care of girls. I had forgotten how much naughtier boys are than girls and how much more inquisitive they are. If you tell a girl not to do something they generally won't do it, but if you tell a boy it's like an invitation to keep doing it! It sounds awful, but girls are easier to look after.

Families with both boys and girls have to cater for everyone, and this can be great, as you are more likely to avoid falling into the trap of never taking girls to play football, or failing to encourage boys to sit still with a craft activity for more than five minutes. Childcarers can focus less on what is right for each sex – catering for everyone's needs will have the end result of making it easier to encourage all children to have a go at everything their brothers and sisters are doing. Perhaps we need to be wary of Smug Mothers of Both.

# The live-in or live-out debate

The live-in/live-out debate rages on. For some families, the live-in option is a clear winner; for others it is something that they will not even consider. Often, it is an option that will be looked at when the time is right, or as the necessity arises. It is really important to take a hard look at your family and your lifestyle, to try and figure out if you are able to accommodate the needs of live-in help. You may surprise yourself with your decision.

We thought we'd never have live-in help – we didn't initially like the idea of having someone else in our home. Then we had twins and everything changed. The balance tipped for us – we needed the help, so were willing to accept the compromises that that help would make necessary. We went from not even considering a live-in arrangement to signing up a live-in au pair in a matter of a few short, busy, stressful months. We had tried various live-out options, but found that at that time in our lives, an extra pair of hands in the house was worth changing our attitudes for. The children doubled up, a spare room was created and we survived the next stage.

So, even if you are sure you don't want live-in help, or it is something you have never considered before, it is a good idea to be open to all your options, just in the back corner of your mind.

Live-out help comes with all its own advantages and disadvantages, too. Care provided away from home (also under the live-out umbrella) and childcare providers who come to your home on a daily basis to provide care for your children can be such a clear choice for some families, while for others it can prove too disjointed or expensive to fit well into their lives.

## Live-in help

Live-in help tends to be a more affordable option, on the face of it, than live-out help. You will pay a lower weekly rate to a nanny or mother's help if they live with your family, than if they live out. However, you are providing a room and board, and all the costs that are associated with that are yours to take into account.

You will be giving up a room in your house (all live-in help requires, as a minimum, a separate bedroom) which could otherwise be used to spread out your children, or even provide an income by renting the room to a lodger. You will be shopping for an extra person in the household – which may or may not become a significant cost depending on how much your live-in helper eats. Some families report tiny appetites; others record a significant increase in their weekly spend on groceries. It is so important not to be mean over what your live-in can help herself to – there are a succession of dreadful stories about au pairs being limited to only eating rice or pasta and put on a vegetarian (cheaper) diet by their host families. Please, don't become one of these families. Always be generous. You will create a happier atmosphere and a happier relationship with your live-in help if she is able to feel on an equal footing in the kitchen.

As well as giving up the room and providing free access to your store cupboard, fridge and freezer, there are other costs associated with having live-in help. More time on the phone (mobiles are definitely to be encouraged), more internet usage and, quite likely, higher utilities bills as extra heating, light and water is in consumed in your home. Your electricity bills can go sky high as even more laundry goes through your machine, just when you thought it was already at breaking point.

> **Nicola is a nanny working in London, over in the UK from Australia. She loves her live-in role**
> 
> I trained in Melbourne in Children's Services and worked in a childcare centre. When I first arrived in the UK I signed up with an agency that

specialises in placing nannies from Australia and New Zealand. They were great and able to reassure families about my qualifications and experience, as it was all familiar to them.

I really enjoy living in as a nanny. We all get along well and I really feel part of the family. Arriving on my own, it was lovely to be able to have a home straight away. I can also save a lot of money. The hours are long and sometimes a bit blurry — the children will still knock on my door at the weekend — but my family are very aware of that and make sure that I stop work at the end of each day. Sometimes I'm around at weekends and I'll naturally be playing with the kids. The parents say, 'You're not supposed to be working!' but I don't feel that I am.

I think in a live-in job you have to realise that your relationship with the parents is as important as your relationship with the children. We all need to live in the same space, share the kitchen and so on. As a live-in I have to respect the family's house rules. I think it would be difficult for a family if a live-in came back at three in the morning.

> In a live-in job you have to realise that your relationship with the parents is as important as your relationship with the children

I have also worked in live-out roles and it is completely different. You have such a different relationship with the parents — it's as if you hardly know them. I might see one parent in the morning and the evening, but everyone's in a rush and it's hard to build a relationship that way.

---

It is not just the financial costs that need to be considered when thinking about hiring live-in help. There is the emotional cost to think about, too. Are you the kind of family who is prepared to make the investment in time and energy to welcome live-in help? Even a live-out nanny or mother's help requires some of your time to make her feel settled into her role and you should remember to take this into account when considering your options. A live-in helper, however, will require more of you and your family in terms of emotional and pastoral support. She may be young, inexperienced, living away from home for the first time and be used to having her parents to turn to for support – you could find yourself fulfilling this role. Perhaps this is an argument for hiring a live-in who is older and more experienced in the role – though it is inevitably much harder to find someone of that description. Nannies and mother's helpers often tend to prefer to live-out once they have gained some experience, got to grips with the language (if necessary), settled into a new city or town and found friends to flat-share with.

Are you the kind of family who is willing to embrace the needs of a young person living in your home? Even if you are able to provide separate accommodation within your home, you are likely to be drawn in and will undoubtedly play more of a role in your nanny's life than you would in the life of a live-out helper. You must decide whether the benefits outweigh the cost.

## Stanley is a father of two boys, living in London. He and his wife chose to have live-in help while the boys were young.

Our second child was on the way when we decided to consider live-in help. My wife was going to stay at home full-time and look after the children. I believe that looking after two children full-time is too much for one person and that it is essential to receive some help through family or paid help.

> The most important goal was to get lots of help when my wife needed it, for her sake and mine

We had no family nearby. Whilst my wife was the key decision maker on choosing live-in help over daily, from my perspective, the most important goal was to get lots of help when my wife needed it, for her sake and mine. For me, live-in help provided two key benefits. Firstly, it is cost effective. This meant we could supplement the live-in help if needed. Secondly, it is flexible and therefore could be utilised when needed the most. Instead of having someone come in for a block of time *each day, my wife could divide the time into two or more sessions so that it was available at 'in-demand' times, such as breakfast, dinner, bathtime or bedtime.*

It is easy to find lots of arguments against live-in help, but there are families who could not manage without it. If you need to travel for work, or have a schedule which makes it difficult to guarantee being home by a certain time each day, you may need to rely on the flexibility that live-in help can offer. You will need to be up-front at interview stage if this is your primary reason for hiring live-in help – if your hours vary you will need to find someone to help who is willing to be flexible, too. Live-in nannies can expect to work for 10-12 hours a day – you will need to pay compensation for extra hours worked, at a rate agreed by you all in the early stages and included in a contract signed by both parties.

Some families, where both parents work long and difficult hours and need to travel at short notice, find they even need two nannies to cover all eventualities. Perhaps one will live-in and another will come in for a number of hours during the day to give the live-in a break. Alternatively, a night nanny can take over from the day nanny.

Live-in help is an obvious choice when you find you need help at different times of the day – particularly if your crunch times, as so many parents' crunch times are, are early morning and early evening. It would be expensive and difficult (though not impossible, of course) to find someone willing to come for two hours in the morning and three hours in the afternoon. We found at our crunch time that a live-in au pair, who went to school and out with friends during the middle of the day, was the perfect solution for us, and absolutely worth giving up a room in our house for.

Live-in help can have great advantages for the children, as well as for the adults in the family. The children are likely to form a lasting bond with someone that they see all the time. There are, of course, boundaries that have to be clearly defined for a happy relationship – the children shouldn't be allowed to wander into their live-in nanny's room, for example, without being invited, particularly when she is off duty. This is especially important, as the live-in nanny, mother's help or au pair will really need to feel she can have a break from the family. Your children will very likely get along well with someone who lives with you and with whom they see you having a good relationship. There are less likely to be tears when you go out for an evening (or even away for the weekend), leaving your live-in helper in charge. The children will be always safely within their comfort zones.

### 10 qualities that make a candidate suitable for a live-in post
- Flexibility • Experience • Youth • Enthusiasm • Similar interests as host family • Discretion • Siblings • Tidiness • Generosity of spirit • Tiptoeing ability late at night

## Virginia, 40, lives in London and has three children. She used to work long hours and travel extensively and needed two nannies to cover her childcare needs.

Soon after I'd had my first child I went back to work in the City. I started work at 6.45am and travelled a great deal. I needed a nanny to work from 8am to 7pm and another nanny to work 7pm to 8am. My husband could do a lot of the nights and early mornings but sometimes he would be travelling, too, so we needed this arrangement to cover all eventualities. It worked really well but it was a bit crazy — I would have to look in the laundry to see what my son had been wearing during the day. The two nannies used to overlap a little and talk about how my son had been. They had very different roles.

I think it's good to change your childcare every so often. We started off with a maternity nurse to guide us through the first weeks. We were the first of our friends to have kids so weren't really sure what to expect. Our first nanny was a traditional nanny. At one stage we had a male nanny, which was perfect at the time. He was a teacher so came to us in the afternoon and evenings. He would take my son to the park and prepare unusual foods — most memorably sushi. They'd have supper under the table covered in blankets; they had a really nice time and I could go to the gym in the evening or have dinner with my husband. I found the relationship easy with a male nanny — very straight-forward. We have had our current nanny for four years. I now work much more child-friendly hours. We are a good team.

I advise my girlfriends with nannies to make sure the contract stipulates working hours a little longer than you strictly need. If you get home at 6.30pm and the nanny works until 7pm, this allows you a half-hour overlap for you and the nanny to spend some time together, download what's happened to your kids that day and also see how your children and your nanny interact. We have learnt from experience that 6pm is the witching hour — have as much help as possible at that time of day!

> *Make sure the contract stipulates working hours a little longer than you strictly need*

## Live-out help

A lot of the advantages of live-out help are the other side of the disadvantages of live-in help. When you employ a live-out nanny, mother's help or after-school babysitter, you will be able to shut the front door at the end of a busy day and call your home your own. If you decide to send your child to a day care nursery, you will return home at the end of the day to find your house undisturbed and just as you left it in the morning. Whatever the stresses and the strains of the day, you will be able to cuddle up with your family in private and regroup to face the next day.

There will be no need to account for all the extra costs and sometimes unpredictable expenses of having an extra person living in your home. However, these cost savings will most likely be more than made up for by the extra expense of hiring live-out help. After all, live-out childcare providers have to take all their living and housing expenses into account when negotiating their salary. A live-out nanny in a city can earn up to 50% more per week net than a live-in nanny. An hourly rate for a mother's help or au pair will quickly add up to more than the cost of a live-in mother's help or au pair – especially when you add in the cost of an occasional evening's babysitting.

You may find as parents that you are all able to have more clearly defined roles in your children's lives if you hire live-out help. The children will, from a young age, be better able to distinguish between the care that they receive from someone who comes into the home, or who cares for them outside the home, and the care that they receive at home, separately, from you as parents. The boundaries of childcare will be clearer for all concerned, if you choose live-out help.

Slightly different approaches to childcare will matter a little less if the childcarer lives-out (as long as you are comfortable with the differences). A nanny may insist that a child eats up all her vegetables, broccoli stalks and all, whereas you may take a slightly more lax attitude (or vice versa). Then, if you are all sharing Sunday lunch together, this could be awkward for the adults and confusing for the children. You will be able to avoid this kind of conflict if you live separately from your childcarer – until you extend an invitation to Sunday lunch. You can, of course, try to impose your rules and hope that the live-out nanny will follow them – they are your children, after all.

## Julia chose live-out help to support her busy family life

With two small boys and four older stepchildren we didn't have the space to donate a bedroom for the sole use of a live-in nanny or au pair. Also, we would have had the problem of teenage boys and pretty young au pairs living under the same roof! It was much easier to have the house to ourselves, the food there when I needed it — no ingredients crucial for the dinner party missing from the fridge. My husband also appreciated coming home and having the kitchen to ourselves and more importantly the television when he wanted it!

> When our helper arrives she is fresh and ready for the day and I am ready for her to be involved

Live-out help suits us all so well. I appreciate the help so much — when our helper arrives she is fresh and ready for the day and I am ready for her to be involved.

A disadvantage of live-out help can be that your nanny is itching to get away at the end of her working day – just as you were keen to leave the office half an hour earlier. She may make a run for the door as you walk in, and you could find yourself faced with the mess from tea time and tired, fractious children who still need to tidy up their toys, have a bath, be read to and tucked into bed, just when you are at your most tired at the end of a busy day. Ideally your live-out nanny will work a slightly longer day to allow you some cross-over time.

It can also be harder to find time to talk through any worries or even just the events of the day with your nanny, when you are crossing each other on the doorstep. Live-out nannies will usually keep a diary so that a line of communication can remain open with the parents. The diary might include details of where the children went, what they ate, when they took a nap and who they played with that day. It will also be a place for the parents to write messages for the nanny, that might otherwise be forgotten in the morning rush. As well as a diary, though, it is important to find a regular time to sit down and catch up properly with your nanny, so that any real worries or concerns from either side can have a proper airing.

Live-out help also encompasses care provided outside of the home – nurseries, childminders and after-school clubs. In these cases you are keeping your home to yourself, by having all your childcare needs catered for elsewhere. You will drop off and collect your children from the centre or childminder's home and come back to a quiet, tidy house at the end of a busy day. You will only need to find a way to reserve enough energy to come home to manage bathtime, storytime and bedtime at the end of a busy day.

## David, 50, lives in Oxfordshire. His son went to a childminder, and subsequently to an after-school club

Our son went to the same childminder on and off for nearly ten years. He thinks of his childminder as more of a friend than anything and he has almost become an extra member of her family. In the last three years he has moved on to an after-school club, along with the childminder's son.

The arrangement suited us all, because the childminder had a boy of the same age as our son, as well as two older boys. We liked the idea of the personal touch of a childminder. Both my wife and I had a commute to work and worked a long day — we were looking for flexible childcare, for long hours, where our son would be happy.

Our son felt like one of the family with his childminder. To this day, he takes off his shoes before he enters a house — a habit he learned at the childminder's. When we went to the childminder's wedding, some other guests thought he was another member of her family. They all really got along well.

Our son started at the after-school club three years ago. He would be there from about 3.30pm until we could collect him at around 6pm. They played a little sport, did some arts and crafts and some cooking. They had a computer with games and a Playstation, which of course he loved. Sometimes they would watch a video.

We are very happy with the way our childcare worked out. Our son has made good friends and had a good experience in each setting.

> Our son felt like one of the family with his childminder

# section THREE

# how to go about finding your childcare

**14** LOOKING FOR CHILDCARE

**15** CHOOSING THE RIGHT CHILDCARE AWAY FROM HOME

**16** CHOOSING THE RIGHT CHILDCARE AT HOME

## HOW TO GO ABOUT FINDING YOUR CHILDCARE

You are getting closer to figuring out what sort of childcare is likely to suit you and your family's needs. We have had a close look at the different sorts of childcare on offer, and encouraged you to try to examine your family to assess what you all really want. You are hopefully getting a fuller picture of what sort of person or place you would ideally like to find. Now is the moment to proceed with your search.

Make sure you are clear in your own mind about what you are planning to look for and hoping to find at this stage, by writing everything down and keeping your lists to hand. Lists will help to clarify exactly what you want, and will help you remember some of the things that you definitely don't want. Show your lists to your partner and best friend – there might be some glaring omissions or mistakes that you didn't spot.

## Five lists to start off with

### What you want

Write down what you think you want in terms of childcare – the type of care, setting and person that you are going to start searching for. At this stage, continue to try and remain open-minded about alternatives.

### What you definitely don't want

The reverse of the above – a chance to think of characteristics or situations that you definitely want to avoid. Keeping an open mind *is* important, but there may just be some childcare situations that you know are not going to be right for you.

### Days and hours you will be working/ have decided you need the help for

Write down the days of the week and the number of hours (including the times of day) that you need childcare for. Putting this in black and white will help you avoid getting into a muddle later on.

### What to look for during a tour at a nursery or childminder's house

We'll be looking later on at the many points you will want to watch out for when taking a tour. Make your own short list of the things which are most important to you.

## What to look out for at interview

You will be interviewing to find a candidate that you are going to be able to have a good working relationship with, not just someone who passes all the tests on paper. We make our suggestions for how to conduct interviews later on in this section. You might find it helpful to have a list of the five characteristics you are looking for in your nanny/childminder/mother's help or au pair, to keep in mind at interview.

## Getting on with the search

Now you just need to find your dream childcare. It really can be straightforward when you follow a few simple guidelines. This section is split into chapters to help you move forward with your search. Chapter Fourteen contains practical advice on how to go about looking for your childcare, in all sectors. Chapter Fifteen guides you through making your own assessment of a nursery, childminder or after-school facility. In Chapter Sixteen you will find advice on how to conduct interviews with nannies, mother's helps, au pairs and maternity nurses.

There are a few key and obvious routes to looking for childcare. Talk to friends and let them know you are looking. Word quickly spreads – our first (hugely successful) au pair came to us by word of mouth. If you are looking for help at home, contact the relevant agencies in your area. Try to isolate the ones which specialise in the type of childcare you are looking for. Go through the internet listings and as well as looking at who has placed advertisements, you could place your own. We will highlight some of the most popular sites for you to visit. Check your local newspaper listings and consider placing an advertisement locally in the press or in targeted national magazines, for example in *The Lady*.

If you are looking for childcare outside the home, start by contacting your local Children's Information Service (or FIS) for details of nurseries and childminders in your area (details of these are included in Section Six at the back of the book). The Children's Information Service, accessible through your local council or the Direct.gov website, will be an invaluable source for your search for childcare away from home.

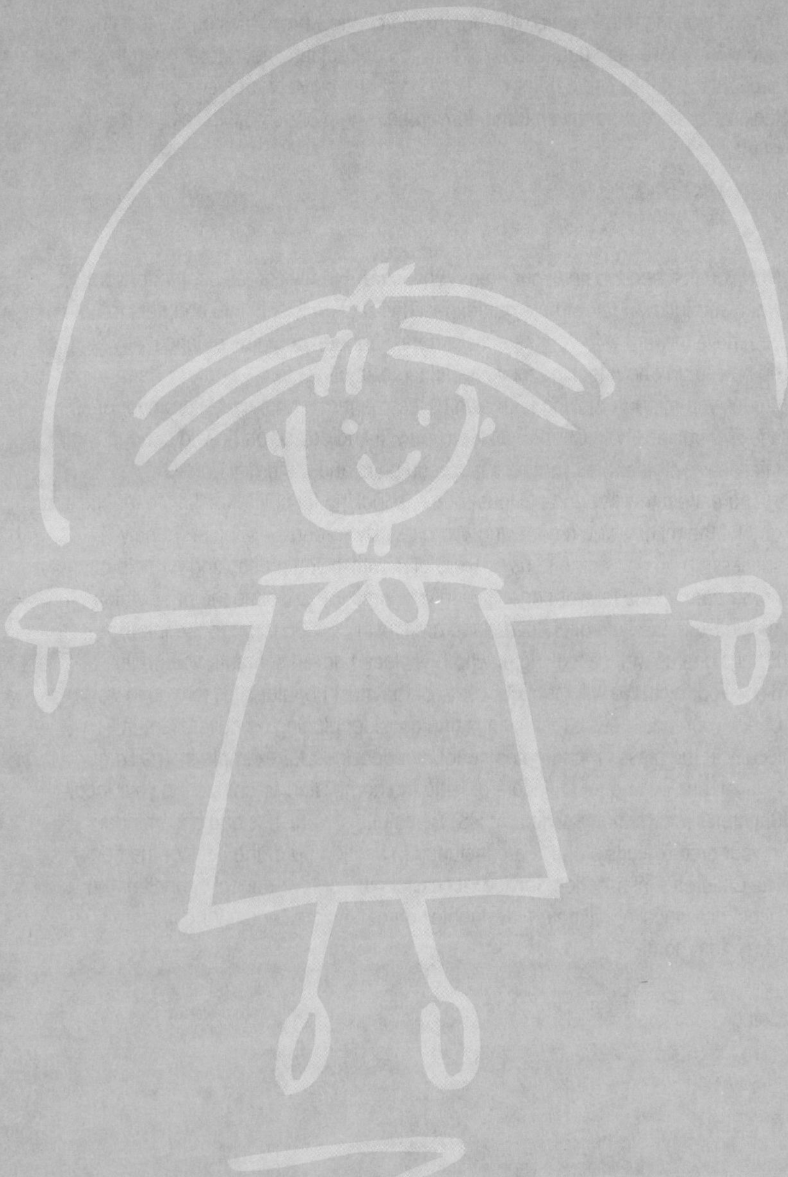

# Looking for childcare

There are several tried and tested routes to finding the childcare of your dreams. In this chapter we look at the different options and how they will work best for you. The methods listed below are the most successful routes to finding nannies, au pairs, mother's helps and other help at home. In this chapter we will also look at how to find local childcare services in your area, plus you will find special sections on how to look for a maternity nurse and a babysitter. We discuss:

## Word-of-mouth recommendations

A word of mouth recommendation can be a great way to find childcare. Personal experience can count for a lot, and in the case of nannies, au pairs and mother's helps, you may save yourself a fee. But, following a word-of-mouth recommendation for a mother's help or nanny means that you are taking that first step towards potentially hiring someone without any of the guarantees that would come from an agency's introduction. A candidate put forward by an agency should have first undergone initial reference checks before being introduced to clients. An au pair introduced by a friend, or friend-of-a-friend, comes without any checks. You have the reference of someone you know to go on, but be sure to ask the questions you have prepared to ask any referee, rather than just going on the say-so of a friend. Don't be lulled into a false sense of security. You should interview as thoroughly as you would any other candidate.

When you take a recommendation from a friend or acquaintance for a nursery or childminder, treat it as an introduction. Be sure to ask pertinent questions, and go on your own to visit and make up your own mind.

## The potential pitfalls of word-of-mouth recommendations

The most obvious ways for this to go wrong are over habits and discipline. A particularly fastidious family with strong views on disciple recommending a nanny to a family without those shared values (or even more problem-laden, the other way round, the messy, laid-back family recommending help to the tidy, highly organised family) will clearly not be a good match. It will be difficult for the family and is also likely to be hard for the nanny who has suited one family so well, to adapt to another, completely different arrangement.

> Five questions to ask your friend about a recommendation for nanny/au pair/mother's help role before calling the candidate:
> - How long have you known this person?
> - How did you meet?
> - What exactly does she do for you?
> - How is her timekeeping?
> - If live-in, what are her habits?

There are other obvious contrasts to make – noisy personalities or quiet souls, outdoorsy or indoorsy types. These issues all go back to figuring out who you and your family really are, that we looked at in Section Two – hang on to these principles even when taking advice from a friend. You know what and who will suit you and your children best.

When looking for childcare away from home and taking a friend's advice, you face similar potential pitfalls. One kind of nursery will appeal very strongly to one family and be totally wrong for another. Families are bound to be looking for different things in a nursery – one will be wowed by the walls crowded with artwork and shelves spilling over with toys, while another family will prefer to see clear space, lots of light and supreme cleanliness. Nurseries can sometimes fall into efficient and creative categories and you and your friend or acquaintance may have different views about what makes the best environment for your young children.

You are unlikely to agree in all things, even with your best friend. You are likely to be best friends because you are different! Don't fall out over childcare.

Before going ahead with making contact with a friend's recommendation, go through this quick list of questions with your friend, to see if you have a chance of compatibility with the childcarer being put forward.

## Agencies

An agency will endeavour to find the best childcare match for the family that is looking for help. The agency will be working for both sides to achieve a successful outcome. The agency is also a business, interested in matching up families and childcarers successfully, to earn their commission.

Most agencies will have nannies and mother's helps on their books. Some will also place au pairs and maternity nurses; otherwise you can find agencies that specialise in one particular area of childcare (see Section Six). Au pair agencies tend to be a separate breed, specialising in placing au pairs, sometimes offering expertise in bringing au pairs to the UK from a particular country.

> Five questions to ask your friend about her recommendation for a nursery, childminder or after-school club:
> - How long have you used this childcare provider?
> - How established is the nursery/club/childminder?
> - What is the ethos of the childcare provider?
> - What does your child do all day?
> - Is the provider flexible over hours and days of the week?

Despite the huge effect of the internet, which now gives easy access to parents and childcare providers to advertise their vacancies and services, agencies are still a popular route to finding childcare. Agencies have to offer high standards to appeal to parents who could readily access the internet and take on the search themselves – they must earn their fees. Appointing an agency to undertake a search for your perfect childcare will inevitably make your life easier, as a lot of the work involved in weeding out candidates and carrying out initial reference checks and background checks will be done for you. Agencies will usually have some candidates already on their books, and will be able to place target advertisements to attract the right candidate to a particular role, if they don't have anyone suitable at the ready.

Agencies will occasionally charge a registration fee as well as a placement fee when you have agreed to hire a candidate that they have introduced to you. The placement fee will vary but you can expect it to be around 15% plus VAT of the net annual salary for a permanent placement.

A good agency will offer much more than just the initial introduction – if you can find one of the agencies that will work hard for you, it can be well worth the extra initial outlay. You will probably be asked to sign a contract with the agency agreeing to their terms and conditions and to the fee that you will pay them when they introduce you to a candidate who ends up filling the position.

## Finding an agency

You may wish to use a local agency, but this is not essential. If you do want to go local, search online directories for agencies nearby and look at your local press for advertisements from local childcare agencies. Ask around, among friends and acquaintances, for agency recommendations. Ask why they recommend this particular agency and about any successful placements that they have made through the agency.

## What an agency should offer you

Look for a full service – make the fee worth paying. Ideally you will be able to meet with an agent (an advantage of using a local agency) so that you can give a very clear impression of who you are and what your needs are. All agencies will ask you to fill in a detailed form giving information about the position you are looking to fill, the salary you are prepared to pay, the benefits and perks that you are offering, along with details about your family and lifestyle.

Give as much information as possible; this will help enormously with a good match. Agencies work hard to match families up together as a successful outcome ensures their reputation and their commission.

An agency should interview prospective candidates (where possible) to assess their suitability for the role in question, before arranging meetings with families. Agencies should also carry out thorough background and reference checks. However, candidates will not be guaranteed by the agencies. Families are expected to carry out their own reference checks to support their choice.

Agencies should be able to provide you with several suitable candidates to interview. Try and be sure that you are being offered real alternatives, rather than dummy candidates to fill up interview spots. A weaker candidate will reflect well on the candidate the agency is keen for you to hire and won't offer you a real choice.

After agreeing on a suitable candidate for the position to be filled, the family will usually be left to make the financial arrangements, with guidance from the agency.

The agency should also be able to give advice on drawing up a contract between the family and the appointee.

The agency should offer some guarantee against the placement being a disaster in a short space of time. Look for a clause in your contract with the agency about this. Ideally you will be offered one replacement candidate if the original placement fails within eight weeks of commencement, as long as some straightforward and reasonable criteria have been fulfilled. These criteria might include informing the agency of the failure within a specified timeframe, as well as showing that the working conditions of the candidate were as agreed prior to commencement. Fees are high, but ensure that your agency offers this service and it can make the fee worth paying.

## Corinna has a background as a nanny and now works at an agency placing nannies with families

My job is all about trying to source good candidates and then matching them with the right family.

I have worked at the Nanny Service for 13 years now. We are an established agency and nannies and families tend to come back to us, so we have quite a lot of repeat business. Children go to school, a nanny gets married or the family moves house — there are a number of reasons why nannies and families might be looking for new work or help. If a placement has gone well, families and nannies will come back to us the next time, and recommend us to their friends.

We have a number of contacts in Australia and New Zealand — colleges and agencies — that we've worked with for many years. Their candidates will have all been police checked and reference checked before they come to the UK. We also find candidates by keeping an eye on the appropriate websites — we will occasionally pull in a girl who is advertising herself as a nanny to see if she is of high enough quality for us to place her. We're pretty hot on CVs — we will only consider the girls who have something special to offer. We put the girls through a rigorous interview process — I dig deep at interviews.

> We put the girls through a rigorous interview process — I dig deep at interviews

I'll ask about a girl's personal life, what she likes to do at the weekend, even boyfriends. If we like a candidate we will proceed with references and check their qualifications. We are very selective.

We are looking for candidates who are going to grow and become fantastic nannies; someone wanting to get into the field with a qualification and who loves children. They have to have a good personality and present themselves well. We are not interested in candidates who are only interested in money, or who are fussy about exactly what they do for a family. Within reason, I'd expect a nanny to be helpful other than just with the children. For example, if the family has run out of milk, the nanny should buy some more when she is out. Australians have a particularly good reputation. They don't have to be asked for anything and tend to have a terrific work ethic.

On the other side of the equation, families register with us and let us have their wish list. They might be looking for someone with newborn experience, a good understanding of English and a driving licence. We then search for the right nanny for that family. The family is invoiced when we can all see that the placement is going to be successful.

We are careful with our placements and things rarely go wrong. If a placement isn't going to work out, it is usually obvious pretty quickly. We will encourage the nanny to stay until we can at least find a temporary nanny to

> It is very satisfying matching people up

fill in. Temps are brilliant. They know what they are doing and hit the ground running.

We recommend that parents call us six weeks before they need a nanny to start. We don't want to waste anyone's time, so when we send a candidate for *an interview, there is a very high chance that that nanny will be offered the job. It is very satisfying matching people up.*

## Au pair agencies

A specialist au pair agency will usually be introducing families to a candidate who is not yet in the country. Agencies work in different ways, but often a UK-based agency will work closely with a particular agency abroad. Some will have a list of available candidates on their books; others will advertise vacancies as they arise, with details of the family and position included in the advertisement. This draws in applicants who are interested in a specific position, leading to a good start in the matching process.

An au pair agency service should include checking references and carrying out police checks as well as a face-to-face interview with a partner agency in the au pair's home country. A good introduction from an agency will include photos, a full CV from the applicant and a letter to the host family. Some agencies will ask for the same from the host family. This is a good sign – the agency is taking both parties' interests into account.

You must ensure that you will be able to conduct an interview over the phone. You need to listen extra carefully when interviewing this way, and be very precise about your family and what you are offering. It is very easy to cross wires, especially if the potential au pair's language skills are not strong. Make an arrangement to call at a convenient time, and plan for a second (and even maybe a third) phone call so that your partner or a friend or relative can have a chat, too. See Chapter Sixteen for our interview tips.

When you have made your choice, you will be asked to make a written offer, including the full details of the duties to be undertaken by the au pair and the benefits you are proposing. When this has been accepted by your au pair of choice, you will need to send a letter of introduction (the agency will help you with what this letter needs to include) and pay your agency fee.

The family will be required to collect the au pair from her arrival point in the UK. You may offer to pay for her travel, but this is unusual in the first instance. If the arrangement works out, you may like to offer to pay or share the cost of her trip home at Christmas or for the summer holidays.

There are obvious pitfalls involved in bringing an au pair over from abroad without meeting first. It is entirely normal to choose an au pair on paper, once she has passed the agency's checks and you have spoken to her a couple of times on the phone, and the next thing you know, you are collecting her from the bus station or airport. It is becoming more common for families to look for au pairs who are already in the UK, through local advertising or websites, to try and avoid the potential problems involved in hiring without meeting. However, au pairs who are already based in the UK are often looking for a slightly different role for their second job (moving up to a mother's help or nanny, for example), as well as often looking for more money and perhaps a live-out position, so that they can flat-share with friends they have made here. There is a ready supply of au pairs wanting to come over to the UK with the security of a family to live with – hiring sight-unseen requires a leap of faith but can have terrific results.

The British Au Pair Agencies Association (BAPAA) is an association of agencies within the UK which works to ensure a high standard of services to families and au pairs. BAPPA agencies provide a thorough screening procedure and on-going support for families and au pairs. They will also give guidelines to au pairs and host families on how everyone can get the most from the au pair experience.

## What marks out a great agency?

You can separate the great from the good or average by looking at the level of care and attention that is given to your application and at the level of after-care that is being offered. If you feel you are only being asked stock questions about the position you are looking to fill and about your family, you are unlikely to end up with tailor-made childcare. The time after a childcare appointment has been made can also set agencies apart. A great agency will follow up properly, making sure that all sides are happy after an initial settling-in period has been completed.

All agencies should check references, but a great agency will provide evidence of this, and will have up-to-date CRB checks on all the people on their books.

A great agency may offer further training and professional development. This might include opportunities for their candidates to go on a first-aid course, and other workshops or courses to keep their skills fresh and up to date.

A stand-out local agency would introduce your childcarer to a network of other childcarers in your area. This is especially important if you are bringing an au pair over from abroad.

A great au pair agency might provide a service whereby an au pair is able to speak to the agent in her home country to try to sort out problems which have not been overcome within the placement, perhaps due to communication issues. Au pairs often arrive in the UK with poor language skills, which can lead to problems with their host family. This kind of aftercare can be of great benefit.

## Charlotte, 38, is a qualified nanny who now works for a nanny agency

I studied for my NNEB qualification at college. The course covered all the developmental stages of children from birth to five years, and offered placements for practical experience. I enjoyed meeting the other girls on the course and built up a good network of friends who were interested in the same career.

After college I worked in a nursery, and stayed for three years. From there, I worked as a nanny for a family with two children who I had looked after at the nursery, and stayed with them for seven years. After more positions as a nanny, I now work as a consultant, drawing on my years of experience, matching nannies with families.

> Qualifications show that a nanny has chosen this career path, rather than fallen into it

Qualifications are a great thing to have. While they are not essential to be a good nanny, they show families that a candidate has had that experience and made that commitment — that the nanny has chosen this career path, rather than fallen into it. Qualifications really help to reassure parents, but of course, qualifications alone can't make a good nanny. A nanny's suitability for her chosen career will always come down to her personality and nature. If you can find a candidate with a real, genuine love for children, who has some experience under her belt and a qualification, you are in luck!

*I always advise families to try to be as clear as possible from the outset about what they are looking for in their nanny. We discuss expectations and working practices with clients. Problems usually arise over a personality clash or over differing ideas about bringing up children — parents need to be very careful about who they hire to try and avoid these pitfalls.*

## Using the internet

The internet has introduced a whole new way to look for childcare. It is naturally a great resource for finding out about local services, checking Ofsted reports on nurseries, as well as finding local childcare agencies. It also offers a worldwide network in terms of searching for your dream childcare directly – the world really is at your fingertips.

There are numerous websites which have sprung up to help in the search for perfect childcare. These might specialise in au pairs, nannies, nanny shares or maternity nurses.

You will find a much fuller list of websites to search in Section Six.

---

**Five popular websites to visit when looking for childcare**

- www.bestbear.co.uk
- www.childcarelink.gov.uk
- www.gumtree.co.uk
- www.bapaa.org.uk
- www.nightnannies.co.uk

## Joanna has two girls and has hired holiday nannies and after-school nannies through websites

I first used the Gumtree website five years ago when I was looking for a nanny to take on holiday with us. I didn't place an ad of my own, I just contacted some of the girls who were offering their services. I spoke to a few and interviewed only two. The one I employed, a school teacher from Tasmania, was fantastic.

I found another school teacher the following summer — this time a New Zealander. I used the same approach, and again she worked out well.

I do think that the Gumtree is great for finding girls to help out during holiday periods — certainly quite a lot of qualified teachers (who are perfect for school-age children) seem to advertise this way.

Just over two years ago, when I needed after school childcare I decided that as my needs were quite specific (two or three days a week only) it was better to place an ad of my own. The response was huge — more than 60 responses in the first day. This is where the Gumtree approach requires quite a lot of work on your part — weeding out the responses which are not appropriate to your needs. I found it quite humbling to see how many well-qualified people are willing to take on just a few hours' work a week. This time I interviewed four girls, and the one I employed, an art student, stayed with us for the next two years.

> I do think that the Gumtree is great for finding girls to help out during holiday periods

I am now on to my fourth Gumtree find — another New Zealander, who is able to provide very flexible help for our family in the short-term. I found her through her ad. I did place an ad myself, but did not have such a big response *(possibly because I was only looking for someone for one or two afternoons a week)* and didn't find anyone I liked amongst the replies.

I would certainly recommend Gumtree to mothers looking to find help for school-age children, who don't necessarily want a nanny, but do want to find a way of finding girls who may be able to provide flexible childcare, particularly in the school holidays. The caveat is that you must be prepared to check references and trust your own judgement.

## Advertising online

When figuring out where to place your advertisement online, imagine you are the person you are trying to attract and look where they would be looking. Post advertisements in the obvious places, as well as in the less obvious. For example, if you particularly want to find a Kiwi nanny, post an ad on a website targeted at Kiwis in the UK rather than on a more broad-based childcare website.

Be as precise as you can be in your advertisement. On some websites you will be able to write one line outlining your post, which will then click through to a full advertisement. Make sure that this line will draw in the candidates you are looking for, by highlighting the things which are most important to you. In your full ad, you will need to give details of what the job is, when you need your help to start, whether you are looking for a share and the area in which you live. Specifics can be saved for later – you don't want to put all your personal details or give detailed information about renumeration online in your initial approach.

### Tailoring your online advertisement

What kind of person do you want to reply to your advertisement? Make sure that you advertisement is appealing to the right people. Is there a particular kind of person who will be happy with your family? This could depend on where you live for example, how accessible your home is to transport links, how long it takes to get to a city centre. You can promote the things near you that will suit the type of person you are looking for. If you are hoping for a quiet, stay-at-home kind of nanny, don't advertise that you are only 25 minutes from Piccadilly Circus, but instead mention local parks and leisure facilities. Send out the right signals, so that you will be appealing to the kind of person you want to attract to the job.

Be specific about your dates and when you need the help to start. Try to start an internet search at least one month in advance of when you actually need the help.

Internet listings are relatively immediate, but you don't want to start too early (the candidates looking online are often looking to start as soon as possible) or leave it too late (and run the risk of not finding help in time, or not having enough time to check it all out thoroughly, or to find the best candidate).

### Dealing with responses to your online advertisement

It is quite standard to ask for references, CVs and even photographs to be emailed with the first response to the advertisement. This will help you to weed out the replies as they come in. If you require a high standard of English, you will be able to send the replies with lots of mistakes in the written English straight to your trash.

You might like to have a list of preliminary questions prepared to send out to each reply that you like the sound of – and ask for replies to be returned within a specific timeframe. This will allow you to make direct comparisons of your various applicants, helping you make the decision over which candidates you will progress to the next stage.

If you like the sound of the applicant on paper (or screen), it's time to make a phone call. This will undoubtedly help you to shed a few more candidates from your long-list, getting you towards a shortlist of candidates to meet with face to face. Go through your list of questions to ask on the phone (see Chapter Sixteen) before inviting a select few for interview.

## Bonita, 34, has one child and lives and works in south-west London. She advertised her nanny share position on the internet

Until my daughter is older and able to express herself, when we think she will benefit from nursery, we prefer for her to have individual care. A nanny share is a cost-effective way to achieve this.

*We prefer for our daughter to have individual care*

Anne and I met at a postnatal group and became good friends. One of the reasons we were drawn to each other was that we have a shared experience of living in a city which is not our own. We don't have the same support networks as some of the other new mothers we met. We don't have parents nearby who are willing and able to babysit, and instead had to rely on babysitting services. Anne and I also live in the same area and our babies seem to get along well. It was an organic process — we started out babysitting for each other, sometimes during the day so the babies could spend some time together as they keep each other entertained.

Anne suggested that we try to set up a nanny share. Sharing is extremely tricky and there's lots of detail to be worked out. We had a lot of discussions and in retrospect we should have had even more meetings, particularly some involving our partners. Finances were a contentious issue. Anne and I would come to an agreement that the fathers would then pick apart. We weren't both going to be needing the nanny for the same amount of time, so there were lots of wrinkles to iron out.

> We should have had even more meetings, particularly some involving our partners

It was a steep learning curve for both of us. We posted an ad on Gumtree and were deluged with responses. As I was returning to work first I had more of the responsibility because it was more urgent for me. I did two rounds of advertising, checking CVs and arranging interviews. We soon learnt that when you find someone you like, you have to move quickly to make the appointment, which can be tricky in a share.

> We posted an ad on Gumtree and were deluged with responses

The nanny we have now hired interviewed well and comes across as being a calm, centred person. We are still in a settling in period, but so far it is all going well.

I think there are lots of benefits to a nanny share. The fact that the babies know each other and are accustomed to playing together is good. I can also *imagine a situation where perhaps Anne or I needed to work late one evening and will be able to help each other out and let the nanny go home. We can give each other the back up that all parents really need.*

## Print advertising

Local newspapers and magazines and perhaps some appropriately targeted national media, can be a good resource in the search for childcare. You will either be able to find advertisements from individuals or agencies, or place your own advertisements to draw in the candidates you are looking for.

If you wish to advertise your position and childcare requirements, a local newspaper or magazine is a good starting point. Although the turnaround time can be slower than if you use the internet, you will be attracting applications specifically from your local area, which may make the recruitment process (and the settling in period) easier. While the internet has replaced much of the need for print advertising, you will be able to reach an even wider audience if you use both.

Local newspapers and magazines (and indeed, websites of local newspapers and magazines) are also a good source of local childcare information. You will find advertisements from local agencies and childcare providers including nurseries and sometimes childminders, in the appropriate classified or listing sections.

If there is a free magazine in your area especially aimed at parents, this can be a great source of information and a perfect place for you to feature your advertisement. If you are not aware of these publications already, you will most likely be able to pick one up at your local nursery or playgroup.

When you decide to place your own advertisement, keep it brief and to the point, while trying to give a flavour of yourself and your family, as well as a clear description of the help you are looking for. It's best to add a phone number with specific times to call, to avoid being inundated at all hours. Don't advertise your rate of pay, or your address, but do mention your local area.

## Noticeboards

If you are looking for childcare at home, you could get straight to the source. Write your own advertisement and put it where it will be seen. Figure out where the nanny or au pair you want to hire will be during the day and make sure she sees your ad.

The noticeboard in our local park café is always heavy with advertisements pinned up by local families looking for help, as well as with the reverse – advertisements placed there by au pairs and nannies looking for a family or just a few extra hours work. Local noticeboards are also a good place to advertise to other families that you are looking for a nanny share in your area.

With permission, you could also place ads on the noticeboards at local playgroups, nursery schools, primary schools or community centres. You can also look for others' advertisements on noticeboards at doctor's surgeries, libraries and shops. Our local organic supermarket always has a selection.

### Getting your advertisement noticed

An advertisement on a noticeboard needs to be instantly eye-catching, appealing and quite specific. If you are looking for an au pair, for example, state briefly where you live, how many children you have, that it is a live-in role with a certain number of hours a week. When writing an ad for a nanny, state which days, the hours and how many children you are looking for care for and whether it is a sole charge or shared care role. Use a few words to describe your family and mention any pets or special interests. You could write your name and number a few times on the bottom of the ad on tear-off strips with a one line job description. Check on your advertisement regularly, in case all of these strips have been removed and you need to replace the ad with a new one. Again, it is best not to mention payment on your advertisement – wait to see if you are interested in any of the applicants before talking terms.

Use coloured pens, highlighters, stickers, coloured paper or children's artwork to make your ad stand out from the crowd and check on it regularly to make sure it hasn't been covered up by other, newer, shinier advertisements.

### Finding local nurseries, childminders or after-school clubs

When you first start to look for childcare outside of your home, ask for a comprehensive list of registered childcarers from your local Children's Information Service (or FIS). For contact details of your local Children's Information Service, contact ChildcareLink on 0800 096 0296 or see their website www.childcarelink.gov.uk. All day care nurseries, childminders, crèches, pre-schools and after-school and holiday clubs must be registered with Ofsted and will therefore be known to your local council.

Look at the list of childcare providers with a map to hand and decide how far you are willing and able to travel. Be realistic about this. You have got to be able to manage your drop offs and pick ups with your work schedule and/or other children's schedules. It is unrealistic to sign up with a nursery nowhere near your other daily routes (however much you like the look of it) and doing so will just make your life more complicated – not the idea of good childcare at all.

## Sarah, 41, from Essex, puts her daughter in a nursery near to where she works

Emily has been going to a day nursery for two days a week since she was three months old. It has been very positive for her to mix with other children. I hate leaving her at the door, especially if she is crying, but I know she is happy there and stops crying as soon as I go. I've seen it with other mothers! This nursery was recommended to me by a friend. It is in a good location for my work, but the most important thing to me is that the children look happy. Once I see happy children, I go down my checklist — cleanliness, staff, food and so on. If there are no smiling faces, there is really no point.

> The most important thing to me is that the children look happy.

I think that children have an enormous capacity for learning. I'm not trying to push my child, but I think she benefits from being in a bigger environment than home two days a week. She enjoys all the toys and activities on offer, as well as the computers and the sandpit. There is a very structured day; I think even babies can benefit from structure and routine.

In the case of after-school clubs, your choices will be limited to whether a club can arrange collection from your child's school. If your children are pre-school age, you could use the information to try to plan ahead a little (although everything is always subject to change and shouldn't be relied upon too much if you are looking far ahead.

Statistics show that availability of places at day nurseries is high in some areas. Demand is still strong, but there is a rising volume in places, which means that more are available. This is certainly easing the pressure on nursery spaces in some areas; however, places at the most popular nurseries can still be hard to come by.

As well as being listed with the CIS and usually having details online, childminders often place advertisements in *Simply Childcare*, a newsletter which is available only on subscription. Log on to www.simplychildcare.com or call 020 7701 6111 for subscription information. Childminders, other childcare providers and parents seeking childcare may all place advertisements. With enough people reading it, good matches can be made. This publication (and its sister website) are particularly useful if you are looking for the odd day of childcare – providers will often advertise small gaps to fill odd spaces.

Find out well before you need the childcare when you need to register your child with a particular nursery, childminder or after-school club. Childminders will usually have spaces which open up irregularly, so it may just come down to luck and timing whether a place is available with your first-choice childminder. Nursery spaces will come up more regularly – as children move up through the nursery and leave from the top, more spaces are created at the bottom. The most popular nurseries always fill up quickly and you will need to register your interest early on.

## Sue, 42, lives on Merseyside and uses an after-school club for her three children

The club was already in the school when my children started. Before that we had used a mixture of childminders and nurseries. I liked this club because it offered continuity; it was on the school premises so my children didn't have to go anywhere. The facilities in school are good and it's quite rural; there's a lovely field to play in. They were also with children that they know from school and could play with, which they like. I wouldn't want to use it five days a week because I think sometimes my children just want to go home. For two days a week it's great and has been a real godsend for me.

The children go straight from school at 3.15pm and the club closes at 6pm. Normally, they have a healthy snack when they get in — carrot sticks, fruit or toast and when the weather is good they can go out to the playground. There are lots of different things they can play with; footballs, games, rollerblades, hockey sticks and beanbags...

I've always been quite happy with the club because there are different activities to do and although the children have to behave it isn't really strict. I think the children need to let off a bit of steam after school when they've been trying to be good for six and a half hours.

*I think the children need to let off a bit of steam after school*

The children really enjoy the club — I often find that I'm breaking my neck to get there to pick them up and then they ask me if I can come back a bit later because they're busy!

## How to find a babysitter

Unless your regular nanny or mother's help has babysitting written into her contract, or you have a live-in au pair who will offer you two nights' a week babysitting as part of her deal, you will need a list of regular babysitters.

If you are new to parenthood, you may be in that stage of thinking that the cost of the baby is balanced by the fact you hardly seem to go out anymore. However, the stay-at-home phase (and the cost-savings) won't last for ever – you will eventually want to leave your precious bundle with a babysitter and rediscover the world outside your front door.

In a dream world, you will have four or five babysitters that you can call on regularly. Three is good going. Having a list like this to hand has many benefits. Your child or children will be happy to be left with different people if they are used to it – if you only ever use one babysitter you will feel trapped when that person isn't available. Family is, of course, the best place to start – our own precious first bundle was only cared for by aunties, grannies and godmothers for the first six months of her life. It was only when we moved abroad that we suddenly had to branch out.

If you are searching out babysitters for the first time, start close to home. Use your local network of friends, neighbours and ask fellow parents at school or nursery if they have any recommendations. (You must be prepared for some acquaintances and even friends to be a little cagey. Good, available babysitters are a little like gold dust, particularly around Christmas time!) Older children of friends who live locally are a great option – if his or her parents are home when they come to babysit, you have the advantage of an adult nearby who could come and help out in an emergency. Often, nursery nurses or nursery teachers make great babysitters and, if you use one from your child's own nursery, have the added advantage of being well-known to your children already. Even if you find one reliable babysitter, you are off to a good start. You will be able to expand your list by asking if she has any friends who like to babysit, too.

## Babysitting agencies

There are some agencies which specialise in babysitting. Their hourly rate is usually close to what you would be likely to pay privately (anything from £5-£10 an hour seems to be the going rate, depending on who you have to do the babysitting and where you live). An agency will charge a booking fee for each evening's babysitting on top of the hourly rate. You are able to request a sitter that you have liked previously, though the agency will not be able to guarantee that you will be able to have the same sitter again. Your children will need to be used to (or swiftly become used to) meeting different people and accepting different babysitters, if agency babysitting is going to work for you. You can find a list of babysitting agencies in Section Six.

## Safe babysitting

There is no legal minimum age for babysitting. However, you as the parent are responsible for the welfare of your children until they are 16 – if you leave them with a young sitter who is inexperienced you will be held responsible if things go wrong. (And, of course, as well as being legally held responsible, you would never forgive yourself.) Parents must use their own judgement over whether a sitter is mature enough to cope with any situation that might arise. A mature fourteen-year-old could be suitable (especially if her parents are over the road), but sixteen is generally considered an appropriate age to be responsible for younger children.

Always ask for and check references when using a babysitter for the first time, if the babysitter is not already known to you. A young babysitter is unlikely to have comprehensive references – you must let common sense prevail. Babysitters should be able to provide you with phone numbers of other families they have babysat for – try to speak to at least one of these families and ensure that the sitter has experience with children of the same age as yours.

## Babysitting circles

This is rather an old-fashioned idea, but, like book groups and knitting, one that is making a comeback. Once you begin to go out again, not only are you spending the money you were saving on going out, but your evening just got a whole lot more expensive, as you pay the babysitter at the end of the night. You can try getting together with a group of friends, neighbours or local parents from your baby group or nursery, to help each other out with babysitting. Each family starts with three vouchers, one of which they use to 'pay' another member of the group when they receive an evening's babysitting. You earn vouchers by offering babysitting. The vouchers continue to move around the group, as you all babysit for each other for free. Although the thought of going out every now and again to babysit for a friend, leaving your own children and partner at home may seem strange at first, it can actually be rather a lovely way to spend the evening, hopefully quietly sitting in a friend's house, away from all your own ironing and admin.

## How to find a maternity nurse

The two best routes to finding a maternity nurse are by word-of-mouth recommendation from a friend, or by using the services of an agency. You probably have a short window of opportunity to find the maternity nurse of your dreams. The popular maternity nurses can be booked up to nine months in advance – repeat bookings are common and the maternity nurse from the first time around can be one of the first people an expectant mother will call when she finds she is pregnant for a second time. If you move fast, you are likely to have a selection to choose from. Leave it late and there will be slim pickings. However, due to the uncertain nature of a maternity nurse's work and dates constantly shifting around (albeit a little) you may well be lucky and find an absolute gem available at short notice.

Agencies will have a list of maternity nurses that they can send in an emergency – this could be to help out when you had anticipated going it alone, only to find you desperately need an extra pair of hands, or to help out by filling in the gap if you have booked a maternity nurse but have delivered earlier than expected, or if you would just like a week's help at short notice. In the same way that temporary nannies can be a godsend, a stand-by maternity nurse can help your family through some difficult times.

## Sarah, 41, lives in Essex and hired a maternity nurse to help with her newborn daughter

I hired a maternity nurse when I realised I was suffering from post-natal depression. I am usually a confident and outgoing person and nobody thought it would happen to me. However, after years of fertility treatment, a caesarean section, and problems with breastfeeding, I found the early weeks of motherhood very isolating.

The maternity nurse was recommended to me by a friend. She was fantastic. She was experienced enough to cope with my emotions which were running high — I cried a lot. She mapped out each day and kept a record in a daily diary, to help me build a routine. She recorded all the feeds and nap times, as well as nappy changes, to see a pattern emerge. She also helped me to identify the different cries my baby made. She was strict, but I needed that since I was all higgledy-piddgedly and didn't know what was going on. The maternity nurse showed me how to do everything and I just glided along behind her doing as I was told. She was a massive support to me. I was lucky in that I had a lot of family around to support me as well, but often family are wary of interfering. I needed somebody to interfere.

I hadn't imagined we would have a maternity nurse before it became a necessity. I think that we appreciated her help so much that it was easy to live with her for that short period of time. I missed her when she left but she was such a help to me. She was very positive and encouraging — she would even congratulate me for doing something well. It was like having a live-in teacher.

> She was experienced enough to cope with my emotions

# Choosing the right childcare away from home

## A note on checking that providers are registered

All childminders and day-care providers, including playgroups, pre-schools, private nurseries, crèches and after-school clubs for children under eight, must be registered by Ofsted Early Years (or in Wales, by the Care Standards Inspectorate).

Check that a childcare provider is registered by asking to see a registration certificate, or by contacting Ofsted. In England, childcare for children aged eight and over, or care for children of any age that is based around one or two activities, or is provided in the child's home (e.g. nannies), does not have to be registered by Ofsted. The provider of this care may choose to register on the voluntary part of the Ofsted Childcare Register.

Ofsted reports provide detailed information based on the annual inspections. When Ofsted inspect care that is registered on the Ofsted Childcare Register, they will produce a letter confirming whether or not the registration requirements have been met. These reports are accessible to the general public.

Ofsted inspect quality and standards of care provided by each childcare provider. A registration with Ofsted gives parents an indication that the provider is meeting certain criteria and standards. In their written reports, the Ofsted inspectors are assessing the provider in the following areas:

- **Effectiveness of the provision, including how far the provider is helping children to be healthy, protecting children from neglect and harm and helping children to stay safe.**
- **Organisation of the provision, including helping children achieve well and enjoy what they do, helping children make a positive contribution.**

On publication of an Ofsted inspection report, childcare providers will be given areas for future improvement, which will be followed up at the next inspection.

Childcare providers with Investors in Children Quality Assurance schemes accreditation have shown a commitment to quality childcare that is of a high standard. Where possible, you may prefer to choose one of these providers.

# CHILDMINDERS
## Choosing the right childminder

Start by arming yourself with a list of registered childminders from your local Children's Information Service (or FIS). Childminders can list their own details on the council website, giving a brief description of their location, the kind of care they are offering, usually including times of day, days of the week, and whether they are able to collect from local schools. The information listed will also include details of the number and age of children that they are registered to care for. Childminders give a brief outline of the facilities they are able to provide, and the activities that they regularly enjoy with the children in their care.

You can narrow your search depending on the criteria that suit you – this may be the childminders closest to your home or work, the childminders who offer the school collections that you need, or the childminder who states that 'messy play' is her favourite activity. Contact the childminders that you are interested in on paper, to enquire about spaces. Childminders are restricted as to how many children they are able to look after, so getting a place with your top choice childminder may just come down to timing and luck.

You may strike gold and have an instant rapport with the first childminder you meet, who lives around the corner from your home, looks after another child of the same age and has a space available on the days you need the care. Lucky you! You are likely, however, to want to visit a few childminders in your local area before committing to one. Each childminder will provide care in a different way and in a different environment. All registered childminders will adhere to a strict childcare code, but each will also bring to the role their own style and personality. It is so important to find a good match – a childminder with whom you will be able to form a good relationship.

## Elaine, 40, is a childminder, mother and stepmother in Dundee

One of the reasons I went into childminding was because I have my own little girl as well as stepchildren and I wanted to earn money while looking after the children. I was always secretly interested in a career in childcare, although previously I worked as a sales manager.

The children I regularly look after here mix well and my own daughter loves being in the middle of it all. As well as the childminding I also do respite care for foster children and abandoned children. I can get a phone call at seven o'clock at night saying a child needs emergency care. It's been very good for my daughter to see that — she is much more aware that some children don't have a mummy and daddy.

Some days we go to toddler groups or play groups, or we'll just play out in the garden. The little ones usually have a rest in the morning, we have lunch together and it is play time in the afternoon.

I like a lot of involvement from the parents. I'm employed by them and wouldn't want to make their lives difficult so I'll follow their routines as much

> I like the small group care that I can offer as a childminder

as possible. If a child is with me for just two days a week it's not worth upsetting their routine. I try to cater for the different ages — we've got a big trampoline for the older ones after school and a playroom full of toys for the younger ones.

I like the small group care that I can offer as a childminder. It's good to be able to give so much individual attention to the children.

## Visiting a childminder – first impressions count

Your gut instinct will tell you a great deal when you first meet a childminder. Does she look like the sort of person that you would like to take care of your child? Try to take in your first impressions of the childminder's home, as well as her appearance and her smile. Can you imagine your child in this environment, being looked after by this person, all day?

## Registration and other certificates and documents

Ask to see the childminder's documentation. Registration shows that the childminder is serious about what she is doing, and gives parents some recourse should any problems arise.

Ofsted-registered childminders should also be able to display a CRB check (for herself and any other adults over the age of 16 who have access to the house); a first-aid certificate; public liability insurance, and certificates showing attendance at a food hygiene course and a child protection course.

## Heidi, 35, works as a childminder in Reading and is mother of two boys

I've been involved in childcare all my working life. Previously I was a residential social worker. I like being a childminder and being able to give more individualised care in a home environment.

I'm a member of the NCMA and I'm also a network childminder. Every couple of months network childminders are visited, assessed and helped with on-going training. The network provides good materials for us to use.

> Every couple of months network childminders are visited, assessed and helped with on-going training

I have about 15 children on my books and I'm full most days. The youngest child is one and the oldest is seven years old. The best thing about the job is being able to work in my home. My second son is about to go to school and it is great for him socially — he has really benefited. Even my older son enjoys helping with the younger ones. The downsides are that that the mess is in your home and you can't clear up all the time if you are doing your job properly. We keep the bedrooms off-limits.

I know how important it is for children to have continuity of care so before I take a child on I have written information on their routine, likes and dislikes. We have a flexible routine which can be adapted to suit new children. No child has outgrown me yet but if I felt I couldn't offer the activities they needed then it might be time for them to move on.

I write a daily diary for the under-fives. If there is something I need to discuss with a parent I would probably call in the evening. It is always busy at the end of the day and it's not appropriate to try and have a private conversation in front of other children or adults.

## Taking a tour

Ask to see around the childminder's home. You can reasonably expect to be able to see any areas that your child will have access to, including the play area, the kitchen, the bathroom and where your child would be put down for his sleep during the day. Ask to see the outside space – a garden or patio will be a great asset at a childminder's house. Try to take in whether the premises are clean and tidy and what kind of toys and activities are available to the children in the childminder's care.

You will probably start to chat as you look around, but it will be easier to have a proper talk when you are sitting in one place, preferably in the place that the children play all day.

### 10 things to look for at the childminder's house
- Quiet spaces • Safety catches • Clean and plentiful toys • Dressing up box • Little clutter • Tidy kitchen/food preparation area • Lists of phone numbers • Happy children • Sharp edges • Usable outside space

## "Pat, 52, is a childminder in Birkenhead and is keen to help prospective parents when they are considering her

I enjoy looking after children. I get a lot of satisfaction from seeing the little ones develop. I've looked after one little girl since she was six months old and she's four now. It has been lovely to see her grow up. I also like the freedom of being my own boss that childminding offers me. I like to be in my own environment, making my own decisions. I've been a childminder off and on for about 10 years. I work five-and-a-half days a week — I look after two special needs children on Saturday mornings.

I am a member of the NCMA. I think membership is something parents like to see — it shows a childminder has commitment. I enjoy the benefits of legal advice, help lines, their standard contract as well as the stationary and so on.

I invite prospective parents round to have a look at me in action. I ask about their child's routine. I encourage families to settle their child in over a period of time so they all get used to me. In terms of communication, I write a letter to all the parents every three months reminding them of dates when

I'll be closed. I will speak to parents when they collect and fill them in on the detail of their child's day.

I like to have a routine with the children. In the morning we have breakfast, some go to school, the others will have a little singsong, some activities, then lunch. In the afternoon we'll pick up the older children from school and go over to the park if the weather is fine. We have a nice playroom here. There are lots of toys that the children can reach so they can help themselves. I encourage them to tidy them up afterwards. We've got lots of dressing up outfits, and a kitchen area with little saucepans and plates. They love it! The children are always learning through their play.

Children really benefit from continuity. They need to feel safe and they need to see familiar faces. I think they also love the family atmosphere we can offer.

*I invite prospective parents round to have a look at me in action*

## The interview

In many respects, interviewing a childminder is very similar to interviewing another childcarer, such as a nanny (covered in Chapter Sixteen). You should feel able to chat freely during your visit and ask any questions that arise through your informal conversation. This can be a two-way process – the childminder will also be interviewing you. She will want to make sure that she thinks you will both be able to get along well together. The relationship between parent and childminder is an important one. There are eight main areas for discussion, including contracts, before you get on to references.

### What do you do all day?
- Ask the childminder to describe a typical day.
- Are the children able to play outside every day? If there isn't a garden or outside space at the childminder's home, ask where they go to play and how often they are able to go outside.

- How far is it to the local park or playground?
- Is there an opportunity for messy play, cooking and creating? Make sure you have a chance to spend some time where your child will be spending the day. You will have a much better picture of what your child's day will be like with the childminder if you are able to have your chat in the playroom.
- Does the childminder take the children to drop-in playgroups or any toddler groups? Childminders often make use of story time at a local library – is there one nearby and is the childminder aware of the schedule? In some areas there is a drop-in playgroup especially for childminders, run by the council. This gives childminders a great opportunity to meet with others doing the same work, to share ideas and experiences, as well as giving the children in their care a chance to mix with a bigger group of children for a couple of hours.
- Where do the children go for quiet time, or a nap if appropriate? Ask to see the sleeping arrangements. Will your child be able to rest away from the others, or do the children all rest in a room together?

## Other children

The other children who are looked after by the childminder will have a big impact on your child's day. Ideally they will be regulars, with whom your child will be able to form a bond with and enjoy playing with.

- What are the ages of the other children being cared for?
- How does the childminder cope with their different needs and routines?
- How long have the other children been with the childminder?
- Why have previous children in her care left and moved on to other childcare arrangements?

## Other adults

Don't be afraid to ask some personal questions of your potential childminder. After all, you are putting your child into her life.

- Who are the other members of her family?
- Does the childminder have older children around during the day?
- Is the childminder's husband or partner often around the children?
- Are there any other adults regularly in the house?

Other adults who will be in contact with the children need to have a CRB check to comply with the demands of the childminder's registration. It is a good idea for you to meet any other adults who will regularly be around your child. If you like the childminder, you could perhaps arrange to come back and meet any other people who may be around during the day.

### What will my child eat?
You should be able to see the kitchen and eating area during your tour. It is a good idea to discuss healthy eating practices, to see if you have similar thoughts on this issue.

- Are meals and snacks included in the childminder's charges? Do you need to provide any extras?
- What kind of snacks does she offer the children, and when?
- Does the childminder follow a regular menu for the children?
- Will she be able to take the individual likes and dislikes of the children in her care into account?
- How would she encourage a reluctant child to eat?

### Discipline
Parents need to be sure that they share similar beliefs over how to discipline a child for a childminding relationship to work.

- How would the childminder discipline your child?
- Ask about particular scenarios, to find out whether your responses to a particular situation would be in line with the childminder's.
- How does the NCMA code of practice, a pledge to give discipline appropriate to each child's behaviour and age, work in practice?

### Communication
As with all forms of childcare, communication is vital to a successful outcome for you and your child. Take the opportunity to find out more about a potential childminder's communication skills and habits.

- How will the childminder communicate with you?
- Does the childminder keep a record of activities during each day? This is a great method of communication and allows parents to be up to date with what their child is doing.

- Will there be an opportunity to talk at the beginning and end of each day, if necessary? This will also depend on your schedule, as well as on how many other children the childminder is looking after.
- If these crunch points of the day are too hectic for a quiet conversation, how else will the childminder make sure she is able to communicate with you if necessary?

### Emergencies and accidents

Registered childminders are required to keep a record of any accidents, however minor, that take place during the time children are in her care. Parents need to sign the accident record when they come to collect their child.

- How would the childminder cope in an emergency?
- What back up does she have in place to cope with emergencies?
- What would she do if she couldn't reach you in an emergency?

### Contracts

The National Childminding Association has a sample contract which members of the association will usually use. Ask the childminder to show you a sample contract. Any contract should include details on the following:

- Cost of the care provided – how much will it cost to have your child in this daycare setting? What is included in the price (in terms of food, snacks, nappies and other equipment).
- Notice period – how much notice is either side required to give to terminate the agreement?
- Holiday arrangements – how much notice will you be given of your childminder's time off? Usually parents will have to pay for their regular hours of care when they are away on holiday since they are reserving their child's place; childminders don't usually charge when they are unavailable due to being away on holiday.
- Sickness arrangements – what arrangements can be made with regard to sickness? If your childminder (or one of her own children who she cares for with others) is ill, she will cancel the day care and not charge the parents. If your child is ill and unable to go to the childminder's, you will usually have to pay for the day's care regardless.
- Settling-in period and length of contract – how long is the settling-in period, before you all make a formal commitment to each other?

Once a successful settling-in period is completed, how long will you sign a contract for from that point? Six months is usual to start with, moving on to a twelve-month contract after that if all parties are happy.

### References

It is vitally important to check references for childminders. Ask the childminder for the telephone numbers of other parents that she is currently childminding for. There should be no hesitation in her willingness to do this – if there is any you should take this as a warning.

You are able to apply for a copy of the latest Ofsted report on the childminder. The childminder might well freely offer one to you.

### Recall

Make notes as soon as you leave the childminder's home after a visit. Especially if you are visiting a few, you will want something to refer to later on. If you are keen on a childminder, let her know quickly (you don't want to lose the spot to someone else) and arrange to go back for a second visit, with your child if you didn't take him the first time. Try to arrange to bring another adult with you on your second visit – partner, granny or friend – for a second opinion.

## The jackpot

An ideal childminder will be formal in her record-keeping, up to date with all her documents and keen to share them with prospective parents, happy to demonstrate her childminding skills in front of a prospective parent, loving towards the children in her care and attentive to their needs.

# NURSERIES
## Choosing the right nursery, crèche or pre-school

Choosing the right nursery for your child is terrifically important. Research shows that good nursery care can be beneficial for your child – so picking the right place can have an impact on your child's development.

As with all kinds of childcare, try to give yourself a choice. Find out where your local nurseries are, then narrow your search to the ones that are easily within in reach of your home or work. Find out as much as you can about these nurseries before you arrange to visit. Make sure that they are registered childcare providers (this is a legal requirement). You could take a look at the Ofsted reports before you visit. Look at the nursery's website and ask for a brochure to be sent to you.

Pinpoint your top three and arrange to visit each one.

## Taking a nursery tour

When you go for your tour, keep your eyes and ears open. Imagine your child in the facility day after day and try to get a sense of what it will be like for him. Listen carefully to your tour guide but be sure to form your own opinions. Taking a tour of a nursery has many similarities to an interview situation. Be prepared with a list of questions appropriate to the childcare setting. You want to find out as much as possible of the nursery's principles, as well as their practical approach to childcare.

One person will probably give you a tour of the nursery. Remember that this person has been chosen because they are presentable, eloquent and a good face for the nursery, which is trying its hardest to attract your business. Nurseries are all aiming to provide the best care and know what standards parents are looking for – and what parents want to hear. Try to engage your guide in conversation and encourage her to go beyond her stock answers during the course of your tour.

If possible, find an opportunity during your tour to chat with some of the other staff. It is worth asking if there could be a chance for you to speak informally with any of the full-time members of staff, after your tour. Your guide will be well placed to answer your questions about the nursery, its ethos and the facts and figures about the business and day-to-day running of the nursery. You might like to ask some more personal questions of the staff that will be actually be looking after your child.

### Suggested questions for individual nursery nurses
- What qualifications do you hold and where did you complete your training?
- How long have you been working with children?
- How long have you been working at this nursery?
- What do you like about working at this nursery?
- What do you like about working with children?
- What do you think are the challenges of working with children?
- How do you manage troublesome children and discipline?
- Is it possible to come to a babysitting arrangement with any of the nursery nurses, either as a regular occurrence or as an emergency back up?

## Donna, 29, is a nursery manager in Shrewsbury

I love working in childcare. Children are funny and challenging and just really nice to be around. It's really rewarding to see the children progress. The only downside of this job is the pay. It doesn't really reflect the responsibility of the role we take on.

Mornings here are a mixture of child-initiated play and adult-led time. The afternoon tends to be a little more relaxed and informal.

It is so important to have a good relationship with the parents; they're putting a lot of trust in us. It is always difficult to manage a situation when children have had an accident, or been bitten by another child, but if the basis of a good relationship is already there, it is easier to work together to resolve any problems. I have a lot contact with the parents and they can always call me if there is a problem.

I would advise parents looking around to ask about routines and to look at the state of the nursery. Look closely to see how the nursery nurses are with the children. Are the children enjoying themselves? As a parent I would also try to visit at an awkward time. At lunchtime everyone is busy but everything should be running like clockwork. If you arrive for a planned visit, you might not get a true picture. Talk to other parents in your area and don't just pick the first nursery that you see. It's an important decision and shouldn't be taken lightly.

> It's an important decision and shouldn't be taken lightly

I think it is great for children to be looked after in a nursery setting. It teaches them to be sociable and to be used to lots of different people. It is a great preparation for school. It has been a good choice for my own daughter.

## First impressions count

As with most areas of childcare, first impressions do count.

- What does the building look like as you approach it?
- How are you greeted at the door?
- Has the nursery remembered that you are coming for an appointment and is someone ready to show you around?
- Does your guide have all the relevant printed information to hand that you would want to take away – for example price lists, policy documents, sample contracts and terms and conditions?

It is a good idea for parents to visit nurseries together so that they can talk about their experience immediately afterwards. If your partner is unable to make it, bring a friend or grandparent for another set of eyes and ears. Granny might be able to give some insights (though these are unlikely to always be positive, they might prove useful) and she may have made some different observations while you were busy asking questions and chatting to your guide.

It can be hard to ask questions, take in the replies and be able to look around at the same time. You are highly unlikely to be able to look around unsupervised (in fact you should be concerned if you are able to do this), so it is worth asking to walk through the nursery for a second time, without chatting to your guide. This will give you a chance to form your own thoughts.

Take a notebook with you. You can go armed with a list of questions – it is so easy to get caught up in a chat and forget to ask some of the key questions you have prepared, if you don't have notes. You will also be able to record your initial thoughts and first impressions of the place, along with the answers to your questions.

Make sure that you are being shown everything that you want to see and that you should see. At the end of the tour, check that you have seen all the rooms that are used for looking after children of all different ages, all indoor and outdoor play areas, where the children eat and where the food is prepared, where the children rest and even where the children have their nappies changed or go to the loo.

Start by asking about the philosophy and ethos of the nursery. Is the overriding atmosphere one of learning or nurturing? Ask for a brief description and look for a balanced answer. Think about what is best suited to your child.

The questions that you should be asking can be broken down into the following main sections.

## Staff

### Staff ratios

How many children regularly attend the nursery?

Ask about the staff to children ratios. There are legal requirements that must be adhered to, which are as follows:

*1:3 0-2 years*
*1:4 2-3 years*
*1:8 3-5 years*

The ratios include any children of staff or volunteers. Regular volunteers can be included in these staff ratios, but students on short-term placements cannot. These staffing levels must be maintained at all times. Ask how the nursery ensures they will guarantee adherence to these ratios – during staff breaks, nursery outings, holidays, sickness or other emergencies.

### Staff qualifications and experience

Fifty per cent of staff must hold relevant childcare qualifications such as NVQ Childcare Level 2 or equivalent. There should always be one member of staff on duty with a first-aid certificate and all supervisors are required to have an NVQ Childcare Level 3 or equivalent. A CACHE Diploma is the new NNEB qualification for nursery nurses, and shows a high level of commitment to childcare skills from the holder.

There should also be a qualified person present in every room where children are being looked after, at all times. Look for a higher percentage than is required by law, as this demonstrates a commitment to training from the nursery.

- Ask directly how many nursery staff are qualified, and to what level?
- Does the nursery offer any professional development for its staff? Are staff members able to attend training courses to improve their skills and qualifications? How are staff incentivised to stay with the nursery?
- How much experience is there among the staff?

### Staff turnover

- How long do members of staff tend to stay with the nursery? Ask how long specific nursery nurses you meet along the way have been with the nursery.

- How does the nursery recruit new staff? Where do they advertise for new staff members?
- What kind of checks does the nursery carry out on new staff – CRB and police checks should be obtained, as well as references from previous employers and certificates to prove they have the qualifications required of the role.

Ask these questions in an open way – what checks do you do, rather than do you carry out CRB checks? Let the guide fill in the gaps and demonstrate that she knows what the requirements are.

## Michelle, 27, has learnt from experience when it comes to choosing a nursery for her daughter, Rebecca

My daughter was six months old when she went to nursery. I liked the idea of a nursery for childcare as it gives her the opportunity to mix with other children, and I liked the security that I thought her being cared for in a group setting offered me.

I work for the local council, and the nursery was recommended to staff there. The nursery was convenient, my workplace had a positive relationship with it and, particularly as Rebecca is my first child, I was happy to have her nearby.

There were a few problems to start with, but rather than getting ironed out, they escalated. I ended up taking Rebecca out after a year.

The management were inefficient – their accounts were in such a mess that they were chasing parents for money they didn't owe, even threatening them with debt collectors. I contacted Ofsted as there were so many problems – from broken stair gates to security issues – and they are still looking into it all. There were problems with the day-to-day care, too; my daughter had constant nappy rash while she was at the nursery and they gave her cow's milk when she was seven months old, which made her horribly constipated. It never felt like there was an opportunity to talk to the manager on an informal basis. I ended up worrying about Rebecca all the time she was there.

When I was looking for the second time I looked at five or six nurseries. I was so worried about leaving my daughter in a bad set-up again. I feel lucky to have found the nursery that my daughter goes to now.

At the new nursery I can have a chat with the manager every day. She's very visible. I know from experience how important that is. I can pop in and see Rebecca at lunchtime. The first few days I phoned the nursery a lot to check everything was all right — they didn't mind and were very reassuring. The girls working with Rebecca are very competent. There is a broad age range among the carers, which I think is a good thing. There is a balance between youth and experience. The security system is good, with a manned reception desk. Rebecca is coming on in leaps and bounds — she doesn't want to come home at the end of the day! She is busy cooking, drawing and playing all day long. It's great.

> The first few days I phoned the nursery a lot to check everything was all right — they didn't mind and were very reassuring

### Are there any male members of staff?
Nurseries with male nursery nurses are rightly proud of this. Babies and small children enjoy and can benefit from having men around. It is a good sign if a nursery has managed to recruit and keep male nursery nurses.

### Key workers
A key worker is a particular member of staff who is assigned full responsibility for your child at a nursery. The key worker will be the member of staff who

will routinely communicate with parents and be the first port of call in case of any problems.

- Does the nursery operate a system of key workers for the children?
- Will each child stay with the same key worker over the course of her time at the nursery or will she have different key workers as she progresses?
- How many staff will be involved with your child?

## Food, including snacks and mealtimes

Meals and snacks provided by the nursery can be labour saving for parents – a big bonus.

- Which meals are provided?
- Are the meals cooked on site? If not, where are they prepared, and how are the meals transported?
- Is the food organic?
- Are the children provided with snacks? What are they and when are they available?
- What are the children given to drink during the day?
- Does the nursery provide any choice at mealtimes? What would they do if a child didn't eat any lunch?
- How will the nursery cope with allergies to certain foods and religious observances which mean that particular foods have to be avoided?
- How are mealtimes supervised? Are the children all expected to sit down together and wait for each other to finish? Are good eating habits encouraged? You are unlikely to be able to visit during a mealtime, but snack time will give you an indication of what is expected of the children.
- Are all meals, milk and snacks included in the fees? Are parents required to provide milk for babies?

## Nursery organisation

### Structure of the day

- How will my child be cared for and entertained throughout the day?
- Is there a structure and routine to the day?
- Are the children given opportunities for free play?

Age groups
- How are the children split into groups?
- How large are the different age groups?
- Is there much flexibility between groups?
- Will my child always be with the same children and carers as he progresses through the nursery, and so be able to continue friendships with other children and relationships with specific adults?
- How are children settled in when they move up into a different room or group? This can be traumatic for a child, especially if they are spending a lot of the week at the nursery.

Quiet corners and nap times
- Where do the children go to rest?
- Is there a suitable quiet corner in each room, or is there a nap room?
- How is the nap room supervised?
- Are there separate sleeping areas for babies and toddlers?
- How does the nursery avoid children being disturbed by others, when some are likely to be reluctant to have a sleep to order?

Routines
Asking about routines is especially important if your child is very young and will only be attending nursery for a few sessions each week – different routines at home and at nursery might be unsettling. For older children, this will be much less of an issue.

- Are children able to follow their own routines while they are at nursery, or do they all have to conform to the same routine?

Over time, children that spend time together are likely to fall into the same routine. Usually, children will need to eat together and most babies fall into a routine based around their milk and meal times.

Activities
Ask to see the plan for a week for a particular age group. Nurseries tend to be quite structured environments, so they will most probably have one.

- How much free play is allowed?
- How often will children take part in messy play?

- What are the areas that you are hoping your child will benefit from at this nursery and how accessible are these activities to your child during the day?

### Learning
- As the children grow older, is there plenty of opportunity for them to explore new things and start to learn more formally as they reach pre-school age (three and over)?
- Are there opportunities for children to start to learn to read, when they show signs of being ready?

## Nursery facilities

### Inside Space
- Where do the children play, sleep, eat, have their nappies changed and go to the loo? Will they spend the whole day in one room, or will they have the opportunity to move around in different spaces?
- How are the toys and activities set up?
- Is everything clean and well-presented?

### Outside space
Make sure you see any outside spaces. Hopefully they will be in action. If the garden is unused on a sunny day, ask why.

- Are the children able to play outside every day?
- If there is no outside area at the facility, where are the children taken for fresh air, and how often?
- Do the children go to other outside spaces, for example to parks?
- How are they supervised on outings outside the building?

## The bad stuff

### Discipline
- What is the nursery's policy on discipline?
- How do the nursery nurses manage bad and difficult behaviour?

During your tour, try to get a sense of whether the nursery nurses are offering positive reinforcement of good behaviour, rather than sending negative messages.

Nursery workers should ideally be spending a lot of time demonstrating good behaviour and interaction with each other and the children, so the children can learn by example. Nursery nurses should always avoid humiliating a child in front of the other children.

Experienced nursery nurses will question why a child might be misbehaving – is she bored, hungry, thirsty or tired? They will also have techniques for managing bad behaviour at their fingertips, such as talking calmly to the children, asking gentle questions, communicating and encouraging the children to communicate their feelings.

### Illness
- When can a child come to nursery and when must they stay at home?
- What is the protocol for contacting parents if the child falls ill during the day?
- At what point (temperature, upset tummy, general malaise) will they call a parent?

How many runny noses do you see on your way round? Constant colds are a common complaint at nursery – when a number of children are looked after together in one setting it is absolutely inevitable that colds will be a problem, until children are able to build up some level of immunity. Do the staff look like they are on top of the runny noses?

### Accidents and emergencies
- What procedures does the nursery have in place for managing accidents?
- How are they recorded and reported?
- What is the nursery's protocol for dealing with emergencies?
- How would the nursery communicate with parents in an emergency?

### Late collection
- What facilities are there for late collection? Most nurseries will only be insured up to a certain hour.
- How much does the nursery charge for a late collection?
- What will the nursery do in the event of an emergency that, for example, shuts the transport network making it impossible for parents who have to travel to collect on time?

One solution sometimes found by parents is to come to an arrangement directly with the nursery nurses, where the carers take a child home either on a regular or irregular basis. This is organised entirely separately from the nursery, but can give the parents a reliable back-up plan. Ask if this is an arrangement that the nursery has made in the past and is willing to facilitate. Then its effectiveness will come down to you forming a sufficiently good relationship with the nursery nurse who happens to live near your home, or whose home you pass on your way back from work.

### Security
- The security of the children is of the highest priority and your guide should have sensible answers at her fingertips.
- How does the nursery guarantee your child's security?
- What checks are in place for when children are collected at the end of the day?
- Are the doors all properly secure during the day? (There is the odd horror story of children getting out and finding their way to the local park.)
- Is the outside play area completely secure?
- How are visitors checked and how do they access the building? (Make a note of how you are treated.)
- How are children kept safe when going on excursions from the nursery, for example to the park?

### Communication
Communication is so important with a nursery, as with every form of childcare.

- How does the nursery communicate with parents?
- How often are parents able to meet formally and informally with key workers and other staff members?
- Is there an opportunity to chat informally each day?
- Will the nursery be able to let you know what has been happening each day?
- Nursery managers may be available at drop off and collection times to ease communication.
- Are parents able to communicate with their children during the day?

We have come across nurseries with outside phone lines installed in each room. Parents are actively discouraged from calling during naptimes, or from calling too frequently, which can unsettle the children, but can call if need be.

## Complaints procedure
- **What is the complaints procedure at the nursery?**

Parents sometimes want to avoid asking about this at an early stage, not wanting to look difficult, but it is important to know that there is a procedure in place in the event of something going wrong. Of course, you can always resort to Ofsted to make a complaint, but there should be somewhere to go within the nursery's organisation before taking that step.

## Record keeping
From 2008 nurseries will have to follow the Every Child Matters 0-5 programme and keep files on children recording their development and progress against particular measures.

- **What is the protocol for keeping records?**
- **Are the records in keeping with government guidelines?**
- **Can the nursery demonstrate their record keeping?**
- **Who has access to the records?**
- **Are the records readily available to parents?**

Ask the staff how they feel about keeping records. Staff ought to be comfortable about it, even if it is time consuming. Good record keeping allows the nursery as well as the parents to monitor progress. It also helps to ensure that children are being allowed to move on in their development and play, and avoid repeating the same activities for a long period.

## Basic facts and figures

### Registration
- **When should a baby or child be registered?**
- **Does registration guarantee a place?**
- **Is there a deposit to pay and when will you get it back?**

### Fees
- **What are the fees?**
- **Do the fees include all meals, milk and nappies or do you need to provide all or some of this?**
- **What is the minimum number of sessions that you are allowed to sign up for?**
- **How much written notice does the nursery require?**

### Documentation
- Ask for a copy of the contract that you will be asked to sign, should you choose this nursery. Ask to see a copy of the policy document.
- Ask to see the nursery's Ofsted report, registration certificates and insurance certificates.
- Is the nursery part of an official body, for example the National Day Nurseries Association?
- Enquire whether the nursery has gained any kite marks of excellence, especially those endorsed by the government, for example the NDNA's Quality Counts, Investors in People or Investors in Children.

### References
Ask the nursery manager to give you the names and phone numbers of two parents with children at the nursery at present, who will be willing to discuss the nursery with you informally.

Also, leave with the phone number of the person that has shown you around, so that you can call later on with the questions that you forgot to ask during the tour.

## Ella, 28, is a nursery manager in Derbyshire

I've always enjoyed looking after children. It is great fun! The best thing about my job is seeing the children who come as babies grow into little children ready for school.

I enjoy being the manager. We are quite a large nursery, with 70 places, so we have a full-time administrator. My time is spent looking after children, covering for other staff, organising staff and making sure we are up to date with all the Ofsted requirements.

Our staff are all trained and go on extra courses every year. I think that gives parents peace of mind. We think contact with parents is very important — I am available every morning to chat and we write down everything the babies have done each day in terms of their routine so that parents are aware of what sort of a day they have had. We can build up a good relationship with the parents — sometimes they will send us all their children and be with us for years.

We open from 8am to 6pm and we give the children breakfast, lunch and tea. After breakfast the children will have free play with a variety of imaginative toys. Snack time is at 10am. We encourage the older ones to put butter and jam on their bread — one of the things that helps them to become a bit more independent. In the afternoon the children have a messy play time — anything from water, sand to painting and crafts. There is always an opportunity for the children to have a rest in a quiet area.

I would advise parents to look at every nursery in their area before making a choice. Parents have come to us and loved us and others have chosen to go elsewhere. Parents' choice will come down to the nursery which shares their ethos.

> Parents' choice will come down to the nursery which shares their ethos

## Forming your own opinion

As you take your tour, try to make your own observations of the children that are in the nursery and the general surroundings. Your tour guide will be pointing out all the facilities and the well-behaved children – try to stand back and come to your own conclusions.

### Children
- How are the children generally behaving?
- Do they look well-occupied, interested and happy, or are they distracted, unfocused and disruptive?
- Are the children interacting well with each other and with the staff?
- Are the children allowed to direct their own games or are they always led?

### Staff
- Do the staff appear friendly and approachable – both to you and to the children?
- Do the staff look happy, relaxed and confident?
- Are they involved with the children or are they playing more of a supervisory role?
- Are they comforting children that need extra cuddles?
- Do the staff and children reflect the local cultural and ethnic groups – is the nursery appealing to everyone in the community?

### Facilities
- Does the nursery have a warm and cosy atmosphere?
- What is the equipment like?
- Are the toys plentiful and clean?
- Are the premises appropriate for the purpose?
- Is the nursery clean and well looked after, even if a little tired round the edges?
- What is the outside area like?
- How accessible is any outside space for the children?

### 10 good signs at a nursery
- Space • Light • Tidiness • Cleanliness • Smiles • Busy children
- Paintings on the wall • Singing • Chatter
- Interested and engaged staff

## Taking stock

Allow yourself some time to reflect after a tour of a nursery. Try to write down some of your impressions and make further notes that you weren't able to make whilst inside, quickly after your visit, so that you have something concrete to refer back to. It can be quite overwhelming and there is a great deal to take in. Think about whether you enjoyed your tour. What is your gut instinct?

When you get home, reflect again on the following:

- Did the children look happy, entertained, well cared for, relaxed and interested?
- Was there a background chatter around the older children – were the carers talking to the children or just taking care of them?
- Were the children playing with the toys or were they all on shelves?
- Were the staff interacting with each other and with the children?
- What was the general impression of the setting – were the toys plentiful, was the space clean and well organised?

If you have gone alone for your initial visit and you liked the nursery, arrange to go back with a partner, friend or relative for a second opinion. It is also a good idea to take your child on your second visit if you haven't the first time around – watch closely to see how the staff react to your child and whether your child looks interested in the surroundings.

## Jenny is the co-founder of a nursery chain in Manchester

We set up Kids Allowed after I had my second child and was trying to find suitable childcare. I had a full-time career, one daughter about to start school and a new baby and we just couldn't find anything flexible enough to allow us to meet our requirements.

The advantage of nursery care for young children is the social aspect, and that at nursery, even though the children are playing all day, they are also learning through play. I think you can tell the children that have been to nursery when they start school because they're sociable, confident and they've got a good grounding of the basics.

Kids Allowed is very customer focused. We are there to deliver a service for the children, parents and siblings. I think in the past that there weren't enough nursery places to go round. Today's market is much more competitive. You have to know what your customer wants and deliver it to attract the business.

Our Kids Allowed nurseries offer some services which I knew from experience are the things that parents often need. We always have extra staff available at the end of the day in case parents are running late. It's not something parents do on purpose — sometimes you just get stuck in traffic or caught in a meeting. We keep four spaces open every day for parents to ring up for what we call 'short notice service'. If, for example, they usually have grandparents caring for their child one or two days a week and they are unable to at short notice, we can accommodate their child for an extra day. We aim to be flexible.

We understand that it's really hard to get out of the house in the morning with children. When I was using nurseries I had to bring nappies, wipes and make-up bottles and prepare food to bring with me to the nursery. We have included all of this in our price so all parents need to bring is their child!

> It's really hard to get out of the house in the morning with children

We run a parent concierge service. It is on offer to help with the day-to-day things like laundry, ironing, dry cleaning and post. There is someone on reception where parents can drop things off and collect a day or two later. This frees parents up to spend more time with their children — just makes lives a little easier. We also offer parent classes and two-hour workshops on various topics of interest to our families.

The children have a free choice of activities which are planned for them each day. Then there will be some 'directed play' where we set an activity and try to engage the children in small groups. We encourage learning through play but recognise that they are very young. Most of all, we want to make sure that the children go home having had a wonderful day.

I advise parents to look closely during a nursery tour. Is there a warm welcome? Does the place smell nice? Is it clean? Are the staff engaged with *the children and playing with them, or are they all chatting in the corner? Take in the environment — does it give you a warm feeling?*

## AFTER-SCHOOL AND HOLIDAY CLUBS
### Choosing the right after-school and holiday club

After-school clubs and holiday clubs can be such a great childcare solution for school-age children. You will, however, not be as free to choose your childcare provision as you are in other areas of childcare. Parents are restricted in their choice of after-school care by the school that their child attends – which may either offer its own after-school club or which will be catered for by one (or two at most) after-school clubs.

Even if there isn't a choice, it is sensible to go and look closely at the after-school club, as you may have other options for after-school care to choose from, such as friends, family or babysitters.

Holiday clubs are often run at the same centres as the after-school clubs. You will obviously have more choice when considering holiday clubs – only being limited by which ones are convenient for you to drop off your children in the morning and collect from at the end of the day.

### What to look for at an after-school club

#### Collection arrangements

Some after-school clubs may be run at a primary school location. Otherwise you need to consider:

- Which schools does the after-school collect from?
- Are children from other schools able to join in?
- How are the children brought to the club each day?
- What is the ratio of adults to children for the duration of the journey?
- If the children are walked to the after-school club, ask about the route.
- Are the children given reflective vests to wear on dark winter afternoons?

### Staff

Meet as many of the staff as you can to get a sense of how the club is run. If possible, arrange to visit a club while there are children present. Be sure to ask about the experience and qualifications of all the staff members.

- Who is in charge of the club?
- What is the ratio of staff to children? The government requires that the ratio is one adult for every eight children in this kind of setting, to care for children over the age of five. (Four-year-olds in their Reception year at school can count as five for the purposes of this arrangement.)
- How do the staff interact with the children? Are they there purely in a supervisory role, or are they really joining in with the children? Children of primary school age don't necessarily need to be entertained in the same way as younger children, as they are more able to find activities for themselves.

### Facilities

Have a good look around the facility – make sure you see every area that the children have access to, as well as the kitchen, if food is prepared on site.

- Is the club clean, spacious, bright and airy?
- Are there separate rooms or areas for different activities? Some children will need to do their homework when they come to the club after school. How are these children provided for? Is there a quiet homework room or area? Are there any reference books or computers for them to use to assist them with their homework?
- Are there plenty of activities on offer for the children? Are there books, toys and craft activities as well as a television and computer games?
- Ask to see any outside space that is available to children to play. Are they allowed to play ball games? How much are the children able to use the space? Is it suitable for the mixed age group that the centre is likely to be catering for?

### Food

An after-school club will usually provide a snack for the children when they arrive at the club from school, and a meal a little later on in the afternoon.

- Ask to see the menu plans for the week, to get a good idea of the meals that are being provided.
- If your child has dietary requirements, in terms of allergies or restrictions, make sure to raise these with the centre. Are they able to cater for your child?
- Is the food prepared on the premises? If so, ask to see the food preparation area. If not, ask where it comes from and how it is transported.

### Organisation

How is the centre run, in terms of organising the children?

- Is one childcare provider responsible for a certain group of children, or one kind of activity?
- Does the club offer a key worker system?

A key worker arrangement is ideal in an after-school club, as he or she will provide a vital link between your child, his school, home and the club. Messages from school are much more likely to reach you at home if there is one person who always acts as a go-between (alongside your child). Communication between school and parents is a vital role for an after-school club to play, especially when the club is caring for a child every day.

A key worker at an after-school club will also be a friend for your child, give him a person to go to if he is feeling lonely, troubled by a conflict with another child or a friendship gone wrong, or someone to turn to if he is stuck on his homework.

- How does the centre cater for the large age range? Most after-school clubs will cater for children all the way through primary school.
- Do they plan weekly activities for the different age groups?
- Is there a chance for the age groups to mix easily while the children are at the club?

### Discipline

Ask about the centre's policy on discipline. The staff at the centre will be in charge of your children and you must make sure you share values.

- How will the carers deal with disruptive children?
- What is the policy on bullying? This can be a potential problem when children with a large age-range are being cared for at one centre.

### Security
- How does the club guarantee your child's safety?
- How do they monitor visitors to the club, and make sure that the children do not leave the club unsupervised?

### Emergencies
- What protocols are in place for dealing with emergencies?

### Illness
What is the club's policy on illness?

- What would staff members do if your child was feeling unwell upon collection from school?
- At what point do they contact parents?

After a tour, make a note of your early impressions to refer back to later on. What was the overall atmosphere like? Did all the children seem occupied and appear to be happy? Did the staff appear involved? Take your child – what did he think of what was on offer?

# Choosing the right childcare at home

### How to identify the best nanny, mother's help, au pair, babysitter or maternity nurse for you and your family

Conducting interviews is a skill and in this chapter we hope to give you some techniques and guidance to getting the best from an interview situation. We will take you through the various stages of the interview process and discuss how to follow up successfully. We will also look at how to sell your job to the right person, remembering that this is, of course, a two-way street and your prospective candidate needs to like the look of you as much as you like the look of her.

The interview is the best chance you have to look at the candidate before you offer a position of great responsibility. Any childcare role is hugely responsible, and should not be taken lightly. When looking to fill a sole charge position, you are asking another person to assume the responsibility of a parent for the time that they are on duty. A shared care role is also a responsible one, since there are bound to be occasions when your shared care nanny will have sole charge of your children. You must use the interview process to ensure you are confident that the candidate is mature and up to the task.

## First things first

You need to know exactly what you want by the time you get to this stage. Refer back to your lists (see the beginning of Section Three) and to our questions in Section Two to help you think about who you are and what will suit you best. Make sure you are very clear about the kind of person you are looking for and the job that you are looking to fill. Be sure about times of day, days of the week and any times of year that you absolutely need the help (when your candidate cannot take holiday). It is a good idea to have your list of duties to hand, too, so you can see quickly if a candidate will match your requirements.

Having said all of that, always think about honesty, kindness, dependability and decency first. Don't pass up a candidate who demonstrates these qualities just because they don't love football (if that's high up your list). Also, try to avoid making the classic mistake of asking the interviewee whether they are honest, kind, dependable and decent. The answer is always going to be yes! (If you make the mistake of asking and the answer isn't yes, show them the door as quickly and politely as possible.) Ask open questions and leave time and space for the interviewee to reveal herself.

## Selecting candidates

You are likely to have a number of applicants to choose from, whichever way you have chosen to go about your childcare search. Internet advertisements are notorious for throwing up lots and lots of candidates and you may have a bit of trawling to do. If you have chosen to go through an agency some of the pre-selection should have been done for you, to assess a candidate's suitability for the position, but you will still want to check through the paperwork to make sure it is going to be worth your time arranging and proceeding with an interview.

Ask to see a written CV from everyone that is applying for the position. This way all candidates start on a level playing field (and some, who can't be bothered to put one together, will drop away instantly). You can ask for accompanying photographs, if you wish. If you have advertised online, be sure to ask for a phone number so that you can speak before meeting.

Check the CVs carefully, making sure that all the qualifications, experience and other criteria that you are looking for are included. Check the age, nationality and language skills of the applicant, if you have strong feelings about any of these. Read through the employment history, looking out for unexplained gaps.

You are looking for a candidate who, as well as having the right qualifications and experience, is really interested in your job. Beware the candidates who say they are prepared to do anything – they won't have the focus that you need, nor perhaps the commitment if something else comes along.

## Holly, 36, is a qualified nanny

I trained at a private college for two years — a year's theoretical training and a year's practical. Then I came up to London, got a job and lived in with a family. I stayed for a year and a half, before leaving to work as a nursery teacher for about two years. Then I went back to working as a nanny, this time as a live-out nanny.

My qualifications have really helped me in my career. The theory part of the training was useful and the practical part gave me experiences to draw on in my work. My employers have always appreciated my qualifications. Some families are looking for the quintessential English nanny.

> My qualifications have really helped me in my career

I have enjoyed staying in each of my jobs for more than a year, as it has given me a chance to build up a rapport with the children, as well as a good relationship with the family.

The best thing about my job is that each day is different. I enjoy being a sole charge nanny and being able to run my day — obviously within the confines of what the parents require.

I would advise parents to always be honest and open with their nanny. If the parents know that the job is going to change in the near future (if the mother is going to be giving up work, for example, and the nanny's job becomes a shared-care role as a result) parents shouldn't just expect the nanny to automatically fall into a new role, and should be prepared to discuss the future openly.

## Phone first

When you have been through your initial weeding out process, take the time to ask a few questions on the phone before setting up an interview. The applicant should be happy to do this – you will be saving everyone's time if there are obvious reasons why you shouldn't meet.

### On the phone, you should:

- Confirm that the applicant understands the post they are applying for.
- Check that the applicant is fully aware of the hours that it will involve.
- Be clear about where you live, the distance from public transport links, and whether you will be requiring the candidate to drive.
- Inform the prospective candidate about any pets that you have in your household – you could save an unnecessary trip if they turn out to be allergic to dogs or can't stand cats.
- Confirm whether the position is live-in or live-out.

You will probably have covered some of this in your advertisement or job description with an agent, but it is surprising how many people will just apply for everything, rather than being selective themselves at the outset. Save time by being clear on the phone.

## Invitation to interview

You have found someone who looks good on paper and sounds good on the phone. It's time to meet face to face.

If you are bringing an au pair over from abroad, this is as far as you can get until you meet at the airport or bus station. That takes a tremendous leap of faith and you must make sure you have conducted a very thorough interview over the phone. Use the questions below and listen carefully to the replies – you will not have the advantage of seeing them face-to-face before offering the post. It is perhaps a good idea to ask for photographs.

Arrange a time that is very convenient to you for the interview. Don't be pushed into a time that doesn't suit you to accommodate the interviewee – it doesn't bode well for the future. You will want to allow enough time to conduct a full interview

– one hour should be enough for the first meeting. Ideally you will be able to hold the interview without your children in the close vicinity. Babies and toddlers will inevitably be very distracting and older children have very waggly ears. It would be perfect if the children were near enough to come and say hello at the end of the interview, if you feel it has gone well. It will be useful at this stage to see how they all interact before you invite your candidate back for a second interview and to spend some proper time with you all as a family.

It is a good idea to conduct the interview with another person present, if at all possible. Your partner, a grandparent, or a good friend will all be able to make useful comments after an interview. It is probably best if one person asks most of the questions, but another is there to pick up on any areas that might have been missed, as well as to give a general impression of the interview and the candidate after they have left. This is especially useful if you are not used to holding interviews. When arranging the interview you will need to make sure that the time that you arrange is convenient to this person as well.

In the interests of not losing a good candidate, arrange for the interview to be held as soon as it is convenient for all parties. Good candidates will inevitably be interviewing elsewhere and you don't want to miss out.

## Josh, 33, lives in Somerset and is heavily involved with childcare arrangements for his two children

My wife is away a lot. She works in Kuwait and comes home every six weeks. I am able to work from home two or three days a week, and am away for the other part of the week.

When I worked regular hours in Exeter, we put our daughter in a nursery at the top of the road, near my office. The nursery was brilliant, the best thing we've ever done. Our daughter is very sociable and I'm sure this is down to her experience at the nursery. When my job moved to Bristol and my wife's work took her away from home more, we needed a live-in nanny to give us the flexibility. We really rely on live-in help to cope with our work schedules.

*We have found older nannies are the most successful — more self-reliant and independent. We tend to interview as a couple as we are both involved and, in fact, the nannies often see more of me than my wife. I have had to hire by myself, but prefer to make a choice with my wife, for a second opinion — we also tend to ask questions covering different areas. I'm more practical; my wife is more emotional.*

> I'm more practical; my wife is more emotional.

*We had a near-miss once. We had placed an ad in the paper, and the girl we chose came with good references. She was due to start on the Monday at 7.30am, but didn't turn up. Eventually I spoke to her mother to be told that the girl had been down at the police station all night; even her mother said we'd had a lucky escape! After that experience, we stick to agencies.*

### First impressions count

Have a quick checklist of first impressions.

- Does the candidate arrive on time for the interview?
- Is she well presented?
- Does she appear to be calm and relaxed, or does she look harassed and dishevelled?

You will probably have to make a quick assessment of all this on the doorstep – try to make those first moments count.

## The interview

You want to make the candidate feel comfortable so that you can really find out what they are like and whether they will be suitable for the position. Begin the meeting by asking how their journey was, whether they found your home easily. This is also a good opportunity to ask if they are familiar with the area that you live in.

The interview can then be divided into parts, as outlined below. This will help you to follow a structure so that you don't get lost halfway through, and forget to cover some important areas. Following a similar pattern in each of your interviews will also enable you to directly compare candidates.

Try to ask your questions in an open way, to allow the interviewee to express herself and her views, rather than just roll out stock, prepared answers. Make sure you dig deep and ask questions in reply to their answers, picking up on something they have said. Perhaps choose one or two areas to really push the candidate on, and pursue a few levels to find out if she is telling the truth – eye contact and body language are of great importance.

## Job description

Outline the job that you are offering. You will have covered this in your initial advertisement or approach to an agency and again on the phone, but it is a good idea to go over it face to face.

State all the duties that you want to be carried out, especially ones which come outside the usual remit of the role that the candidate is applying for (for example, you might be hoping that a nanny will walk the dog alongside taking responsibility for the children).

If you have young babies, include details of any music groups or swimming lessons that you would like the children to be taken to. If you are looking for help with older children, include details of homework supervision and music practise if this is going to be part of the role. If your children have any particular allergies, diets or special needs, mention this early on.

It is helpful to outline of your children's routines and reiterate the hours and days of the week that the job will be for and any times of year that you absolutely cannot have your childcare absent for.

Finally, confirm the start date for the position and then you can move on to asking your questions; some specific, some more open.

## Past experience

- How long have you been a nanny/mother's help/au pair/babysitter?
- What are the ages of children that you have worked with previously?
- What do you think are your strengths when working with children?
- Which aspects of your previous jobs have you particularly enjoyed?

- What has been the biggest challenge you have faced previously in this role?
- Do you have experience with my particular situation? (For example twins in the family, children with special needs, children coming up for potty training, new baby arriving, children starting school, single parent families.)
- Query any gaps in the candidate's employment history. Ask why these gaps arose, and what they did in their time off between jobs. Make sure that you are satisfied with the response that you get and that you don't suspect something is being covered up. Gaps could be because of illness which might affect the suitability of the candidate for the role you are looking to fill, or could flag something else you would like to know about.

## Training and qualifications

- What qualifications do you hold?
- Where did you undertake your training?
- What do you feel you learnt during your course that you can apply to your everyday work?
- Do you have a first-aid certificate?
- What would you do if a child was choking?
- Can you swim?
- Can you cook? (Or, do you enjoy cooking?)

## Principles

- What do you particularly enjoy about working with children?
- How would you spend the day with my children?
- What difficulties have you come across in this kind of work before, and how have those difficulties been resolved?
- What do you think is the most difficult aspect of childcare?
- How would you discipline my children? (Suggest a particular scenario.)
- What qualities do you think it is important to have for this role?

- What kind of food would you prepare for my child?
- What are your views on television, sweets, treats, computer games?
- How have you avoided having favourites among siblings in your previous jobs?

## Personal

- You can get a lot of information by asking the candidate to describe herself. This is a good open question – listen closely to the answer.
- Are you close to your family?
- Do you have any siblings? Did you help to look after them?
- Who do you live with?
- Why did you leave your last job, or why are you leaving your present position?
- What are your interests outside of work?
- If the candidate is from abroad, ask how long she is planning to stay in the UK.
- If English is not her first language and she is not yet fluent, ask if she is planning to take any further language classes.

### 10 open and revealing questions

- What do you like about being around children?
- How would you praise a child for good behaviour?
- How would you discipline a child for naughty behaviour?
- What is your best experience in childcare?
- And your worst?
- How have you dealt with problems with children of this age previously?
- What are your ambitions?
- How would you manage sibling rivalry?
- How would you cope if one of the children was poorly for the day?
- What would you do on a rainy day in May?

## Live-in roles

When interviewing for a live-in role, make time to go through your house rules – decide beforehand how you feel about your live-in inviting her own friends to the house, either when you and your family are in or out and whether you want to impose a curfew (not unreasonable on week-nights when you are expecting help first thing in the morning). Also, what are your views on drinking? Will you be offering your live-in help access to the house phone and internet for their personal use, or restricting access to some areas of the house?

You will need to ask some extra questions when interviewing for live-in roles.

**10 questions you must ask a potential live-in carer**

- Why do you want to live-in?
- Have you lived with a family before? (To try to get an idea of their expectations.)
- Where do you hope to be in a year?
- What do you enjoy doing at the weekends?
- What do you like to do in the evenings?
- What time do you like to eat in the evening? (Make sure that you are clear whether you are happy to always share mealtimes with your live-in helper, or not.)
- Do you smoke?
- Do you drink?
- Do you know many people in this neighbourhood?
- Do you have a boyfriend/girlfriend? (Discuss whether friends/boyfriends are welcome in your house.)

## If it is all going well...

As the interview progresses, you will be forming an idea of whether the candidate is likely to be a realistic proposition for you and your family. If you feel quite confident that you will not be offering the job, you can whizz through this and wind it all up. If you think the candidate is a realistic proposition, go on to discuss the details of the package.

### The details of the package will include:

- Pay: including tax and National Insurance arrangements.
- Holidays: detail what you are offering in terms of holiday pay, and how much holiday your employee will be entitled to each year. If there are specific times of the year that you absolutely need to have your help available, say this now.
- Accommodation (if applicable): show the candidate the accommodation that you are offering, including a tour of the house and other rooms or facilities that will be available to her.
- Perks: highlight any perks you are offering with the position (such as a car for personal use at the weekend, mobile phone, travel with the family).
- Probationary period: it is usual to suggest that the job would start with a probationary period. Three months is common.

Make sure that if you are keen on this candidate, that you sell your position to her and underline the highlights of what you are offering.

### Any questions?

Ask if the candidate has any questions for you. She should! It is unlikely that you will have covered everything; her questions may also throw some more light on her character. If her questions are about the children, it is usually a good sign; a flow of questions about pay and perks may put you off.

### Winding up the interview

- If you are keen on the candidate that you are interviewing, make sure that she knows it, without making any promises there and then. She is likely to be interviewing with other families at the same time; if she knows you are interested she may be less likely to accept other interviews.
- At this stage ask for all the documentation so that you can get on with checking references. You can also arrange for a second meeting when a candidate can spend some time with your children and meet your partner if she hasn't done so already.
- If you are keen, offer a reference for yourself. The candidate may be interested in talking to your present employee, or a previous

nanny, mother's help or au pair. Allow this conversation to take place privately, so that both sides can say whatever they like. Check with previous employees first that they will be happy to take part in this conversation (obviously it helps if your present helper is leaving amicably – you might prefer to avoid this otherwise) and confirm that you can hand out her phone numbers.

## Instant recall

Try to take notes over the course of the interview and try to make time to write down your initial thoughts as soon as you can after the candidate has left. Avoid holding back-to-back interviews if time allows, as it will be hard not to muddle people up. It will be useful to have something in writing to refer back to, especially if you are interviewing a few candidates.

Concentrate your thoughts on specific areas immediately after an interview.

- Did you have a good rapport with the candidate?
- Does the candidate share your attitudes to childcare and/or do you think she will willingly follow your practices?
- Do you think that you would be able to have a good working relationship with the candidate? This is especially important to consider for a shared care role.
- Do you think that the candidate would be easy to live with (if applicable)?
- Does the candidate have the qualifications that you are looking for, or the practical experience to make up for a lack of formal qualifications?
- How did the candidate get along with your children?
- Did you have the impression that the candidate was interested in being offered the job? Don't waste your time trying to persuade someone to take your job.

## The follow up

Always, without fail, check the references. Make sure that they are valid by phoning previous employers and character referees. Although your needs may be different to those of a potential employee's previous employers, you will nevertheless always glean some useful insights by having an off-the-record chat. The responsibility is entirely with you, as the employer, to be confident that you are hiring a person suitable for the role. There are at present no legal requirements for a person applying for a job as a nanny, though there are associations that applicants may choose to sign up to, though this is far from common. Candidates should not be surprised that you want to check their identity, employment history and qualifications. They should make this all as easy as possible for you.

You could ask a candidate to bring documents with her to interview, or ask for them as a follow up after a successful interview. If you are thinking of progressing with a particular candidate, make sure you have seen the following:

- Two forms of identification, including one photo ID.
- At least two references. One must be from their present or previous employer. Make sure that the references come with phone numbers so that you can follow them through. If the candidate is applying for her first job (and you are happy with that) you should have references from her college and any work placements she may have had.
- A full employment history – complete with dates and job descriptions.
- Original documents showing any qualifications relevant to the job.
- Criminal record check. It is not possible for parents to gain access to criminal records in respect of a potential childcare employee; however, nanny agencies are able to register with the Criminal Records Bureau. They can then ask prospective nannies to apply for Enhanced or Standard Disclosures from the CRB, to assess their suitability to work with children. If you are using an agency, ask if they offer this service. You could ask a nanny directly to show you her disclosure – she doesn't have to show it; you don't have to hire her.

After you have carried out your follow-up checks, steer clear if you have any concerns about a candidate. If you suspect she may be not quite telling the truth, or purposefully trying to mislead you over anything at all, cut your losses and do not proceed further. However desperate you are to make an appointment, it is highly unlikely that an early niggle will go away. In fact, quite the opposite will probably be the case, and the niggle will turn into a bigger problem.

Make sure that you start a search and interview process early enough to leave yourself time to find the best candidate. If you are feeling under time pressure, you are more likely to make yourself believe that a candidate is great and end up hiring the wrong person for the job.

## What to ask referees

You will probably only have a short window of opportunity during a phone call with a referee, to find out as much as you can about a candidate. Always check first whether it is a convenient time to chat, once you have explained the purpose of your call. Arrange to call back at a more convenient moment if necessary. Be prepared with the questions you want to ask the referee and a notepad to write down the answers so you can review the call afterwards.

### Main points to cover with a referee:

- What were the candidate's duties when employed by the referee?
- Did she have sole charge of the children?
- Would the referee recommend the candidate for the job that you are offering?
- How would the referee rate the care given to the children by the candidate?
- What were the candidate's particular strengths and weaknesses?
- How much time off did the candidate have during employment for ill health?
- Was the candidate punctual and reliable?
- Why did the candidate leave their employ?
- What the candidate was like to live with (if applicable)?

### The rules on references

It is not permissible for an employer to write a bad reference. If you give a bad reference and your ex-employee fails to find a new job on the back of it, you may be liable for her inability to find work. It is also difficult to give an unjustifiably good one; if you give a good reference and the employee doesn't live up to the claims, the referee may be liable again. As a result, written references can tend to be rather bland. Always try to read between the lines and always make a call – you will usually glean more information and insight from the referee during the course of a conversation than in writing. (See Section Five for further information on talking to a referee.)

## Second interviews

If everything checks out, invite your favourite candidate (or possibly favourite two candidates) back for a second interview. At a second interview, it is important that the prospective childcarer meets the whole family and has a chance to spend some time with the children. An invitation to Saturday lunch can be a good idea, and is slightly less intense than holding another face-to-face interview, followed by watching the childcarer play with the children. Lunch will give you an informal chance to chat, share food and for you to observe how the candidate gets along in a family situation. She might volunteer to help with the clearing up (good sign) or have terrible table manners (bad sign – this is the person who is likely to be supervising your child's meals). It can be a good way to find out much that you need to.

## Final stages

Your favourite candidate has been back for a successful second visit with your family, has played with your children and met and impressed your partner. The candidate is available to do the job you require starting when you need them to and is keen to work for you at the salary you are offering. And she hasn't been snapped up by another family.

Great! But before you get too carried away, try to reflect calmly before making a formal offer.

- Is your gut instinct telling you to hire?
- Are you entirely confident that she will be capable of looking after your children?
- Have you been thorough in your background checks?
- Are you absolutely confident that she has been honest?
- Do you agree on the principles of childcare that you hold close?

If the answer to all of the above is yes, then what are you waiting for?

## Interviewing after-school babysitters

Be clear from the beginning about the hours involved in the job and look out for candidates who might be using your job as a stop-gap. An afternoon job, particularly if it is only for a few afternoons a week, can be hard to fill. Quiz candidates carefully about what else is going on in their lives and make sure that your job is going to suit them. If they are going to be looking for other jobs to fill up all the hours of the week, then as soon as a full-time offer comes along they are likely to go and take it. While there are never any guarantees that childcare arrangements will last in the long term, you give yourself a shot at it lasting in the short term at least by choosing the right person. To be the right person in this instance, the candidate has got to *want* part-time work, or the arrangement won't last.

---

## " Anne, 30, from south-west London shares her experiences of choosing the right person for a nanny share position

I am going back to work three days a week, and the friend that I'm going to have my nanny share with is going back to work five days a week. Ideally, you would be sharing with someone who requires the same amount of care as you, so you split everything 50/50. But we are good friends and have been able to talk frankly about money and work things out.

> It's too expensive to do it alone!

We chose to go this route for childcare because we wanted our son to be looked after in a home environment, by a nanny, but it's too expensive to do it alone! We would like our son to be able to have a flexible schedule, with plenty of time outside, and we think this is easier to achieve with a nanny than in a nursery setting. Also, this way our children have the advantage of a friend to play with.

My friend and I made a list of the things we were looking for. As well as agreeing on the hours of work and days of the week, we agreed that we wanted someone experienced, with fluent English, a first-aid qualification and an up-to-date CRB check. We advertised on Gumtree and got 80 replies! On close inspection only seven were worth interviewing. Then we learnt how quickly you have to move when a good candidate pops up — they are quickly snatched from the market.

You have to trust your nanny share partner to interview in your absence. Don't do what we did and miss good candidates because you couldn't all manage to get to an interview at the same time. You need to be able to react quickly when good people come up.

> You need to be able to react quickly when good people come up

My advice would be to talk about money early on. You need to be able to do this with the person you are planning to share with and with the potential nanny. I usually discuss money on the phone before an interview, as that way we don't all waste each other's time. You are becoming an employer, so have to remember all the responsibilities regarding sick pay, holiday pay and even possibly maternity leave, as well as the tax and National Insurance payments.

The key is to find someone to share with, with whom you can talk about everything openly. Then this is a great solution — a nanny for your child, in the company of a friend, at a reduced cost to each family.

# section FOUR

# managing your childcare

**17** MANAGING YOUR RELATIONSHIP WITH YOUR CHILDCARE PROVIDER
**18** COPING IF THINGS GO WRONG
**19** THE END OF THE AFFAIR

## Regular check-ups

Find a regular moment to check in and catch up with your nanny, childminder or key worker at nursery – not while rushing in the evening or out in the morning, or while cooking and clearing up the tea, but a proper, child-free moment for the pair of you. If you think an issue has come up which needs addressing, don't wait for the next scheduled meeting, but arrange for an earlier meeting to discuss the problem. Communication is absolutely key to managing any childcare situation.

By keeping communication open between you and your childcarer you will hopefully avoid some of the pitfalls we highlight in this section. Sometimes problems can arise from a simple misunderstanding. Keep talking and most misunderstandings will come to light and be resolved. Just avoid driving your childcarer mad by going overboard and asking how everything is going every half an hour.

## Keep hold of your common sense

It is important to hang on to your common sense when managing your childcare. Although this relationship is different to other working relationships, as it is about your family, perhaps in your home and even maybe live-in, it is still a work relationship from your carer's point of view. Try not to let your emotions get in the way of your people-management skills. When dealing with any problems that may arise, focus on the specific issue without involving any other issues. Maintain a professional approach to the problem.

## Trust

It is so important to try to build trust between parents and childcarer. This doesn't mean that you should be blind, or that you should overlook too much – keep your wits about you. Do check up – don't be subversive or the relationship will fall apart quickly, but don't be taken for a mug, either. This is another hard childcare balancing act. Don't fall into the trap of setting up tricks for your childcarer, but do make sure that everyone is being honest.

A good way to do this is to listen to others around you. Your friends and acquaintances are all likely to see your childcarer collecting your children from school or nursery, or out and about in the park or at playgroups. Every now and again, ask how they think the set up all looks to be going. You could use a more subtle approach and just wait to see if they say anything, but some people might not want to volunteer bad information for fear of saying the wrong thing. You might not hear how brilliantly it is all going, either, if you don't ask.

If your child is at a nursery or with a childminder, listen out for comments from other parents as well as following your own instincts. While every parent who is using the nursery or childminder is likely to have their own experiences of the childcare, there will be some similarities and common themes. However, don't be swayed by other's opinions if everything else is telling you that the provision of care is good. Keep your ears open while keeping your own counsel.

### 10 things your sole charge childcarer needs to know

- How to use the phone
- Your mobile phone number
- To call 999 in emergencies, for fire, ambulance or police
- Your doctor's name and phone number
- Your neighbour's name and phone number
- The address, postcode and directions to your house
- Details of your child's name, date of birth, NHS number, blood group and any allergies or long-term conditions
- The location of your first-aid kit
- Where you keep the spare keys (and how to lock up)
- Location of a torch and fuse box

# Managing your relationship with your childcare provider

In this chapter, we look at each of the childcare relationships and try to foresee the most common pitfalls. Most situations can be resolved, as long as everyone keeps their head. It is a good idea to always keep a copy of the nursery policy, childminder's commitments or agreement that you have come to with your help at home regarding duties. This will be a vital source of information should any problems arise.

## How to manage your relationship with ...your nursey
### The nursery's role

A day care nursery's role is to provide suitable care to enrolled children. Parents will be asked to sign a contract with the nursery which will outline the main points of the nursery's duty. The nursery is legally obliged to provide quality childcare, with strict ratios enforced at all times between the number of children and the number of carers, both qualified and unqualified. Your contract will be your basis for any claim and should include details of what to do and where to go in case of any complaints.

## Potential pitfalls…

- The care in a nursery setting is taking place outside of your home and it is common for parents to feel a little detached from the care that their child is receiving. Nurseries will work hard at communicating, as they are aware that this is a potential problem area.
- Parents are often rushing to get to work in the morning and so drop off as quickly as their children will allow. They are just as likely to be rushing in the evening, to get back to the nursery in time for collection at the end of their working day, then keen to get home. In this scenario, neither end of the day is conducive to stopping for a chat about how things are going.
- A child may take some time to settle into childcare away from the home. The environment is of course totally alien to a child at the outset, which can have the potential to cause some distress.

## …and how to overcome them

- Nurseries will sometimes offer a service where a child's key worker will fill in a daily record sheet, with details of what the baby or child has been doing all day. This might include details of sleep, food, milk, outside time and other activities. Nurseries are required by law to keep full details of each child's development (these records should be accessible to you as parents whenever you ask to see them, by arrangement), but these more informal daily record sheets can be an invaluable contact between nursery and parent.
- It is a good idea to try to hold a regular meeting with your child's key worker. When your child is a baby this is likely to be brief, and will cover the baby's routine, sleep, feeding and settling patterns during the day. As your child grows older, the nature of these conversations will change, and there will be much more ground to cover – including social interaction with other children, response to staff and any teaching, behaviour and discipline issues.

- Try to keep conversations with a nursery light and non-aggressive. If you are upset over something it is even more important to try to remain calm. A strident tone will immediately put everyone's defences up and you are unlikely to make much headway.
- Be prepared when you go to talk to your childcarer. Listen to the advice and information you are getting – it is very easy to stick to your own preconceived ideas and stay focused on your own agenda. Focus on the child you have gone with the intention of talking about. A child's position within a family and sibling rivalry, for example, are important issues, but do not need to be part of every debate.
- In terms of acclimatising your child to the shift to day care, it is so helpful if a parent can spend some real time settling a child into nursery. Rather than dropping and running, your child will be much happier if you are able to spend some, or even all, the time with him during the first few visits. Your nursery should be open to this, and welcome your efforts to help to settle your child in. If the nursery is resistant to you spending this time behind their doors this should be taken as a warning signal.

## Complaints procedures

Every nursery should have a complaints procedure, set out as part of the initial contract that parents are asked to sign when their child joins the nursery. In the first instance, always speak to the person in charge at the nursery that your child attends. This is important, rather than going straight to a more senior person in the nursery's hierarchy (if it is part of a larger organisation), as there may well be a reasonable explanation from the nursery that will resolve the issue altogether. You may be able to raise a concern early that will then be addressed quickly and can avoid becoming a big problem. The vast majority of problems that arise at a nursery will be resolved in this way.

If you feel that your complaint is not being properly addressed or has not been resolved, or you have a more serious complaint about any nursery which is registered with Ofsted, you can call the Ofsted Early Years Complaints Helpline on 0845 640 4040. Ofsted are obliged to follow up any complaints made and will go as far as deregistering a service if they decide that the quality of service provided is not reaching the national standards. Ofsted does not usually get involved in complaints over fees and contractual arrangements.

If your concerns are so serious that you think the safety of your child is at stake, then of course you should remove your child from the nursery immediately and contact the child protection team at your local Social Services, as well as informing Ofsted. It is rare for a problem to get so bad that Ofsted need to be involved.

## ... your childminder
### The childminder's role

A childminder looks after your child in her own home, most likely alongside other children, to ratios set out by the government. The care will be home-based, and children will often go on outings to the park, to collect older children from school, as well as to the local shops. The childminder will engage children in activities while they are in her care. You will hopefully have a pretty clear idea of the childminder's schedule before your child joins her and have had a chance to see her in action with other children.

### Potential pitfalls...

- You might find that you have a different childcare philosophy to your childminder once she begins the day-to-day care of your child. You will most likely have discussed your views when you were interviewing possible childminders, but clashes are still possible and you must decide whether you want to work through these problems or call it quits if you believe the differences in opinion are insurmountable.
- Your child may not get along with all the other children at the childminder's house. If there is a small group of children (as is usual) this can become important, as there will not be many alternative children to play with. The childminder will need to resolve disputes between children, but if your child becomes unhappy and doesn't want to go to the childminder, this will become your problem, too.

### ...and how to overcome them

- Communication is key to keeping your relationship with your childminder a healthy one. Parents will often be rushing in and out at drop-off and collection times, and the childminder is likely to be

busy with other children who are also in her care. Make an appointment to chat regularly, when you both have time to discuss things – once a month would be a sensible amount of time between meetings. Talk informally about your child, how he is enjoying his care and any problems that might have arisen since the last time you chatted.
- If a specific problem comes up, if your child is suddenly unhappy about his care, of course you should arrange for a meeting as soon as possible. Try to have this meeting without your child, or other children, in earshot. A telephone call at an arranged time in the evening can be a good way to talk privately to your childminder. Face-to-face is obviously best, but hard to achieve with a childminder without children present.
- Keep all discussions with your childminder upbeat and non-aggressive. If you are generally happy with the care that your child is receiving, be sure that your childminder is aware of that before you start to talk about the bad news. Look for positive solutions and try to have some of your own answers to a problem up your sleeve, rather than expecting your childminder to resolve everything alone. Ask for the childminders advice for resolving the disputes between children – she will want everyone to get along well, too.

## Helen, 28, works full time and uses a childminder to look after her daughter after school

When Leah started school, I was hoping she would be able to go to the after-school club, but the opening times weren't flexible enough for my working hours. I found a childminder who could manage the collection along with collecting her own children from a different school. She was brilliant and loved her job. I didn't

*I didn't really realise how lucky we were until she moved house and we had to look for another childminder.*

really realise how lucky we were until she moved house and we had to look for another childminder.

I think the new childminder is motivated by money. She charges me from when she leaves her house to collect Leah, not when she actually meets her, which adds an hour each day. She doesn't encourage Leah to do her homework even though I have asked her to. She doesn't really offer any activities — I think Leah watches television most days. I have looked around but there really isn't anyone else available at the moment. I think a childminder is a good solution for after-school care — I will keep trying to find someone who I get on with better.

## Complaints procedures

Again, the vast majority of cases will be dealt with informally between parent and childminder. You should always first go to the childminder with any problems that have arisen – they may just turn out to be a matter of miscommunication or a misunderstanding.

If after a conversation with your childminder you still have serious concerns, you can turn to the Ofsted Complaints Line on 0845 640 4040. All childminders must be registered with Ofsted. Ofsted's guidance notes (see Section Five) and our chapter on Childminders in Section One, give a clear idea of the type and level of service you can expect from a childminder. Ofsted will investigate any complaints in confidence and feed back to you.

If your concerns are serious and you think your child's safety is at risk, remove your child immediately and contact the child protection team at your local Social Services, along with the Ofsted complaints line.

## ... an after-school club
### The after-school club's role

An after-school club has an important role to fill in the life of a primary school-age child. Childcare workers from the club will collect your child from school on the appointed days and look after the children through homework and tea time.

The childcarers at the club will be seeing your child at the end of the school day when he is likely to be tired, but still needs to do homework and interact well with his peers.

The clubs operate on weekdays during term time, and some will also operate as holiday clubs during school holidays. At these times the clubs will run for the whole working day, usually from around 8.30am to 6pm.

## Potential pitfalls...

- It is easy to fall out of regular communication with your child's after-school club, as it is likely that you are rushing in to collect your child at the end of a working day. It is therefore a good idea to schedule regular meetings with your child's key worker to check up on your child's progress and behaviour at the after-school club.
- Your child is likely to be tired during the time at the after-school club. Primary age children often come out of school exhausted and just make it home to curl up on the sofa. A child who goes to a club instead of home after school needs to continue to behave well and interact with his peers, while also getting on with homework. As every parent knows, tiredness can easily lead to bad behaviour, which will cause your child problems at the club, with the carers and with the other children.
- The after-school club has an important role to fill as communicant between school and parent, in particular if the club is collecting the child from school every day. Messages can easily be lost in the transition from child to key worker to parent.

## ...and how to overcome them

- If your child is mature and of a suitable age, you could talk to him first so that you are up to date with how he feels about the childcare arrangement.
- Be sure to arrange a regular meeting with the key worker assigned to your child at the club. It is a good idea to ask for detailed information about how your child spends his time at the club – most children either will be too tired to tell you all about it at the end of the day, or just won't want to tell you what goes on. To ensure that the

arrangement is a happy one, you will need to communicate regularly, directly with the club.
- Ask your child's key worker to make you aware of any difficulties that your child faces in his relationships with the other children at the club, so that you can all help your child to resolve them.
- Tiredness is an issue for children in 'wraparound' day care. The club will usually provide a snack and a meal for children in after-school care. Ask what food is provided, and if you feel it is necessary, send your child with an extra snack to keep him going. Make sure your child knows where he can go for some quiet time at the club, if he needs to catch some rest, would like to relax with a book or quietly get on with homework.
- Organise some sort of communication record between the school and the club, to make sure that messages make it all the way home. Information is often passed from school to home via children – if it's not in writing, there is every chance it will be forgotten by the time the child gets home from an after-school club. Your child's key worker at the club will be an important person to involve in making sure that this communication channel remains open.

## Complaints procedures

Complaints about staff or the care that your child is receiving should in the first instance be made to the person in charge of the particular centre. Most problems will be resolved between parent and key worker and the after-school club manager.

After-school clubs and holiday clubs are required to be registered and inspected by Ofsted and in the event that your complaint is not properly dealt with at the club, you can call the Ofsted Complaints Line on 0845 640 4040. If you believe the care that your child is receiving is negligent and endangers your child in any way, you should remove your child immediately, as well as calling the complaints line.

## ... an after-school nanny or babysitter
### An after-school nanny or babysitter's role

An after-school nanny or babysitter will collect your children from school, perhaps take them to after-school activities and then take the children home. Once at home, an after-school nanny or babysitter can be expected to supervise homework and possibly music practice, play with the children, host play dates, prepare and clear up the children's supper and look after the children until a parent returns home.

## Potential pitfalls...

- After-school nannies and babysitters must be punctual, as persistent lateness in collecting your child from school will lead to problems for your child (including worry and tiredness) and will ultimately bring about a complaint from the school. Your childcarer must be diligent about her role as a messenger between school and parent.
- Make sure that the after-school nanny or babysitter takes this role seriously. It is likely that she will have another job alongside this one, as this role will probably only offer three or four hours' work a day. Try to make sure that your childcarer is committed to your job and try to make it rewarding for her.
- Your school-age children will need to form a bond with an after-school nanny or babysitter, usually within a limited time frame. It can be difficult for children if there is a different person collecting them from school on different days – it is obviously best if you are able to arrange for one person to be in this role.
- The nanny or babysitter needs to be mature enough to establish her authority over the children, even if she is only with them for a few hours each week.

## ...and how to overcome them

- If you hear from the school or your child that your after-school nanny or babysitter is consistently late collecting from school, explain that timekeeping is an important part of the job and that you will have to look elsewhere for help if she is not able to manage the collection on time. Allow your nanny or babysitter a second chance, especially if you are otherwise happy with the care that your child is receiving in this arrangement.
- While your children are probably getting a little old for a daily diary from an after-school carer (and you probably have a pretty good idea anyway of what is going on in the time between school and your return home), it is wise to have some form of written

communication in place. A notebook can be used for her to record messages from school, or to let you know of any other messages or important incidents.
- You might want to consider offering paid holiday if your after-school nanny or babysitter stays with your family for more than a term at school. This is unlikely to have been part of your original agreement, as these arrangements are usually fairly short-term and flexible. However, if you have struck gold and your relationship is going well on all levels (child/carer as well as parent/carer and school /carer) then it is a good idea to reward the nanny or babysitter and hopefully encourage her to stay for longer. We have come across examples of this kind of arrangement lasting three years or more.

## ... your nanny
### The nanny's role

A nanny plays a hugely important role in a family's life. A nanny is expected to act in your child's best interests at all times and to give any children in her care her full and undivided attention. The parent/nanny relationship can be a particularly intense one and, as with most other relationships, respect and communication are vital.

A job description for a nanny will be invaluable when it comes to managing the care that your nanny provides. This should have been worked out and agreed by both sides at the beginning of the working relationship and can be a point of reference from then on. Make sure that this document is clear and precise and includes everything that you expect your nanny to take responsibility for. Avoid the temptation to dress up a job description at the outset – you will pay the price later on. The job description can be part of the initial contract and it would be wise to agree to update and check through the job description at regular future intervals.

### Potential pitfalls...

- There are issues when employing a nanny over how much control the parents either want or should have over the nanny's time. This will largely come down to the individual parent's wishes. Some parents are willing to let the nanny run her own day; others want to be there by proxy, organising each day to the last minute, so the nanny is really filling the parents' shoes as much as is humanly possible.

### 10 things to do on your nanny's first day
- Smile brightly.
- Help her to a cup of tea and show her where everything is for her next one.
- Ask the children to show her around their playroom and bedrooms.
- Make sure she has time with the children on her own to begin bonding.
- Go on an outing with the children – show her how you cross roads with the children.
- Show her where the first-aid kit is kept.
- Give her a list of emergency numbers – including doctor, parents, grandparents (if nearby), a close neighbour, nursery school and schools, including names of any teachers.
- Prepare and eat lunch all together.
- Go over the house rules.
- Congratulate her at the end of the day – finish on a positive note.

- Think in advance about how you feel about your child being taken to other people's houses (and other nannies and children coming to your house). Socialising is important for your children and for your nanny, but it is quite understandable for parents to want to know who their children are socialising with and where. You probably didn't interview your nanny's boyfriend – and it would be inappropriate for your child to be spending the day with him and your nanny. Make sure that this is understood.
- Experienced nannies will want to be trusted and be allowed to bring their own skills to the job. They will also know that it is important to follow the parents' lead and work together in a partnership. An experienced nanny will show her maturity by accepting instructions from a parent, if the parent wishes to give them. Reluctance to follow the parents' programme and an insistence on running her own agenda can be a sign of an inexperienced nanny.
- A nanny is likely to be either qualified or very experienced and will have her own views about how children should be looked after.

During the interview process you will have gone over childcare philosophies and tried to find out whether you and a potential nanny agree on the main issues involved in looking after, caring for and disciplining children. You are likely to have hired the person with views closest to yours, but there are still possible clashes ahead. If you are out at work all day you will need to rely on your own judgement of your child's well-being, along with any feedback from friends who see your children with their nanny, to gain an insight into how well your children are being cared for during the day.

- Even the best relationship between parents and a nanny is likely to have off days. This relationship needs managing with kid gloves for everyone to get the best out of it. Despite the fact that you and your nanny are likely to become great friends, this is, and will remain for the time being, a business arrangement. The nanny is your paid employee and will expect the rights and respect that that entitles her to. She is not your best friend – even if your working relationship ultimately leads to a great friendship.

## ...and how to overcome them

- Try and figure out when you are interviewing and hiring a nanny how you feel about control. How much information do you want your nanny to give you each day? It is reasonable, as well as being quite normal practice, to ask for a written diary from the nanny each day. This should detail how the day has passed, what your child has eaten, where he has been, who he has seen and how he has behaved. A daily record is a good way for parents to be in touch with the daily programme of child and nanny.
- Communication is the buzzword for all childcare arrangements. In this intensely personal relationship between a nanny and parent, it is vital. Arrange a child-free meeting with your nanny on a regular basis. This will be formal or informal, depending on your preference. You might even want to have an agenda, to make sure you cover all the ground. As well as this possibly quite formal meeting, try to chat regularly with your nanny – staying in touch will help a happy relationship. Keep your job description to hand and update it from time to time, in agreement, if necessary.

## Fiona, a mother of three in Shepherd's Bush, shares her tips for communicating regularly with her nanny:

We tend to sit down for a 'formal' chat once a year around the anniversary of when our nanny started with us. There is continual feedback (both ways) throughout the year as well. We choose a time when both my husband and I are around, typically at the beginning of a babysitting evening once the children are in bed. I always schedule it with her in advance and remind her that it is an opportunity for her to discuss anything she is concerned about or would like to raise with us and we will do the same. We do give her feedback about how we think she is doing and discuss anything that (we all) should be doing differently with the children. We tend to also discuss any annual pay raise at this meeting.

> We do give her feedback about how we think she is doing

- Make time to listen to your nanny on a regular basis. Listen to any passing complaints your nanny makes and check that you are not asking more of your nanny than you should. No one can really be superwoman – don't ask your nanny to take on more tasks than you could manage yourself.
- Nannies can be starved of adult company and, while some days your nanny will be keen to get out of the house as soon as you get in, on other days she may want to stop and share details of the day. Try to be understanding about this. Even though you are likely to be tired at the end of a working day and keen to spend some time with your child on your own, accept that your nanny may need some time, too. If you are always sending her on her way the moment you get home, you are missing out on an opportunity to bond with her, as well as an opportunity for your children to see the respect that will hopefully flow between you and your nanny. On the other hand,

don't always keep your nanny chatting when she *is* keen to leave at the end of the day, or you will end up being guilty of consistently making her late.
- Try to pick up on any major differences of opinion in childcare philosophy quickly. A difference of opinion can lead to bad feeling and any problems left to fester will become bigger and more important in everyone's eyes than they need be. Discipline, treats, diet and entertainment are all important child-raising issues that you and your nanny need to agree on.

There are plenty of irritants that can pop up in the nanny/parent relationship. Nannies and parents will almost inevitably drive each other crazy from time to time. (If you and your nanny never have a disagreement, thank your lucky stars.)

Common complaints from parents about nannies:
- **Messiness** – leaving the house untidy at the end of the day.
- **Illness** – taking too many days off sick.
- **Inflexibility over working practices** – it drives parents mad when the nanny leaves a saucepan in the sink, stating that their job is to look after the children…
- **Personal issues** – parents complain if they have to hear too much about their nanny's personal life.

And the other way round – what drives nannies mad about parents:
- Parents often returning late at the end of the day, even when they call in advance.
- Being taken for granted and not fully appreciated for all that they do.
- Nosiness – parents being too interested in their personal lives.
- Parents interfering with the schedule, or overloading the children with too many activities.
- Being asked to take on too many 'housekeeping' tasks.

## Carrie, 25, is from South Africa. She has been working as a nanny for two years

I love nannying because it is so rewarding to see the little personalities grow.

I arrived from South Africa and started helping a family that my sister had been babysitting for. I went to help out on a temporary basis as their nanny had just left and I ended up staying. I had grown up as part of a big family but hadn't had much experience with kids. By the time I was applying for my next job I had lots of experience. The second time around I was able to reply to an ad on Gumtree.

I think children take a little while to settle into a new routine with a new nanny and parents need to appreciate that. Mischievous children will try to push boundaries with a new nanny but will settle down after a couple of weeks.

> Mischievous children will try to push boundaries with a new nanny

I think communication is so important between nanny and parents. I speak to the parents pretty much every afternoon to tell them what the children have been doing and what's happened during the day. Then if a problem comes up, it is easier to talk about it.

At the moment, the older child goes to nursery school in the morning — he is improving his social skills. He enjoys going and it makes him slightly more independent. I think that nursery school is a natural progression — but it is lovely for little ones to be looked after at home.

I have had one bad experience with the family I worked for before this one. The children were very unruly and the mother wasn't backing me up. One day the children were fighting horribly over the computer, so I told them neither of them could play on it. The mother came in and said, 'That's ridiculous, they can play on it if they want to.' I was telling them one thing and she was telling them another. We both agreed I wasn't the right person for the job. It was not a good working relationship.

### Managing your live-in childcare relationship

There are some issues which are particular to live-in nannies. All live-in relationships are complicated, but this one can be almost the most complicated. Your nanny is a professional, and should be treated as such. She has been invited to stay in your home, but you are also making it her home – she should not be made to feel like a guest.

- There is such a lot of give and take necessary for a live-in arrangement to be successful. In an ideal world, a live-in nanny would have a separate entrance, a separate kitchen, bathroom and living room, as well as the pre-requisite separate bedroom. It is, of course, brilliant for all concerned if this is possible. In most family homes, however, the family and nanny need to figure out how best to share the available space. A nanny is unlikely to want to stay long if she is always under the impression she is treading on the family's toes.
- Make sure that you make your views clear about shared mealtimes and evenings. Neither the nanny nor the family are likely to want to eat together every evening, or watch the same television programme together. If you are not going to be spending the evenings together, let your live-in helper know when she is able to cook for herself as soon as the living arrangement starts. It is quite common to put a television in a live-in nanny's bedroom, while making it clear that she is also welcome to join you in the sitting room. She will most likely prefer to be in her own space, if not out with friends, at the end of a long day of childcare.
- Issues of tidiness and cleanliness will be paramount when a nanny is living with you. If she is not fastidious (and you are) it will probably drive you crazy very quickly. It could be uncomfortable in a live-out situation, but worse if you are surrounded by someone else's mess all the time. Comment politely but swiftly if this matters to you, before it becomes a major issue.
- Parents are more likely to become involved in their live-in helper's private life. You will need to set house rules about visitors (overnight or otherwise) and think about whether you want to impose a curfew.

How will you react if it is broken? If you want to set strict rules, have reasons ready. If you are relying on help with young children early in the morning, it is quite reasonable to expect your nanny to not be staying out half of the night before. If your nanny disturbs the whole household in the middle of the night, it's time for a serious talk!

If seemingly insurmountable problems arise and you have hired your live-in nanny through an agency, it is always worth going back to the recruiting agency for advice.

## Natasha, 44, lives and works in London and has two children. She and her husband have had live-in nannies for the last four years

I went back to work soon after having both my children, but strongly wanted them to have the one-to-one care of a nanny at home. If I wasn't going to be looking after my babies, I wanted the equivalent care that they would get with me through a nanny. Also, I wanted to be able to dictate a little bit more about what they ate and their day-to-day activities. I have been very fortunate with the nannies we've had — we have all shared ideas about childcare, weaning, food, discipline and bedtime routines.

It takes time to find a good nanny. It takes even longer if you are looking at a bad time — Christmas, from my experience, is a hopeless time to look.

I think that it is good to have a change of nanny every now and again. It is healthy for the children to get used to different adults. I find that I learn something new from every nanny, too.

I wasn't sure how I'd cope sharing my household with somebody day in, day out, 24 hours a day, seven days of the week. You have got to make some compromises when you've got a live-in. Even little things like people stacking

> You have got to make some compromises when you've got a live-in

the dishwasher in different ways — I have had to learn to be a bit more accommodating and not as rigid about things.

A friend said to me quite early on that there is no right or wrong way to be a parent. I think it's exactly the same with childcare. There's no right or wrong childcare. There is childcare that is suitable for our household that would be completely unsuitable for a different household. There is childcare that is suitable for you at one point in time that may no longer be suitable a year later. My advice to parents is to be prepared to be open-minded and flexible. You might change your views.

*There's no right or wrong childcare*

### Managing your nanny share relationships

There are specific potential problems to be addressed when two families are involved in a nanny share. Complications can arise when one family thinks the other is getting a better deal – though this is often a case of the grass being greener…

- Families need to first of all agree on how much to pay the nanny and to split this down the middle, or proportionately to the number of days' care each family receives. Both families need to be clear about the practical and financial arrangements involved in the nanny share. Both parties will need to take into account where the nanny share will take place, as well as how to split the costs involved in the share evenly. The host family will have extra costs involved due to increased heat, light and food bills involved in hosting the nanny share. The family who are not hosting will make equivalent savings and might come to an agreement with the host family over reimbursing some of the costs for each day. Always be very clear when advertising for a nanny share arrangement about where you would prefer for the share to take place. Once you sit down to think clearly about this issue, it is likely that you will feel strongly one way or the other.

- One family may host the share and think that they have the tough end of the deal, as it is their house which is getting torn apart every day by young terrors. Meanwhile the other family think they are in the harder position of having to deliver and collect their child each day and don't have the advantage of an adult in their house all day to deal with deliveries, repairs and perhaps even laundry.
- Managing your nanny share well often comes down to managing your relationship with the other family involved in the share, as much as managing the relationship with the nanny. Two families may have met at ante-natal classes, or have a friendship that goes back to before anyone had children. The sharing families may have found each other online or through a nanny share service.
- Take time to talk with the other family before you embark on your search for a nanny to share – things will usually work out better if you are able to interview together and agree on whom to offer the job to in the first place. Also, this way the nanny will genuinely feel like the nanny for both families, rather than for one family with another tagging along.
- Both families need to maintain their own relationship with the nanny. This is best done separately from each other, while promising to never comment negatively on the other family in the share. It is easy for this kind of relationship to sometimes begin to feel one-sided – if, perhaps, one family has more contact with the nanny or forms a stronger bond with the nanny. Don't be jealous – try to see the benefits in the nanny being happy in the share, which is increasingly likely if she has an especially good relationship with at least one family. Each family should address any concerns to the nanny privately and avoid presenting a united front, which could leave the nanny feeling ambushed and overwhelmed, unless the issue under discussion is of genuine concern to both families.
- Nanny-share families need to be regularly in contact to make sure that the arrangement is working – this is a childcare triangle, and all sides need to be happy for it to be successful. As well as sharing views on childcare philosophy and principles and making

*(continued)*

MANAGING YOUR CHILDCARE

> sure the costs are evenly spread out, families will need to agree about when to go on holiday and when they can both give their shared nanny time off. Arranging holiday time with a nanny who looks after one family can be tricky – arranging it when there are two families and a nanny to take into account can be like negotiating between superpowers during the Cold War.

## … your mother's help
### The mother's help's role

A mother's help should be just what it says on the tin – a person employed to help a mother. This role involves some childcare, some housework and generally providing an extra pair of hands for busy mothers. It is usually a shared-care role, with the mother at home working alongside the mother's help. This brings with it a whole raft of complications. The mother's help arrangement, along with that of a nanny in a shared care role, can be one of the trickier childcare balancing acts to manage.

A full job description will be vital to keep to hand when managing a mother's help. Be clear about the role from the beginning and give a copy of the job description to your mother's help. Both parent and helper can easily feel disappointed in this working relationship if the boundaries are not very clearly laid out. In essence, a mother's help should be prepared to take on any role that the mother is prepared to perform. But to make the relationship a successful one, there does need to be a balance – parents need to let the helper have some of the fun from time to time.

### Potential pitfalls…

- A relationship between a mother and a mother's help is a real balancing act. You will need to make sure that the mother's help has a 'go' with the children, while making sure you are getting enough practical help, too. You will probably be off to a bad start if you hand over all the ironing, laundry, cooking and clearing up and none of the trips to the park or playtime with the children. Equally, you don't want to go too far the other way and end up doing all the chores while your mother's help skips off to the sandpit on a sunny day with the children.

## MANAGING YOUR RELATIONSHIP WITH YOUR CHILDCARE PROVIDER

- A mother's help is most likely young and quite inexperienced, even if she holds some childcare qualifications. She may have taken on this role to build up her experience under supervision, so that she can move on to be a shared-care or even sole charge nanny in her next job. She should be gradually allowed to take some responsibility for the children. You will probably need to teach her along the way – certainly you will need to show her the ropes of your household and your child-raising techniques. Beware of assuming that your mother's help will be capable of more than is reasonable, especially in the early stages of your relationship. Equally, beware of underestimating her and not giving her enough responsibility. This will end in frustration on the part of your mother's help and probably an early departure.
- If your mother's help is living in with your family, you need to be wary of all the potential pitfalls and solutions we have seen can arise with live-in nannies. The biggest issue here is making sure that you and your children understand that the mother's help must have some real time off. If the relationship goes well, there is a danger that you all get so used to your mother's help being around and offering back-up, that you will forget that she needs some private time. A young and inexperienced mother's help also might not be very good at pointing out when she is due some time off – a good relationship could potentially end in tears.

### ...and how to overcome them

- Try to be fair when sharing out the jobs between you and your mother's help. While it is reasonable to hand over quite a lot of the ironing, it is a good idea to make sure that sometimes you are the one to stay at home while she takes your children on an outing to the playground, leaving the ironing behind.
- When you are all used to each other and your mother's help has had a chance to settle in and get to know you all, try to give her choices where possible. She will appreciate sometimes being given a degree of independence during the day, rather than constantly being given directions.

- Spend enough time with your mother's help for her to feel supported and encouraged. A mother can expect to rely on the help that a mother's help offers, but also needs to accept that there will be an aspect of training to her role, too. You must be prepared to put in some time training a mother's help, for her to be able to give you the kind of help that you need.
- Communicate regularly with your mother's help – find a child-free moment to sit down and discuss how you both feel the role is going. Are you getting the kind of help that you were hoping for? Is your mother's help getting the experience that she was hoping for? What more do both of you want to gain from this situation? By discussing roles you will be able to straighten out any problems early on.
- Be strict with yourself and your children about your mother's help's working hours. Children should not be allowed to wander into your mother's help's bedroom whenever they feel like it, and you should be wary of asking for extra little bits of help here and there, such as just to pop to the shops or go out to collect a child from a playdate. Working hours must be clearly defined, and these should be strictly adhered to. Obviously, having an extra adult living in your home does give you as parents some extra flexibility, but do be sure to give time back to your mother's help if you have gone over at the end of the day or asked for and extra half an hour here and there.
- Keep a close eye on how comfortable everyone is in a live-in situation. You must all find a way to be comfortable with a relationship that involves working together and living together when off-duty. Be frank at interview about your views on cleanliness, tidiness, privacy, time alone for the family, how you want to manage mealtimes and your views on visitors to your home. While making your mother's help feel welcome in your home and making sure she feels that it is her home, too, you need to be clear from the start about your house rules.
- Don't get too bogged down in etiquette and protocol – you will have hired a mother's help because you need support, and the last thing you need is another person to worry about. A mother's help should be just that. A help.

## ... with your au pair
### An au pair's role

An au pair usually comes to the UK to live with a family with the aim of improving her language skills. There are specific government guidelines outlining how many hours an au pair may work each week, what sort of tasks she can be asked to undertake and how much pocket money she should be reimbursed with each week (See Section Five for full details, including a list of countries from which au pairs are allowed to travel to the UK).

An au pair will live in with a family, usually work for 25-30 hours a week and undertake light housework and babysitting. There are responsibilities attached to having an au pair for the host family, which cannot be taken lightly if the arrangement is to be successful.

Always make sure that you have a clear list of duties written out and that your au pair has a copy of her own. Try hard to be generous to an au pair – it is a great arrangement when it all works, and can lead to long friendships for you and your children – if everyone feels they are being respected and well-treated.

### 10 ways to help a new an au pair feel at home
- Make her bed up and give her a tidy room with empty drawers.
- Add a bunch of flowers for a warm welcome.
- Encourage your children to make welcome cards.
- Put a television in her room but tell her she is welcome to watch television with you, too.
- Show her how to get online on your house computer or how to access your wireless network, if you wish to share these facilities.
- Show her around the kitchen – fridge, store cupboards, freezer, tea and coffee-making equipment. Explain on the first day what she is welcome to help herself to. Explain how the oven, grill and the microwave work – save the washing machine, dryer and emptying the dishwasher for the next day.
- Take her for a walk around your neighbourhood – include important local places including the train station/bus stop, the

*(continued)*

MANAGING YOUR CHILDCARE

- convenience store or supermarket, where to get the best cup of coffee, local parks, language schools and the children's regular routes.
- Show her where you are on an A-Z or road map so she has an idea of the bigger picture.
- Bake or buy a cake for tea. Your children could decorate it.
- Encourage her to call her parents on the first evening and make sure she gives out your home number so they can call her another time.

### Lucy explains why she chose to hire an au pair

I had a two-year-old son, another child arriving in weeks, builders in the house (of course!), a husband that worked away from home for half of the week, and a seriously ill father-in-law that we visited as a family often, with additional trips made by my husband separately.

All in all, I was alone a lot, and it was a busy and stressful time. With a second baby on the way and no family to turn to for extra support if we needed it, I was worried about the months ahead. I felt like regular basic household help and pockets of childcare each day would make that extra difference.

> With my husband away a lot, the fact that there would also be someone else in the house with my two little ones and me was reassuring.

As such, an au pair sounded ideal. With my husband away a lot, the fact that there would also be someone else in the house with my two little ones and me was reassuring. Any concerns about having someone live in our house were immediately outweighed by the benefits.

Our first au pair was fantastic and has probably set too high a bar for any help we may have in the future. She was loving towards the children, a welcome companion for me, and proactive about everything — childcare, cooking and general household duties. I think it helped that her mother was a nursery school teacher, and that she had previously worked with another family with two young boys. She had had more exposure and experience with children than me!

We've since had another good experience with an au pair. However, I think it's important to realise that time brings changes. My husband changed jobs, works in London and travels infrequently. The kids are now four and six, and naps and nappies are a thing of the past. Also, the whole family now eats the same food. They are both in school everyday for at least part of the day. Pockets of the day are hectic, but manageable. Our current au pair is leaving soon to join her boyfriend back home. I will certainly miss the regular household help and babysitting flexibility, but the extra pair of hands on a live-in basis is a pure luxury. Also, while she has been a very easy person to live with, if truth be told, I am ready to have our home back to ourselves.

## Potential pitfalls...

- Communication can be an issue here. If you have hired an au pair with poor language skills (and many girls who are coming to the UK for the first time in an au pair role will be here to learn the language and consequently arrive speaking very little English), you will need to make a big effort to help your au pair improve her English-speaking skills. Language skills (or a lack of them) can cause real problems with au pairs when they first arrive. It is of course in everyone's interests to help your au pair improve her language skills as swiftly as possible. Your au pair needs to be able to communicate with your children for a happy relationship to be formed. This is also a question of safety – your au pair needs to be able to cope in an emergency.

MANAGING YOUR CHILDCARE

- An au pair is probably relatively inexperienced and is likely to be in a new country and a new city for the first time. She may be overwhelmed by having to deal with getting to know your family in a foreign language, as well as taking on a new role. The first few weeks are critical for settling in a new au pair. It is likely that your au pair will have grown up doing things differently from the way you choose to run your household and raise your children. She may find your methods strange and will take some time getting used to them.
- Loneliness can be an issue for a young au pair new to a town or city. It is best for everyone if your au pair is able to develop her own network of friends in your local area.

## ...and how to overcome them

- Sit down regularly with your au pair to discuss how things are going, how she is feeling about her role and how she is getting along with the tasks that you have given her. Arrange a child-free moment for this conversation to take place. Be sensitive to the situation – you might wish to speak privately rather than in front of your partner – this will be less overwhelming for a young au pair. Pick your time carefully, too, especially if you have some criticisms to make and be sure that there will be enough time for you to complete your conversation privately.
- Taking time to settle an au pair in at the beginning of her time with you will certainly be time well spent. Try to avoid having a new au pair move in with your family at a particularly busy time, so that you have the ability to spend some time showing her the ropes. Ideally your new au pair will be able to tail you for the first week or two, perhaps even longer if it is her first time in this country or if her language skills are particularly weak.
- Help your au pair improve her language skills – this is worth some time on your part as it will clearly benefit everyone involved in the relationship. You can do this by:
  - Writing instructions down for your au pair if you think she is having trouble understanding you. This will make it easier for her to look

things up later on, or to ask a friend for help. Always be prepared to give the same instruction a few times over.
- Putting a television in your au pair's bedroom. Watching television is often a good way to improve language skills – a television in an au pair's bedroom is a good idea and shouldn't be seen as just a way of separating you all in the evening. It is entirely possible that your au pair will want a break from your family at the end of a busy day, as well as being likely that she will want to watch something different from you.
- Encouraging your au pair to go to a local language school. This will give her a formal framework for studying English, as well as an opportunity to make some friends in your local area. You might offer to help by listening to your au pair read aloud, or by expressing an interest in her homework assignments. Reading aloud to young children can also help language skills enormously – our three-year-old was very happy to correct pronunciation!
- Make sure you take plenty of time to acquaint your new au pair with your expectations and let her grow used to your way of doing things. It can be disheartening to find yourself starting all over again with a new au pair, but you will know from experience that this can be a fantastic arrangement for the right au pair with the right family. A relationship with an au pair can improve very quickly, with patience, kindness and thoughtfulness.
- Try to ensure that your au pair has a social life – through introducing her to other au pairs in your local area. Language school can be a good place to meet up with other au pairs with local families. Some agencies will also offer a service whereby they will put au pairs in touch with each other. Encourage your au pair to live her own life in her free time, within the constraints of sharing a home with a (most likely) young family. If your au pair wakes up the whole household when she comes home in the middle of the night, you need to talk. If she perfects the art of creeping upstairs quietly and then managing her workload perfectly well the next day, there should be no cause for concern.

## Responsibilities of the host family

In most childcare situations, the parents play the role of employer, or client. With au pairs, the situation is rather different, as the family offers to 'host' the au pair, to welcome her into the family. It is a great balancing act, which requires constant attention. The au pair relationship can be a very successful one, with careful management.

Both sides need to be realistic about their expectations – the parents need to accept that they are not hiring a nanny or a housekeeper, nor, indeed, a combination of both, but are asking a probably young and quite inexperienced person to come into their home to help. The au pair needs to realise that the parent's motives are not entirely altruistic – the au pair has been engaged to help and she should not consider the parents in the host family as surrogate parents. However, the host family must accept that they may have to support the au pair emotionally in times of need.

Au pairs are often young and new to the country and may not have a support network around them, which can lead them to rely on their host family quite heavily. The host family undertakes to welcome the au pair as part of the family. While au pairs who come through an agency will have been briefed on allowing the family to spend time alone together, it is important to be clear early on about how much time you all want to spend together. It is not unusual for host families to eat with their au pairs a couple of nights a week, but most will not expect to do so every night.

The role of the au pair within the family is important to consider, more than with other forms of childcare, as she is likely to be a presence when she is not on duty. The family must be careful not to take advantage of this and, equally, the au pair should try to behave as part of the family when she is not on duty – by helping with the washing up and being a friendly face around the house. If you find you have a moody teenager locked in her bedroom, you are probably not getting the help you need.

## … your granny
### Figuring out a family member's childcare role

Blurring the lines between family and employment can be a recipe for disaster. Financial issues, potential to abuse goodwill and fear of treading on toes are all major concerns. Yet, finding care for your children from within your own family is a popular and hugely successful solution for many parents.

If Granny is providing your childcare, managing this situation can be tricky. You will be asking your mother or mother-in-law to take on a childminding role, while having a familial relationship, too. There are all sorts of issues surrounding this – mostly to do with what you feel comfortable asking your mother/mother-in-law to do for you and your family. Of course, the same issues arise if you are asking your sister or a friend, too.

You must treat a family member in a childcare role as a formal childcarer and be sure to stick to timetables and rules as if your mother (or other family) were a regular employee. Of course, the confusion and potential for trouble is that she *isn't* a regular employee and you will need to figure out how you are all going to deal with this.

On paper, it's perfect if your Mum offers to look after your children for you while you work. But do think hard before embarking on this arrangement and try to anticipate every tricky issue that you think you might come across. You might argue about the right way to raise children. It could be a dispute over diet, sweets, television, playmates or table manners. There will be other, personal issues, that you know you and your family tend to disagree about and which could well come into play in this childcare situation – you know best how you and your family function.

Talk through these issues beforehand, and try to be honest with each other about how you will feel if any conflict arises. Plan in advance, if possible, for how you will find your way past these problems. Are there some issues on which you can agree to disagree? How much leeway will you give to make the childcare situation work? There are so many advantages to children being cared for from within their own family group – you are probably willing to let some things be done differently from the way that you would insist from another childcarer.

> Kim, 32, lives in Derby, has one child and works full-time. She has used family members and a childminder to help her with childcare.

I went back to work when my son was six months old. Initially he was with his grandparents, but when my mum went back to full-time work when he was nine months' old, he went to a childminder.

I think I went into it a bit blind; we decided we wanted to have a family and we didn't really think of all the implications. We had to ask the grandparents.

The advantages of using grandparents are that you know the kind of care they're going to give your child — it is the care you had when you were young. Also, your child will most likely have their grandparents' full attention. The disadvantage is that grandparents tend to spoil their grandchildren! I also felt sometimes like I was putting on them a bit. We did ask if they'd mind and they said no; my mum wasn't working at the time and was able to help out. My mother-in-law and my stepmother were both working part-time, so they were able to help look after him. It took a bit of organising.

You need to have a good relationship with your parents and be able to communicate with them. You need to be able to say what you think. You also need to be sure that they are willing and able. If you are planning to rely on family long-term, make sure they know this! Some grandparents might feel they've done their bit in bringing their own children up and don't want to do it again.

We switched to a childminder when my mum went back into full-time employment. I think it was heartbreaking for her, because she didn't know how to break the news to me and I think she was worried I would be upset. As luck would have it, my best friend's sister was just in the middle of registering to be a childminder. I've known her all my life so we are very lucky — I knew I could trust her. She has three children of her own — they are all well-mannered, nice children. She had clearly done a good job with her own. She lives five minutes' drive away so now my son goes to her. It is very convenient.

My son starts school this year, and I don't want to have to pay for a full-time place at the childminder's as he'll be at school from 9am to 3pm. My childminder can't be flexible because she wants a child full-time, so we are going to revert back to asking grandparents for help again. It should all work out because my father-in-law has since retired and says he is happy to help, and my mother-in-law will be retiring next year. My colleagues at work are willing to swap shifts with me — it all takes some organisation.

## Potential pitfalls...

- If granny is looking after your children, there are likely to be some generational issues that may crop up and potentially cause problems. Methods of childcare always vary between generations. Trends and practices change. While your parents will naturally have your children's best interests at heart, it is important that you all agree on the methods of childcare that you would like to be followed before any regular childcare arrangement begins. If your relative says she just would prefer to do things her own way, and you feel strongly that you would like things to be done your way, then it's probably best to avoid argument by not having her as a regular childcarer. Differences of opinion are likely to occur in the areas of discipline, treats, television and computer access.
- Payment may cause embarrassment when childcare arrangements are made within families. Don't be shy when talking about money – if you are after a formal childcare arrangement that you can rely on, it is sensible to offer to pay. Your family member or friend may

- refuse to accept payment point-blank – in which case you will have to be a little more creative with ways in which to recompense her.
- There may be logistical headaches to overcome when asking a family member to look after your children. Grannies are often happier to look after young children in their own homes (rather than in the child's home), but you will want to make sure that her home is baby-proofed in the same way as your own. You will also need to set Granny up with all the equipment she will need, to avoid constant lugging around kit between homes and potentially (or constantly) leaving things behind in the wrong house.
- It is important in this kind of arrangement to remember the things that make other childcare arrangements successful. One of the main issues is communication. Family members offering childcare and parents need to stay in touch over the childcare as much as any other childcare arrangement. You should put in place methods of communication in the usual way, so that you know about your child's day and keep in touch with how the situation is going. Hard feelings can develop quickly (and can be fiery, especially within family) if communication doesn't flow easily.
- It is easy for the family carer to feel that they are being taken advantage of, or being taken for granted in this situation. Parents are likely to be delighted with this childcare solution – granny really can be a brilliant answer to all childcare conundrums. But it is so important to remember to say thank you – all the time. If feeling beholden isn't your style, you may want to look down other avenues.

### ...and how to overcome them

- Discuss all issues of childcare well in advance of when you need this kind of childcare arrangement to begin. Make sure that all parties are in agreement about the methods of discipline to be used – it will otherwise be too confusing for your children to be expected to behave one way on one day of the week and another way on other days. Older children can cope with this, but young toddlers will find this too muddling, and the confusion could lead to worse behaviour. As well as discipline, talk about diet, routines, and safety issues.

You as the parent must feel confident enough to set your own rules around all of these areas. You should be able to expect the family member who agrees to look after your children to take your beliefs on board.

- If your family childcarer doesn't accept financial recompense for helping you out with your childcare needs, be sure to thank her in other ways. A bunch of flowers will always be well received. An afternoon off when you are able to arrange it will probably be appreciated even more, especially if it comes with advance notice. A treat – something that your family member wouldn't spend money on for herself, an evening out or a voucher for her favourite store, are all ways to recognise the time and effort that she is putting in on your family's behalf.
- There are practical measures you can take to keep this kind of family childcare simple. Granny will probably be happy to give up a cupboard in her kitchen so that she has everything to hand for when the baby is dropped at her house. It will make sense for her to keep a supply of nappies, bottles, books, toys and other age-appropriate paraphernalia to hand to entertain your child while he is in her care.
- Communicate regularly with your family member – about how they feel about the situation, whether it is still working for them, as well as on a more day-to-day level. A notebook that travels between homes with the child can be extremely useful – carers and parents can write daily messages and let each other know about routines, oddities, general information or requirements for the next day. This is also an easy way to avoid repeating lunch and supper on the same day.
- Make sure that your family childcarer doesn't feel that you are taking advantage of her. The best way to avoid this is to make sure that you *aren't* taking advantage of her generosity and the fact that she is family. Certainly avoid asking more of a family childcarer than you would feel comfortable asking someone from outside your family. Make a point of saying thank you – sincerely and often – possibly even more often than you would to another childcarer.

> It is important for everyone in this situation – but particularly for granny and her grandchildren – that granny can be granny from time to time. Visit grandparents as grandparents at the weekend and let them be in their natural role – dishing out treats and sweets and spoiling and enjoying their grandchildren. If your children only see their grandparents in their 'childcare' role, they may miss out on the great relationship that can be formed across the generations.

Family childcare arrangements require a great amount of flexibility and goodwill to be offered by both sides to be successful. Try to keep the arrangement as formal as is reasonably possible, to avoid taking advantage of a family member's generosity.

## …your maternity nurse

### The maternity nurse's role

A maternity nurse will come and stay with a family for the period of time immediately or very soon after the arrival of a new baby. A maternity nurse's role is to help the mother recover from the birth, to help her get used to life with a new baby and to help establish feeding and sleep routines for the baby.

### Potential pitfalls…

- Families are welcoming a maternity nurse into their home at a particularly emotional time. The new mother's hormones are all over the place and everyone is most probably sleep-deprived and prone to tears. Emotions run high and it is easy to strike out at anyone within close range.
- A maternity nurse has a fine line to tread – between being helpful and being too bossy. She has to quickly assess how much of a lead the new mother wants her to take, as well as try to establish routines for the baby, while letting the mother feel in control.
- Occasionally parents will have thought that they wanted a maternity nurse, to find that when the time comes, the situation doesn't suit

them at all. It is very hard to predict how you will feel after a birth and occasionally new parents find they resent another adult 'intruding' on their time with their newborn.
- This is a live-in role at a very intense time and new parents will be quite likely to be dealing with sharing their home for the first time, at the same time as getting used to a new baby and their new role as parents. All the live-in complications can arise – it is entirely possible that parents and maternity nurse might all get under each other's feet. Maternity nurses usually expect to eat meals with the family, but will be sensitive to parents' need to be alone at times, too.
- If you are already a large family, problems can lie ahead over what role, if any, the maternity nurse will play with your older children. Most maternity nurses prefer to keep their role very defined, just to help the mother and baby; others will be more flexible over this. If a maternity nurse feels she is being asked to be nanny, cook, chauffeur and maternity nurse all rolled into one, she may well feel fed up.

## ...and how to overcome them

- It is best if families have had a chance to meet with the maternity nurse before the baby is born – ideally you will have been through an interview process and chosen the candidate that you feel will best fit into your home environment and meet your needs. The maternity nurse, who is most probably experienced in this anyway, will have had a chance to meet you before you are in your postnatal state and will be able to recognise your mood swings for what they are and respond to them accordingly.
- Hiring a maternity nurse with experience is likely to make this process pass more smoothly. A mature, independent woman who is used to the role will have seen it all before and be able to cope with whatever is thrown at her (though not in a literal sense!). Experienced maternity nurses will be able to 'read' the parents to judge how much input they want or need – and will also be able to deal with the situation which may occasionally arise when parents ask her to leave early so they can continue their bonding process alone. A much more frequent occurrence, however, is when the

parents ask the maternity nurse to stay on longer than the original booking. An experienced maternity nurse, who is most likely booked up ahead, will be able to explain gently why she can't and instil the new parents with the belief that they are ready to continue alone.

- If you are having trouble adjusting to the live-in aspect to this arrangement, talk openly about this with your maternity nurse. It is worth explaining that a live-in situation is new to you (if that is the case) and that you are having trouble getting used to it. Again, a mature maternity nurse will be familiar with this situation and will be able to give you some space. She will certainly appreciate your honesty, rather than having to be a mind reader and interpret the stony looks herself.
- Make sure you have addressed the question of what the maternity nurse will be prepared to do with regard to other children in the household. If your hopes and expectations are not being met, speak with the maternity nurse about this as soon as you can, to avoid any bad feeling developing. You may find a maternity nurse who *is* willing to help collect older children from school and playdates, prepare their supper and give them a bath, as long as this all fits in with the routine that she is establishing for the new baby. Ideally, it should – the maternity nurse is, after all, there to set you up so that you will be able to cope when left to your own devices later on.

## MANAGING YOUR RELATIONSHIP WITH YOUR CHILDCARE PROVIDER

### 10 tips for a healthy relationship with your maternity nurse

- Meet before you have the baby.
- Interview as you would a full-time, live-in nanny/au pair/mother's help.
- Don't expect the maternity nurse to do everything.
- Try not to feel upset when she takes the baby/babies away from you so you can rest/play with other children. That is what she is there for.
- Agree to order take-out food at least once a week to give everyone a night off from cooking and clearing up.
- Ask if you can take it in turns to empty the dishwasher – don't bear grudges about having to do all the housework.
- Give her a quiet place, away from the baby if at all possible, so you can all have a breather from each other.
- Enquire after her own family but try to keep conversations brief – too much talk is a regular complaint from parents.
- Be sensitive
- Respect her guidance while remaining confident about your own desires.
- Make the most of her being there – it is probably going to be brief.

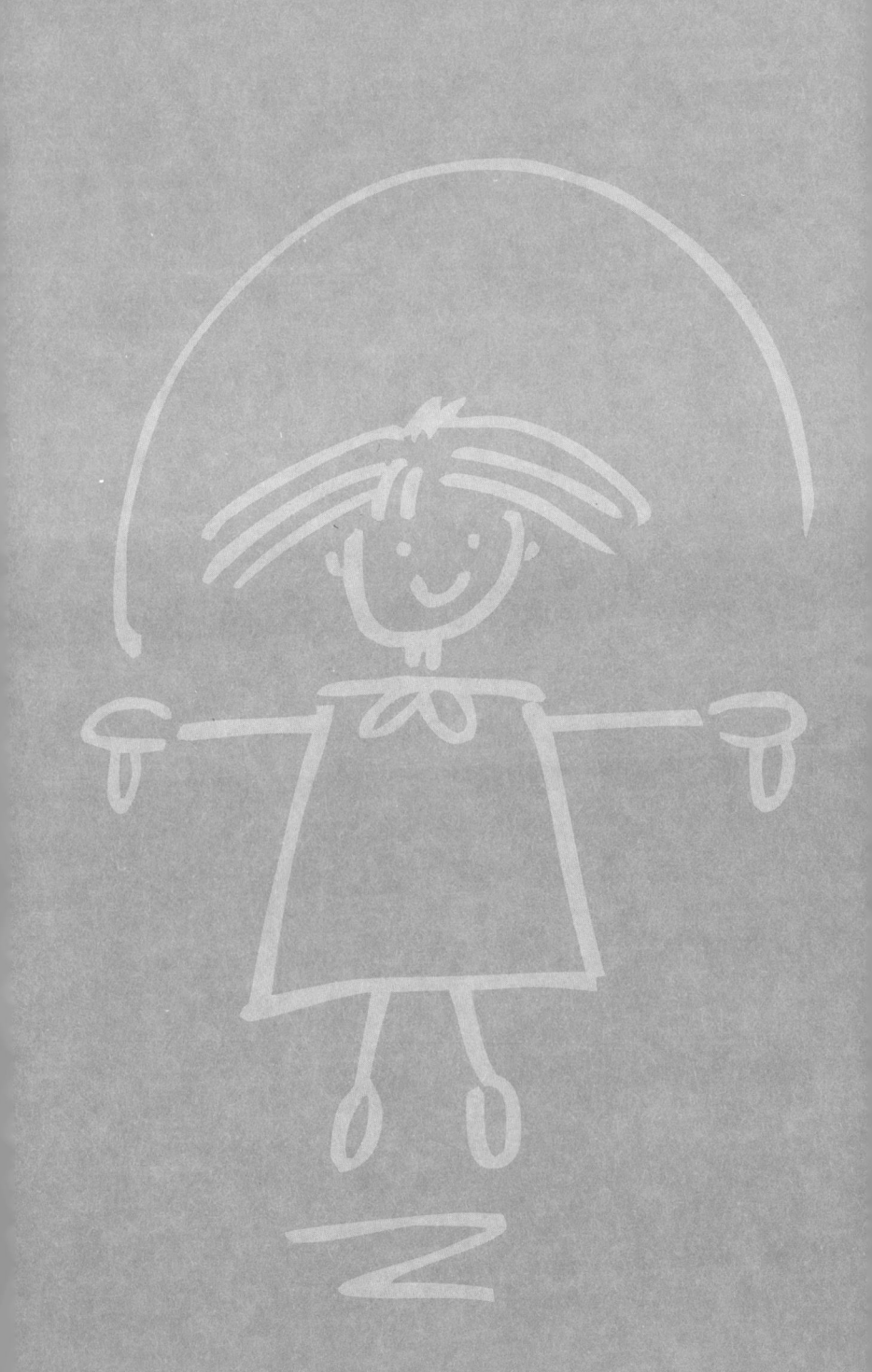

# Coping if things go wrong

## Reasons for childcare to go wrong

There are many different reasons for things to go wrong. If you are alert to the different problems that might crop up you will be well placed to deal with them quickly. Some problems can be resolved or managed, as we have looked at in the previous chapter; often a simple misunderstanding can stand in the way of a good working relationship and can easily be straightened out. Other problems may be deep-rooted, and will be a warning that the arrangement does not have a good chance of working out in the long-term.

## Lack of Enthusiasm

If a childcare giver is not particularly enthusiastic about childcare (and managed to conceal this fact at interview), this will start to become apparent over a relatively short period of time. Of course, this is easier to spot if you are around for some of the time that your carer is looking after your children and harder to spot if you are not. Again, communication is the answer. Chat about how the day has gone and listen out for signs of boredom on your carer's part. A happy attitude is so vital when looking after children – someone who is down in the dumps is the wrong person to be caring for your children. Looking after children can be stressful and there are some very monotonous chores – it certainly doesn't suit all people.

If your childcarer is not enthusiastic this will also be reflected in your children's attitude towards her. Children are inevitably drawn towards the people that take an interest in them.

## Misunderstandings

Misunderstandings can usually be resolved easily enough. As long as no one has said anything they will later regret, most misunderstandings can be ironed out. Misunderstandings can commonly occur when childcarer and parents do not share their mother tongue. When a new au pair arrives in England, for example, communication can be problematic and all sorts of potential muddles lie ahead. Ask a childcarer whose English is basic to repeat instructions back to you to make sure they have been clearly understood – and encourage attendance at language school.

## Mistakes – 1

There are different kinds of mistakes with different consequences. Burning the fish fingers or forgetting to buy milk can usually be put down to scattiness. Everyone makes little mistakes from time to time in their workplace. As long as a childcarer's mistake has not endangered your children in any way, it is a good idea to try to be accepting and move on. An after-school babysitter arriving fifteen minutes late, as a one off, to collect your children from school is not the end of the world. Forgive and forget, especially if you are otherwise happy with your childcare arrangement.

## Mistakes – 2

The second category of mistake is the one you the employer can make – hiring the wrong person, or choosing the wrong nursery or childminder. It is likely that if this happens, you will realise very quickly that things aren't going to work out. This will happen to everyone at some point – don't beat yourself up about it and try to just resolve the situation as quickly as possible. If the mistake is obvious to everyone (and if it is bad, it most likely will be) your arrangements will probably fall apart very quickly. Try not to take this to heart and concentrate on what went wrong, so that you can use the experience to your advantage next time around. Usually this kind of mistake will come down to a personality clash – a difference of views on childcare and a different approach to looking after children.

## Mistakes – 3

The big ones. If you discover that your childcarer has been dishonest, in any situation, act immediately. Whether the dishonesty concerns money, concealing something that has happened during the day or covering up an accident, once you know that you cannot trust the person providing your childcare, you should bring the relationship to a close, as soon as you practically can. You have to be totally confident in your childcare provider to feel comfortable leaving your child in her care.

## Sue, 42, from Merseyside, has had some mixed experiences with childminders

I had one childminder who was so unprofessional that I wouldn't have recommended her to anyone. Sometimes I'd take the boys there and she wouldn't even have got out of bed — I'd wake her up and she'd come to the door, bleary-eyed in her dressing gown. Another childminder was recommended to me and she was fantastic — completely geared up for it with the patience of a saint. She had climbing equipment in her garden, and took the children out on trips to the park. From my experience, if you pick up on something which doesn't feel right, follow your instincts. When you find someone you like, you've struck the jackpot.

*If you pick up on something which doesn't feel right, follow your instincts*

## Keep in touch with your children

Your children's relationship with their carer needs managing, in the same way as your relationship with the carer needs to be looked after. If your children are happy with the care they are receiving, the arrangement has improved chances of success.

Talk to your children – try to be indirect, but ask them about their day, what they have been doing, where and with whom. Try to keep in touch enough to know if they are happy with the situation. Clearly this will be easier with older children, but there is definitely something to be gleaned from younger children too. Remember, as well as asking questions, to leave some silences which may be filled by your children. Wait to listen to whether they offer any information. The answer to 'How was your day?' is almost always, 'Fine.' So don't always ask; wait to see if anything is offered.

If your children are unhappy, you will know. If the reluctance to be dropped off at nursery or the childminder's house continues, even when they have had a good amount of time to settle in, it is worth asking some questions – of the key worker, the childminder and perhaps other parents, as well as your child. If your child continues to cry every time you leave him with his nanny or your mother's help or au pair, it's time for a chat with your carer. You will know your child enough to know if it is taking him too long to settle in – a confident child will usually just walk into a new childcare situation if all is well; a clingy child could need a few weeks to settle in. If the tears last after the first month, you need to start asking why.

As your children get older, they will be more interested and able to express an opinion about who is looking after them. While it is clearly the parents' choice, it is vital for a good relationship all round that the children and carer get along well. Listen carefully to any complaints your children may have about their childcare – while all children like to exaggerate, there is likely to be more than a grain of truth in most things that they tell you.

Try hard to resist the temptation to probe your children for information – they will see you coming a mile off if you start asking too many questions about the way your mother's help behaved in the park, rather than did they have fun? By listening to the description of their day you will gather whether your mother's help played with them or spent the afternoon on the phone.

At bedtime we used to talk about the five (or three, depending on how late it was) best things that day and the one thing we didn't like. You can also talk about plans for the next day so that it is less obviously a grilling session about what has already been.

## Your child's development

Are you happy with your child's development? Do you think your children are getting what they need from their childcare? Are your children keeping up with their peers, in terms of speech and social development?

It is a good idea to be up to date with the stages that your children should be going through, in a broad sense, to be aware if your child's development is falling far behind (though bear in mind that children all develop at different rates and don't panic if a contemporary from a toddler group starts talking before your child). An experienced childcare provider will be aware of this, too – this is something you will be able to work on together. Your child falling behind could flag a potential problem with your childcare – or could signal a development issue that it would be wise to follow up.

## Back-up plans

You need to be prepared for things to go wrong in your childcare arrangements. If, for example, your child's regular care is with a childminder or nursery and your child is ill but you still need to get to work, you will need to call for help at short notice. If a child is sick it is obviously better if he can be cared for by someone he already knows.

Family is the obvious route to go here – lots of cuddles from Granny will get him through the day. However, for many parents this isn't an option, and you need to have something else up your sleeve. The next best solution is to call on good, local friends to help you out in an emergency. If you can arrange a reciprocal agreement with a friend, then no-one needs to feel guilty, and both mothers can feel confident that if they can't work from home for the day there is an alternative. Perhaps even come to this arrangement with two friends, so you have two places to try in an emergency.

You can find yourself in the same position if your childminder or nanny is sick and can't take care of her charges. A good childminder will have made some provisional plans to cope in this situation and will have arranged for a couple of local childminders to shoulder her workload in case of ill health. Childminders need to adhere to strict ratios, so all the children from one childminder would be unlikely to be able to be placed together. Even if your childminder has made some provision, you would be well advised to have your own back-up plan too.

A nanny employed privately by one family is unlikely to be able to provide the family with any short-term solution in case she is taken ill or needs to go away in an emergency – her nanny friends will be busy with their own charges and employed by other families who won't be thrilled at the prospect of their employee looking after extra children for the whole day. Family or friends are the best places to go for short-term help, on odd days. A good relationship with a childcare agency can help here – most agencies have temporary nannies on their books.

Then there is the kind of back up you need in case your childcare arrangements fall apart all together, not just for the odd day. If you decide that the nursery is failing in its duty of care, or that your nanny is incompetent, you won't want to leave your child in that situation while you go through the (sometime long) process of finding new childcare. This is where temporary nannies come into their own. Nanny agencies will have a list of temporary nannies on their books, who can be drafted in to help out in emergencies. Nannies who specialise in temporary jobs are often superb, are experienced at landing on their feet and quickly assessing a situation and can be relied on to give you the support you need as a family. This kind of calm, assured help will be just what you need to get you through a rough patch, and give you the space to reassess what you want for your long-term childcare solution.

# The end of the affair

## All good things come to an end

Even great working relationships with nannies, mother's helps and au pairs come to a natural end at some point. There will come a moment when it is time for your nanny to move on. This may be to another job with different or greater responsibilities, home if she has been living in the UK temporarily, or sometimes back to college to improve her skills and qualifications. Childcare is not always a vocation – sometimes it is a means to an end, or just a way to earn some money to travel or while deciding what other career path to follow in the future. It is possible to make positive decisions about moving on to new childcare.

## Children outgrow their childcare

Children can outgrow their childcare in two ways. If they have been looked after at a day care nursery, this will usually only provide care for children up to five years old, until they start school. The child will have to move on to another form of childcare to wraparound the school day and during the school holidays.

After-school clubs and holiday clubs can be the next step up for school-age children. If this form of childcare is used, it could in theory last until the child is 12, or leaving primary school. In practise, it is unlikely that the same after-school and holiday clubs will be able to cater for your child for this long. Being in the same environment for a number of years will not be stimulating for your child as he grows physically, emotionally and developmentally. He could outgrow the activities on offer and, while it may be beneficial for him to be among the older children at the centre, he may tire of always being around younger kids. He may also have repeated the activities on offer a number of times. You are likely to have to find an alternative as he grows older.

A child could stay with a childminder as he grows older – if the childminder offers a pick-up from his school, until he is old enough to travel by himself. Similar problems may arise, as with after-school clubs – while there can be great benefits in staying with the same carer for a number of years and forming a strong bond, an older child may not find a childminder's home, surrounded by younger children, the most stimulating place to be. Again, parents may need to look for alternatives as their children grow older.

## Childcare moving on

Au pairs, mother's helpers and shared care nannies may all be building up their experience to move on to a job that comes with more independence and responsibility. The time will come when they feel they have learnt all they can with your family and they should move on, to build on their experience in a new setting. While you may be very sorry to see your help go, it is hopeless to try to stop this happening. It is good for people to want to move on and develop – and even good for children to see this happening. Ideally, we all want our children to be looked after by ambitious, interested people – who are unlikely to want to stay in the same job for too long.

Try to make sure your children understand that is it normal for a nanny, au pair or mother's help to move on at some point. While you want to avoid talking about this every day and making the children anxious that their childcare is going to change at any moment, let them know that this arrangement won't last forever. Encourage your children to understand that it is exciting for their au pair to move on, or for their nanny to go travelling. If a childcare arrangement is ending amicably, involve the children by holding a farewell tea party, make good luck cards and have a fond farewell.

## Families change

Childcare needs change as families evolve. Families might move house and go to the countryside or move into a town or city. Both will most probably involve changes in childcare arrangements. New nurseries, childminders, babysitters – whole new networks will have to be found.

Family situations change. Parents may split up, which could involve a change in childcare, either because of a change in financial circumstances or living arrangements, making the previous childcare unsuitable to the new situation. A death in the family could alter the family's childcare requirements. A new baby will change family dynamics and parents' needs.

Children grow up and go to nursery and then to school. It is impossible to plan too far ahead – try to look just a little into the future and around the next corner, if you can pull it off. Anticipate your needs if you can, but don't get stuck into one way of thinking.

So much is unpredictable and unforeseen – it is important to enjoy good childcare while it is working well for everybody, but also important to recognise when a situation is no longer offering the best solution. Be bold and make the changes where necessary, rather than letting a good situation turn bad because it no longer suits everyone involved.

## Bad things tend to come to an end rather more quickly...
### What to do when things go wrong

If a bad situation has arisen in an otherwise happy arrangement, make time to talk things through. This should obviously be a private conversation, which will need to take place with children well out of earshot. Try to find out what is at the root of the problem. If your childcarer won't tell you, you are off to a bad start. If she is prepared to talk, there is hope.

If your conversations with your childcare provider take a turn for the worse, keep talking to see if you can resolve the issues. While hoping for the best, start preparing for the worst. Put some feelers out, in case you need to make some rapid changes.

If a bad situation arises in a childcare arrangement that you have not been feeling 100% happy with, it is probably another warning sign that you need to make some changes. Constant niggles and things going wrong are unlikely to get better, unless this is right at the beginning and they are obvious teething problems.

When things have really gone wrong, cut your losses. If your childcare is outside of your home and you are extremely unhappy with the care being provided, either at a nursery, childminder or club, give notice and take your child away as soon as you are able to make alternative arrangements. At home, trying to persuade a nanny, mother's help or au pair or babysitter to stay when things are obviously coming to an end is never a good idea. Offer to pay a month's wages (check your contract), and suggest that you carer leaves at the end of the week or month – depending on how bad the situation is and how quickly you think you will be able to put temporary childcare in place.

Always be prepared to use a temporary solution to fill a gap, rather than trying to string out a poor situation to get you to your next childcare arrangement. You will be able to think more clearly with a good, if temporary, arrangement in place. Dragging out a bad situation can bring you all down with it.

In all instances, put your children's welfare and your sanity high up your list of priorities and phone an agency for temporary help.

Remember to be mature – parents have to be the grown up in this situation. Don't show your children you are upset and always try to avoid them being drawn into a bad situation. It is best for everyone involved to close this chapter and move on in a positive frame of mind, to happier childcare arrangements.

## 10 signs that things are going wrong

- Your happy, bright and bubbly children develop black moods and unhappy faces.
- A frosty atmosphere may develop between you and the carer.
- A breakdown in communication.
- Rudeness or unpleasantness towards parents or children from the carer.
- Bad behaviour from your usually well-behaved and well-balanced children.
- Poor communication or understanding between carer and children leading to an unhealthy relationship.
- Moodiness or sulky behaviour from your childcarer.
- Bad reports from friends who see your carer and children out together.
- Outright arguments between you and the carer.
- Persistent lateness or ignoring of house rules on your carer's behalf.

## Learning from bad experiences

What went wrong? If you are able, it is great to have a debriefing session with your departing nanny or other childcarer. If things have ended badly this may be unpleasant and you may decide you don't want to know what she really thinks of you all. If you don't trust her judgement (or trust her to be honest) this won't be worthwhile. However, if you have generally gotten along, it is a useful conversation to have. It will help you with your future childcare arrangements.

If a situation turned out badly, it is a good idea to make a list of where you think you might have gone wrong, to hope to avoid making the same mistakes another time. Ask yourself questions such as these:

- Did you hire the wrong person for the job?
- Was the person you hired too young or too old?
- Were you expecting too much of your childcare?
- Did you advertise the job honestly? Should you describe the work in a different way next time to make sure you attract the right candidates, with whom you will stand a better chance of having a successful working relationship?
- Did you have a personality clash? Can you figure out why?

The main thing to remember is not to take a childcare arrangement going wrong to heart – we all make mistakes and we all get over them. The right childcare for you and your family is out there, somewhere.

### Do as you would be done by in your childcare relationships

- Remember that respect and trust are key.
- Avoid confrontation but keep communication open.
- Ask questions, and leave plenty of space for answers.
- Try to control your emotions and keep things in perspective.

**And don't**
- Forget your manners.
- Shout, humiliate, embarrass or harangue.
- Say something you will regret.
- Expect anyone to be a mind-reader.

## The end of the relationship

When it has all come to an end and you have said your goodbyes, look back on the good times. There will definately have been some, unless it all went wrong horribly quickly and is just best forgotten all together. It is great fun to pop into your childs old nursery to show off a new school uniform. You are likely to be able to stay in touch with a childminder, too, especially if you all stay in the same area.

A nanny, au pair or mother's help is likely to have been playing a big role in your family's life, particularly if she has been with you for a while. It is great to stay in touch, especially if you have all got along well and your helper is going to be staying in the local area. Apart from all the positives about continuity for the children, making sure they don't feel abandoned and so on, it will be great to add to your list of babysitters. An old nanny or au pair coming back to babysit can be a successful arrangement for all concerned.

Of course, if a nanny is returning to her home country, it is a little trickier to stay in touch. Special bonds can be maintained through email and children love receiving letters (and can usually be persuaded to even write one themselves given that they might get one back). It's fun to see an old au pair's pictures of her own baby a few years down the line.

When you part ways, always give a reference straight away. It is so easy to say you will send it and then get wrapped up in all the other things that are going on in your life and simply forget. It is an important document to give your nanny, au pair, mother's help or babysitter. Keep in mind the kind of references you like to see when writing a reference for your departing helper – what are the pertinent things to mention about this particular carer? Be generous, think of the positives and always include your phone number.

## A Final Word

We hope that our advice and the experiences that are shared in this book help you to find the right childcare. Remember that childcare is an individual choice. Only you can know what will be best for you and your family. We hope that this book helps you make the right decision. Having good childcare helps us all to enjoy the time that we have with our children and can make the early years even more fun and successful than we know they already will be. Good, reliable childcare arrangements make for happy children and happy families.

# section FIVE

# technical questions

- COST OF CHILDCARE
- CHILDCARE VOUCHERS
- TAX
- CONTRACTS AND LETTERS OF EMPLOYMENT
- LEGAL OBLIGATIONS OF EMPLOYERS AND EMPLOYEES
- INSURANCE
- HEALTH AND SAFETY ISSUES
- OFSTED
- CHILDREN'S INFORMATION SERVICE
- VISAS AND WORK PERMITS
- GOVERNMENT GUIDELINES FOR AU PAIRS
- CRB CHECKS
- QUALIFICATIONS
- CHILDCARE RATIOS

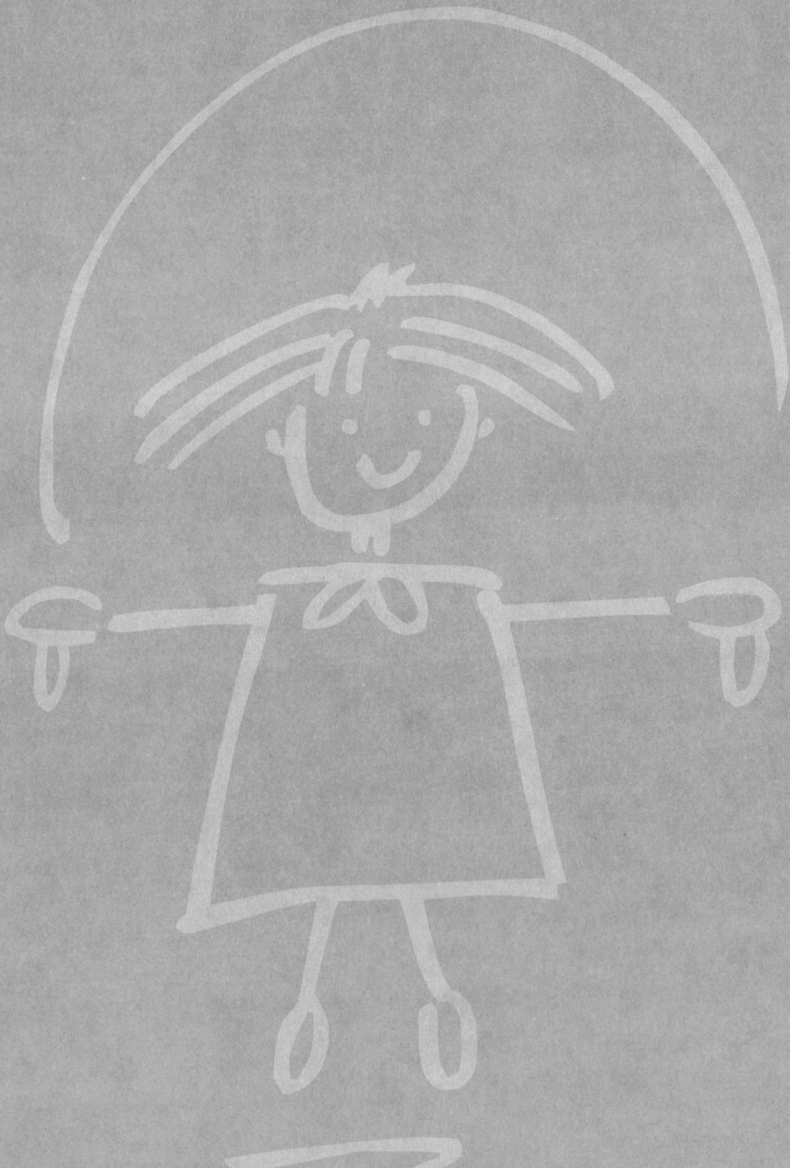

# Technical Questions

By now hopefully you've decided on the perfect person or place to look after your child – at the very least, you have a clear idea of what type of childcare will suit your needs. Now it is time to find out how to actually go about formally employing someone. This part of the book will focus on some of the nitty-gritty admin stuff – from information on whether you are liable for tax (and how to pay for it) to tips on the legalities involved and what to look out for in a nanny contract. It will also include information on who you are permitted to employ and what the varying types of qualifications mean.

## Cost of childcare

Cost is clearly one of the most important factors in deciding what type of childcare suits you. Whether you are going back to work or need some extra help at home, a big factor in your decision-making will inevitably come down to whether your chosen option is affordable.

Working parents often view paying for childcare as an 'investment' for the future as, for some, paying out as much as they earn in the early years means they can maintain their skill in the workplace. In Section One we examined the different childcare options available – the following cost grid will give you a quick guide to the likely costs for each type of childcare though, naturally these will vary.

## TECHNICAL QUESTIONS

| Type of childcare | Hours/ day | Hours/ week | Cost/ day | Cost/ week | Hidden cost/ Advantage |
|---|---|---|---|---|---|
| Day Nursery | 10 | 50 | £29 – 60 (average) | £150 – 300 | No hidden cost. Meals and nappies may be included. |
| Childminder | 8–10 | Varies | £4 – 7/hour | Varies | No hidden cost. Childminder is self-employed. |
| After-school club | 3 | 15 | £8 | £40 | No hidden cost. |
| After-school nanny/ babysitter | 3–4 | 15–20 | £21 – 40* (£7 – 10/hour) | £100 – 200 | No hidden cost. Tax/NI liability if paying over £100/week. |
| Babysitting | Varies | Varies | £6 – 10/hour | n/a | Taxi home if no car or bicycle. Food if an early start. |
| Holiday clubs | 5 – 6 | 25 – 30 | £20 | £100 | No hidden cost. |
| Nanny live-in | 10–12 | 50 – 60 | £50–60 | £250–300 | Board and lodging cost. Some babysitting included. Tax/NI not included. |
| Nanny live-out | 10–12 | 50 – 60 | £70 – 100 | £350 – 500 | No hidden cost. Tax/NI not included. |
| Mother's help live-in | 10 | 50 | £40 – 50 | £200 – 250 | Board and lodging cost. Some babysitting included. Tax/NI not included. |
| Mother's help live-out | 10 | 50 | £50 – 60 | £250 – 300 | No hidden cost. Tax/NI not included. |
| Au pair | 5 | 25 | £12 – 14 | £60 – 70 | Board and lodging cost. Two nights babysitting included. |
| Au pair plus | 7 | 35 | £16 – 18 | £80 – 90 | Board and lodging cost. Two nights babysitting included. |
| Maternity nurse | 24/6 days | 144 | £80 – 150 | £500 – 900 | Board and lodging cost. Maternity nurse is self-employed. |
| Night nanny | 10 | 50 | £75 – 130 | £375 – 650 | Introduction fee of £150 – £175. Nanny is self-employed. |

TECHNICAL QUESTIONS

According to the national childcare charity, Daycare Trust, the typical cost of a full-time nursery place in England for a child under two in 2007 was £159/week or £8,368/year, which is an above-inflation 5% increase on 2006.

The figures in the chart give you an idea of what you will pay, as a basic rate, for different types of childcare. Of greater interest, however, is the real cost to you once tax and National Insurance contributions (NI) have been calculated.

| Net pay/week (what you pay for your childcare) | Gross cost (what it actually costs you) |
| --- | --- |
| £100 | £100 |
| £110 | £113.11 |
| £120 | £129.33 |
| £130 | £145.81 |
| £140 | £162.03 |
| £150 | £178.51 |
| £160 | £194.73 |
| £170 | £211.21 |
| £180 | £227.43 |
| £190 | £243.90 |
| £200 | £260.13 |
| £210 | £276.60 |
| £220 | £292.83 |
| £230 | £309.30 |
| £240 | £325.52 |
| £250 | £342.00 |
| £260 | £358.22 |
| £270 | £374.70 |
| £280 | £390.92 |
| £290 | £407.40 |
| £300 | £423.63 |
| £310 | £440.11 |
| £320 | £456.33 |
| £330 | £472.81 |
| £340 | £489.03 |
| £350 | £505.50 |

*Figures provided by Nannytax.

TECHNICAL QUESTIONS

The majority of nannies will talk in terms of net pay; i.e. what they want to earn in terms of cash each day/week. This can be really confusing, particularly if you are paid a monthly salary, which is a gross sum per year. The grid above will give you an idea of how much your nanny will actually cost you. For instance, if you agree to pay your nanny £250/week net it will actually cost you £342 in total, including tax and NI for your employee and employers' NI. Please note that the table should be used as a guide only, as each employee situation will be slightly different.

As this grid is for guideline purposes only, figures are rounded to the nearest pound. It is based on 2008/2009 tax and National Insurance rates for a person on a standard tax code (Tax and NI thresholds are both £105/week). The total gross figure comprises gross pay plus employer's NI contributions.

## Childcare vouchers
### What are childcare vouchers?

If you are a working parent then Childcare Vouchers are one way that your employer can help you with your childcare costs. They were developed by Accor Services in 1989 and over 200,000 parents are now benefiting from them. Childcare Vouchers only became tax and NI exempt in April 2005 and since then they have become one of the most popular forms of family-friendly employee benefit that an employer can offer. If your employer gives you childcare vouchers you will not pay tax or NI on the first £55/week or £243/month (for tax year 2008/2009), if you are a standard rate tax payer. This means standard rate tax payers can save more than £962/year while higher rate tax payers can save as much as £1,195/year. Watch out though, if your employer gives you the option of choosing more than £243/month, you will have to pay tax and NI on anything over this amount. And remember, it's not just for mums! If you have a partner you can both join the voucher scheme and double your savings.

### How does the childcare voucher system work?

Ask your employer if they offer childcare vouchers. If they do, great! If they don't, then try to persuade them to start a scheme. Your employer can either run the childcare voucher scheme themselves or pay an outside childcare voucher company (see the list below) to administer one for them. You will either get the vouchers direct from your employer or from the childcare voucher company. Many childcare voucher companies use e-vouchers, which are issued through their website.

Childcare vouchers can be given to you in addition to your salary but many employers offer them through 'salary sacrifice.' This means that you exchange a specific amount of your salary for childcare vouchers. Your contract must be amended if you agree to 'salary sacrifice' as you have formally approved a cut in your taxable income. There is, however, a slight restriction on taking childcare vouchers in this way. A 'salary sacrifice' cannot reduce your pay below the National Minimum Wage (NMW). You are not obliged to take the maximum allowance of £55/week. This means you can take a lower amount in vouchers so that you don't fall below the NMW. But watch out – childcare vouchers may affect your tax credits entitlement.

## How do I use the vouchers?

You can use them to pay your childcare provider e.g. nanny/childminder/nursery who can then claim the value of the voucher from the voucher company (usually done by direct payment into their bank account). If your employer administers the scheme itself then your childcarer will claim the money direct from your employer.

The great thing about the scheme is that you don't have to use the vouchers in the week or month they are provided, so you can save them up for times of the year when you may need more childcare – such as over the summer holidays. Paper vouchers are usually valid for one year and electronic vouchers generally don't have an expiry date – just remember that vouchers cannot be backdated. If your day nursery fees are due on 1 June and you receive your first voucher on 21 June, you can only use the childcare voucher for your next fees due on 1 July.

## Can I get vouchers if my employer offers directly contracted childcare or a workplace nursery?

If your employer offers directly-contracted childcare the same limits of £55/week or £243/month apply. Workplace nurseries refer to childcare that is provided by your employer at – or near – where you work. You will not have to pay any tax or NI on this facility. You cannot get childcare vouchers if your employer pays you cash for your childcare; pays the childcare bill; or pays the child's school fees.

## Will the vouchers affect my tax credits?

Entitlement to the element of Working Tax Credits (WTC), which gives specific support related to childcare costs, will in most cases be affected. It is a good idea to

## TECHNICAL QUESTIONS

find out what kind of support you could get through WTC before you join a salary sacrifice scheme.

If you are on a higher income, childcare vouchers may affect your entitlement to Child Tax Credit (CTC) or may cut the amount you can get. Higher earners will generally be better off accepting childcare vouchers as they will make the greatest savings on tax and NI. Visit www.hmrc.gov.uk for more on the current income thresholds. If you want to know whether you would be better off with tax credits or childcare vouchers, you can use the online calculator on the site or call the tax credit helpline on 0845 300 3900.

### What kind of childcare can the vouchers be used for?

The vouchers can be used to pay for any form of legal childcare but the first £55/week you get in vouchers will only be exempt from tax and NI if the vouchers are used to pay for registered childcare. Check if your childcare provider will accept them. It does not cost your nanny/nursery anything to receive payment through childcare vouchers but beware – not all childcare providers choose to take them and they do not have to by law. Make sure you agree how you will pay for the rest of the childcare if the voucher does not cover the whole cost.

Childcare vouchers can be used to pay for a wide range of childcare:

- Day Nursery
- Nursery School
- Childminder
- Crèche
- Pre-School
- Nanny
- Au Pair
- Out of School Club
- Holiday Play Scheme

To make sure that you can benefit from the tax and NI-free part of your childcare vouchers then your chosen childcare provider must hold a current registration certificate or an approval certificate with an expiry date. You will need to quote the 'registered' childcare Unique Reference Number (URN), which you will find on your childcarer's latest registration certificate. The approval organisations include:

TECHNICAL QUESTIONS

England: OFSTED Childcare Register (compulsory and voluntary)
Self-certified
Wales: Childcare Approval Scheme
The Care Standards Inspectorate
Northern Ireland: Local Health and Social Services Trusts
Scotland: The Care Commission

Unfortunately, childcare provided by granny does not qualify. The only exception is when a relative is a registered childminder and happens to care for a child who is related to them but whose main paid childminding is for children they are not related to. In this case, the care provider must care for the child outside of the child's own home.

## How does my child qualify?

All children up to the age of 15 (until 1 September following their 15th birthday) will qualify for you to receive the tax-free childcare vouchers. If your child is disabled then you qualify for the vouchers for an extra year. The child must be your child, step-child, or a child for whom you have parental responsibility. They do not have to live with you for you to be able to claim vouchers.

## The main childcare voucher providers are:

Accor Services
Care4
Sodexho Pass
Busy Bees Childcare Vouchers

## Also offering voucher services:

Abacus Voucher Solutions
Allsave
Bringme from Lloyds TSB Registrars
Chamber Childcare
Cheshire Childcare Vouchers
Childcare Account
Childcare Options Ltd
Children's Links Childcare Vouchers
Early Years
Employers for Childcare

TECHNICAL QUESTIONS

Fair Care
Family Matters
FenniesVouchers.com
Fideliti
Gemelli Childcare Vouchers
Imagine Co-operative Childcare Vouchers
Kiddivouchers
Kidsunlimited
Leapfrog Childcare Vouchers
Premier Employer Solutions
TEDS eVouchers
Tiny Teddies Childcare Voucher Company
Voucher Solutions
Willow Childcare Vouchers
Your Staff Benefits Childcare Vouchers

## Tax

When you take on a nanny or a mother's help and pay her more that £105/week (tax year 2008/2009) you become an employer and will have to pay tax and National Insurance contributions (NI). If, however, you pay your nanny below the threshold but she has another job, then you may also have to pay tax. If you do not register with HM Revenue and Customs (HMRC) then you could face a hefty fine and back payments.

One of the easiest ways to deal with this bureaucratic headache is to employ a payroll agency to do it all for you. There are several companies that will look after all the tax and NI issues; a selection is listed below:

Nanny Tax (www.nannytax.co.uk)
Taxing Nannies (www.taxingnannies.co.uk)
NannyPaye (www.nannypaye.co.uk)
PAYE For Nannies (www.payefornannies.co.uk)
Salix Payroll Services (www.salixpayrollservices.co.uk)

For a fixed annual fee most agencies will ensure that your employment responsibilities for pay are met by issuing payslips and telling you when and what to pay to HMRC. A good payroll company should also keep you up-to-date with tax rates and other changes that may affect your employment responsibilities. Some will give

TECHNICAL QUESTIONS

you sample nanny contracts and help you with any pay-related issues. A few will also provide employment law support. In summary, most good payroll agencies will:

- Register you as an employer with HMRC and then deal with all the paperwork on your behalf
- Provide weekly or monthly payslips
- Keep complete payroll records
- Process a P45 every time a nanny joins or leaves you
- Send you a quarterly summary of the tax and NI due and show you how to pay it
- Prepare and file (most do this electronically so that you benefit from the HMRC cash rebate) an employer's annual return and employee's pay and deductions summary with HMRC at the end of each tax year
- Sort out any sick or maternity pay

## How to do the tax yourself

If you like number crunching or are just feeling brave then you may consider working out the tax and NI for your nanny yourself. Be warned – it isn't straightforward, as most nannies tend to agree net pay, while tax is calculated on gross pay.

- Firstly give HMRC's new employer helpline a call on 0845 607 0143. If you are a pro and have more than three years payroll experience you should call 0845 714 3143. They will register you as a new employer.
- If you have agreed net pay with your childcare provider then call your local tax office for them to turn it into a gross amount.
- One important thing to remember is that you must pay your child provider at least the National Minimum Wage per hour. For the latest rates visits www.hmrc.gov.uk/nmw.
- Once you have the gross figure then you need to call the helpline again and they will help work out the tax and NI. There are many different factors that will influence how much tax your employee will pay including if they have come from a previous job. Their tax status will also change if they have another source of income or you provide benefits in kind such as a car or health insurance.
- You can pay the tax and NI on the 19th of each month, or quarterly if your monthly payments do not exceed £1,500.

TECHNICAL QUESTIONS

- To help you set up your payroll and calculate tax and NI, request an interactive employer CD–ROM. If you don't fancy using a computer then you can order paper copies of everything you need. You must keep accurate records of how much you pay them and what deductions you have made as well as any expenses and benefits that you have given.
- At the end of each tax year you will need to complete and send your Employer Annual Return to HMRC. This will include the deductions you have made from your employee, your employer's NI contributions, the payments you have made to HMRC, the payments you have made to your employee and any statutory payments.

If you employ someone who says that they are self-employed you must check that this is actually the case. You can check by calling the new employer helpline or by using the employment status tool on www.hmrc.gov.uk/calcs/esi.htm.

### Which other childcare employees (beside nannies) do you need to pay tax and NI for?

If you are employing someone to look after your children in your home (e.g. a mother's help) and you are paying them more than £105/week (tax year 2008/2009) you will need to pay tax and NI.

### Tax credits system

If you are responsible for at least one child or young person that usually lives with you, you might be entitled to Child Tax Credit (CTC). If you work, but are on a low income, you may be eligible for Working Tax Credit (WTC). You don't need to have children to claim this but there is a childcare element. Neither CTC nor WTC affect Child Benefit payments.

### What is Child Tax Credit, and can I claim?

CTC helps low-income families with the cost of bringing up children. You don't have to be working to claim CTC. Whether you are eligible and how much you get depends on your family income. To check the current income thresholds visit www.hmrc.gov.uk or call the tax credits helpline on 0845 300 3900.

You don't have to be the child's parent to claim but you have to be the main person responsible for them. You can claim CTC if the child is:

- Aged 16 and under, up to 1 September after their 16th birthday.
- Aged 16 but under 20, if they are in full-time education or attending approved training.

If the young person is aged between 16 and 17 and they are not in full-time education, you can still claim CTC providing they don't have a job or training place and they have signed up with the careers service or Connexions Service (or Northern Ireland Training and Employment Agency).

## How much CTC will I get?

The amount you get depends on a number of things including your and your partner's income and the number of children in your family. The CTC payment is made up of two parts (for 2008/2009 tax year):

- Family element paid to any family with at least one child, worth up to £545/year.
- Child element paid for each child in the family, worth up to £2,085/year.

You may also get more if you care for a child under one or a disabled child.

## What is Working Tax Credit and the childcare element?

This supports people on a low income (employed or self-employed). Extra help for parents is available through the childcare element of the WTC. This element can help with 80% of your registered or approved childcare costs – up to a maximum amount of £175/week for one child and £300/week for two or more children for the 2008/2009 tax year. So if you have one child in childcare you could get up to £140/week, while if you had two or more children you could receive £240/week.

In order to qualify for the childcare element of WTC, a few conditions must be in place:

- Lone parents must work 16 hours/week or more
- Couples must both work at least 16 hours/week or one partner must work 16 hours or more if the other is incapacitated, in hospital or prison.

If you get childcare vouchers from your employer to cover some of your childcare costs then you cannot claim for the amount covered by the voucher. As a result childcare vouchers may affect your eligibility to both the childcare element of the WTC and CTC; see the section on childcare vouchers above for further details.

## Contracts and Letters of Employment

### Who should get one and why?

If you are employing someone to look after your child it is best to formalise the arrangement with a contract, or at least a letter of employment. Your nanny will appreciate the fact that you have gone to the trouble of giving her a contract as it shows that you recognise her as a skilled employee and it encourages a proper working relationship. A contract has to meet minimum standards of employment such as the number of days' holiday per year. It is also much better to know where you stand from the outset rather than finding out, at a later date, that you are liable for maternity pay. Having a contract will also help prevent any misunderstandings.

### What about a verbal agreement?

Verbal contracts are legally binding but they are much more difficult to enforce as it is one person's word against another's. Even though employment law applies without this piece of paper, having a contract that is personal to you is much better as it brings much more clarity to all situations.

### Where will I get a contract?

Many of the nanny tax payroll companies and some nanny agencies offer their customers sample contracts which you can adapt and use. There are a number of internet sites that sell legal documents including au pair invitation letters and nanny contracts for a fee on line. You can also buy templates from associations such as the Professional Association of Nursery Nurses (PANN) at www.pat.org.uk or the NCMA for childminders. Of course you can use a lawyer, although this may prove expensive.

### When should we sign a contract?

It is best to agree with what you will put in the contact before your nanny begins working for you. By law you should give her a 'statement of employment' within eight weeks of the start date. However, it is much better to do this before she starts work. You should both sign two copies and keep a copy each.

## Twelve key things to put in a contract

This list is by no means exhaustive. It covers the basic points that should be included in an employment contract. Employment law is constantly changing so make sure you are aware of the latest minimum standards of employment.
- Names and addresses – both yours and your nanny's.
- Date and start date – seems obvious but don't forget!
- Job description – who they are looking after and where, as well as what she is expected to do (e.g. caring for your children as well as doing their cooking and washing/ironing).
- Hours of work – include which days she will be working for you as well as the basic hours. Build in flexibility concerning overtime and babysitting.
- Salary – include details of when it will be paid and when there will be an annual review as well as details on expenses, use of a car or benefits including any accommodation or meals provided. Also reference overtime and babysitting rates.
- Holidays – by law she is entitled to 20 days paid holiday/year (amend if she is part-time). Put a note in about choosing holiday dates. Normally each party chooses 50% of the holidays. Nannies don't have to work bank holidays but you must pay her for four of them. All eight bank holidays must be paid from April 2009 if it is a normal working day.
- Sickness and sick pay – your nanny is entitled to statutory sick pay after the first three days of absence. You may want to add into the contract that you will pay the first three days.
- Maternity pay – explain that you will pay the government statutory maternity pay. Add in if you will pay over and above this.
- Pension arrangements – add this in just to be clear even if there aren't any.

- Confidentiality – even if you aren't a film star (yet) it is worth asking her not to disclose anything confidential about you or your family.
- Disciplinary and grievance procedures – state how you will take action, e.g. verbal, written then dismissal. Explain reasons for likely dismissal, e.g. unsatisfactory standards of work, loss of driving license. List reasons for instant dismissal, e.g. cruelty to children.
- Termination – state the probationary period and the notice period. You may want to give alonger notice period than legally required to give you time to find a replacement.
- Other points to consider – requirement for first aid training – specify at whose experse. CRB check or acknowledgement or requirement if able to apply.

## Au pairs

The au pair scheme is a cultural exchange programme, not a contract of work. When you invite an au pair to come and live in your home you should have already sent her an invitation letter or a written offer. This letter may be required by the British Consulate in the au pair's home country to obtain the visa. If your au pair has come from a non-EU country on the UK's au pair scheme the invitation letter must meet the conditions of the scheme including hours and pay. It is a good idea to give her some information outlining duties, hours of work and free time, babysitting requirements, pocket money, holiday pay and notice period. You should also draw up a daily timetable to show exactly when she will be helping you.

## Sample welcome letter for au pairs*

Your Name
Your Address
Your Email Address

Date

Au Pair's Name
Au Pair's Address

Dear

Further to our telephone conversation, I am writing to confirm our invitation to you to be our au pair from the date [estimated date] for a period of _____ months.

We live in [your area] which is a [village located on the outskirts of Woking with excellent road connections via the A3 and M25 Orbital Motorway to London]. We have a _____ bedroom [detached house] which is located in _____. You will have your own bedroom with [an ensuite shower room].

As mentioned, my [husband] works as _____ and I _____.

We have [two] children; _____ aged [10] and _____, aged [6]. They both attend school in our village, which is a 10-minute walk from our house. They both love [sport and are very into football, swimming etc]. We [are all animal lovers and have a lovely friendly dog].

As our Au Pair [Au Pair Plus] you will be expected to help out in the home for _____ hours a week and your pocket money will be _____ a week. Your duties will be light housework and looking after the children. As discussed, we will require you to babysit for [two] evenings a week.

You will have plenty of opportunity to study [and attend language school if required]. There is a [good sports centre nearby and also many shops, restaurants, cafés and cinemas]. There are [good public transport facilities] within walking distance from our home.

We enclose some photographs of our family, our home and your bedroom which I hope you will find comfortable.

We are looking forward to you joining us and we await confirmation for your date and time of arrival. [Naturally, we will be at the airport to collect you.]

Should you require any further assistance or you have any queries, please do not hesitate to contact us.

Kind Regards

_____

*Sample welcome letter for au pairs provided by BAPAA.

TECHNICAL QUESTIONS

## Sample au pair duties/house rules (to be sent or presented after receipt of the welcome letter)*

Here is a timetable of when we will need your help.

| Day | Morning | Afternoon |
| --- | --- | --- |
| Monday | 8.00 – 9.00 | 15.00 – 19.00 |
| Tuesday | 8.00 – 9.00 | 15.00 – 19.00 |
| Wednesday | 8.00 – 9.00 | 15.00 – 19.00 |
| Thursday | 8.00 – 9.00 | 15.00 – 19.00 |
| Friday | 8.00 – 9.00 | 15.00 – 19.00 |
| Saturday | Free | Free |
| Sunday | Free | Free |

*Sample au pair duties/house hold rules provided by BAPAA.

### Babysitting

We will need you to babysit up to two evenings a week and we will arrange this in advance with you. This might sometimes be at weekends but we will make sure that you get time to go out at the weekends too!

### Looking after the children

In the morning, we need you to help with breakfast and take our two children to school. Please be extremely careful crossing the roads and always hold their hands. In the afternoon you will need to collect the children from school, supervise them at home and cook their tea. The food will be something to heat up that we have prepared or something very simple for you to prepare. We are fairly organised and will make sure that you know what to cook each day. The children can only watch TV once they have done their homework and eaten tea. They both love to play in the garden, do arts and crafts or play board games so please try and encourage this type of activity rather than television. If the weather is nice you can always take them to the park straight after school.

### Household help

- We have a cleaner who comes in once a week but we will need your help too.
- The dishwasher – please help to load and unload as needed.

- Ironing – with two children we have lots! So please try to do about 30 minutes when you get back from school with the children while they are doing their homework.
- Kitchen floor – please vacuum the floor every evening after tea and mop it when you see it needs it (probably every other day).
- Change the children's bedding every Monday.
- Playroom – please help to keep it tidy and encourage the children to help you.
- Clothes washing – we will show you how to use the washing machine so that you can do your own laundry.
- Bathroom – make sure that you leave the bathroom clean after you have used it.

## House rules

- Security – Make sure that you lock the doors, windows and set the alarm every time you go out. Let us know when you are going out so that we know whether to set the alarm or not.
- Telephone/computer – please do not use our home telephone. It is very costly to phone abroad. We are happy for you to use the computer/internet; just make sure you ask us first and please don't download any programmes onto the computer without asking.
- Friends – please ask us first if you want your friends to come round and make sure that this is in your free time. If your friends are here in the evening please make sure they leave by 23.00.
- Pocket money – we will give you £65/week in cash each Friday.
- Smoking – we are non-smokers so we don't want any smoking in the house or in front of the children.

## Childminder contracts

Your childminder is self-employed and should give you a contract to sign. The National Childminding Association of England and Wales (NCMA; www.childminding.org) has a registered childminding contract, which you can buy on their website (www.ncma.org.uk). The Scottish Childminding Association (SCMA; www.childminding.org) and the Northern Ireland Childminding Association (NICMA; www.nicma.org) both supply contracts. The contract should set out the partnership between childminder and parent and covers hours, fees, holidays and retainers.

TECHNICAL QUESTIONS

## Nursery contracts

If you decide to send your child to a nursery you will be asked to sign a contract. Nurseries often call these their 'terms and conditions'. You might also have to pay a registration fee – usually non-refundable – to put your child on their waiting list.

Once you have been offered a place you will usually be asked to pay a deposit or to simply pay by direct debit one month in advance. Most nursery contracts should include:

- Details of the registration fee – usually paid when the registration form is returned.
- Details of what kind of deposit is required – normally paid once you have been offered a place for your child. It is usually only returnable if you give the correct notice period.
- Fees and payment information – including how/when to pay (usually by monthly direct debit in advance), late payment charges, fee increase notice period, and whether they accept childcare vouchers.
- Opening hours and holidays – i.e. information on when the nursery is open (normally 8am to 6pm Monday to Friday for 51 weeks/year) and when it is closed (usually at Christmas and on Bank Holidays). Most nurseries won't reduce your fees if your child is absent while the nursery is open.
- Cancellation/termination policy – one calendar month's written notice is usually required.
- Rules regarding employing nursery staff – many nurseries will ask you to agree not to employ members of staff while your child is at nursery and for a certain period after you have left. Some nurseries will make you pay a recruitment fee if you do poach their staff!
- What to do if your child is sick – this includes information on how long to keep your child off if they are ill and details of their refund policy (should they have one) for non-attendance. The nursery will also explain what they will do if your child becomes ill at nursery – e.g. you will be asked to collect your child, your GP may be called or, in an emergency, your child will be taken to hospital.
- Information regarding collecting children – details of who is authorised to collect your child as well as late collection fees.
- How to go about reducing/increasing the number of sessions – e.g. notice period required and the minimum number of sessions your

child can do. You aren't normally allowed to swap your booked sessions for other days.
- Information regarding siblings – some nurseries offer siblings priority on their waiting list while others may offer a discount if you have more than one child in attendance.
- Suspension – this is incredibly rare but it is often stated in the contract that if the nursery considers a child's behaviour unacceptable then they reserve the right to request that the child is removed from the nursery immediately.

# Legal obligations of employers and employees

## What are your obligations as an employer of a childcarer?

Besides the tax and NI responsibilities of employing a nanny you will also need to meet minimum standards of employment. Here are some of the key duties you will have to fulfil when employing a nanny; if you want to find out more contact Business Link on 0845 6009006 or visit www.businesslink.gov.uk.

- Written statement of employment – like a contract, which must be issued to your nanny within eight weeks of her start date.
- Payslips – you must give your nanny regular payslips showing her earnings and tax/NI deductions.
- National Minimum Wage – she is entitled to this unless she lives as part of your household.
- P45 – you are required by law to give your nanny a P45 (summarises pay and tax received) when she leaves.
- Holidays – you must give your nanny four weeks holiday. This should be pro-rated if she is part-time. You must also pay for four bank holidays – this rises to eight in April 2009.
- Hours – nannies are exempt from measures concerning working hours. You must however allow her rest breaks.
- Sick pay – if your nanny is unable to work due to sickness then she is entitled to Statutory Sick Pay after the first three days of absence. Whether you pay these first three days or not is entirely up to you.
- Maternity rights – your nanny is entitled to maternity leave and may be entitled to Statutory Maternity Pay if she becomes pregnant while

working for you. She is also entitled to return to work after her leave, under the same terms and conditions as previously.
- Redundancy pay – if your nanny has been employed by you for two years or more she is entitled to redundancy pay.
- Notice period – you must give your nanny one week's notice if she has been with you for more than one month. If she has been employed for two years she is entitled to two weeks. This increases by one week for each year worked until she has worked with you for 12 years.
- Liability insurance – as an employer you must make sure you have employer's liability insurance to cover you against any accidents in the home or during working hours. It is often included in household insurance but double-check. Don't forget to include your nanny on your insurance if you want her to drive your car. If you have a nanny share you may have shared liability but it depends how the share is set up so check with your payroll agency or take legal advice.

## Where do employers and employees turn in case of problems with employees/employers?

If you have both signed a contract then this might clear up the problem easily. Sometimes talking to someone independent about the problem can help. If you use a payroll agency try calling them as the chances are they might have come across the problem before. Many now have legal departments that will give you advice to both employers and nannies. If the situation turns nasty then you will have to seek legal advice either from the legal arm of your payroll agency or from a lawyer. You may also wish to consider contacting ACAS (Advisory, Conciliation and Arbitration Service) for advice on employment relations on 08457 474747. Alternatively, visit www.acas.org.uk.

## Professional negligence – what to do in law if things go wrong with a childminder, nursery or nanny.

If the person or place is Ofsted registered then Ofsted should be the first point of contact. Otherwise, contact the legal arm of your payroll agency or a lawyer for advice.

## Insurance

### What is liability insurance?

Liability insurance protects you against accusations of negligence made against you. So if your actions, or lack of action, result in an injury or damage to property then you could be held responsible and have to pay compensation. For instance, if a child falls off a climbing frame and the childcarer was not supervising the child properly, they could be liable and might have to pay compensation.

### Who should take out insurance?

#### Parents
As an employer of a nanny or mother's help you must make sure you have employer's liability insurance to cover you against any accidents in the home or during working hours. This type of insurance is often included in household insurance but check to make sure.

#### Nannies and Mother's Helps
There is no legal obligation for a nanny or mother's help to have public liability insurance unless she is on the Ofsted Register. A nanny or mother's help could potentially be sued either by the parents or by third parties if she is responsible for causing an accident, making it a good idea to for nannies to have their own public liability insurance. A public liability policy doesn't just protect the nanny if the children in her care have an accident due to her negligence; it also covers third party and third party property. For instance, if the children in a nanny's care caused a priceless vase in a museum to fall and break, the museum could then claim against her insurance if she was found to have been negligent in her care for the children. A number of companies specialise in this, such as Morton Michel and Nannyinsure.

#### Childminders, Nurseries and After-school clubs
All need to have public and employers liability insurance. Parents should ask tosee the schedule of insurance which would list everything the person/club is insured for.

## Health and Safety issues
### What are the government guidelines for day care and childminding?

Government guidelines for health and safety are included in the 'National Standards' for childcare providers and the childcare provider must meet these criteria. The national standards for health and safety are:

- **Safety** – the childcare provider must take positive steps to promote safety within the setting and on outings. They must ensure proper precautions are taken to prevent accidents. They are responsible for health and safety matters for the premises, staff and children as well as ensuring that staff have an understanding of health and safety requirements. The standards include guidelines on: gas/electricity; security; supervision; outside area; water; hazardous plants; fire safety; outings and transport and insurance.
- **Health** – the childcare provider must promote the good health of children and take positive steps to prevent the spread of infection and appropriate measures when they are ill. The standards include guidelines on: hygiene; animals; sandpits; food handling; medicine; first aid; sickness and smoking.

The childcare providers – full and sessional day care, crèches, out-of-school care and childminding – must also comply with other legislation including food hygiene, fire and planning requirements. These requirements are for England but are similar throughout the UK.

From September 2008, the Early Years Foundation Stage (EYFS) will replace the National Standards for Under 8s Daycare and Childminding in England. All early years providers in Ofsted-registered settings attended by young children – birth to five – must meet the EYFS's welfare requirements. The new requirements include: safeguarding and promoting children's welfare; ensuring that suitable people are looking after children; making sure the premises, environment and equipment are suitable; planning and organisation; and guidelines for documentation.

### What do providers need to display to show that all the criteria have been fulfilled?

The childcare provider will have an Ofsted Registration Certificate, which confirms that the person or organisation is registered with Ofsted to provide childcare. This certificate sets conditions or limitations on the registration and some of these may relate to health and safety issues.

Private nurseries are inspected by their local Environmental Health department either before or soon after they have opened. The inspectors will look at health and safety, food standards and the threat of infectious diseases. Each nursery is risk-rated and will be inspected somewhere between every six months and two years, depending on their rating. The nursery will have a copy of their inspection. Public nurseries are inspected by their local council. If you want to see the official local authority hygiene ratings for a nursery, visit www.scoresonthedoors.org.uk.

Childminders are not always checked by Environmental Health – whether there is a requirement to be checked will depend on their local authority.

## Ofsted

### What does Ofsted do?

Ofsted (Office for Standards in Education, Children's Services and Skills) inspects and regulates care for children and young people, and inspects education and training for learners of all ages.

Any person who looks after children for more than two hours a day must normally register with Ofsted if they provide care for children under eight. Some people are exempt from registration, such as nannies or those providing activity-based provision such as sports coaching. Childcarers working in their own homes must register as childminders, while those working on non-domestic premises must register as day-care providers. Inspection reports on childminders, nurseries, crèches, out-of-school clubs, holiday play schemes or playgroups are published on their website – www.ofsted.gov.uk. If you have a query or a complaint you can also call the Ofsted helpline on 0845 640 4040.

### What is the Ofsted Childcare Register?

The voluntary part of the Ofsted Childcare Register (OCR) was introduced in April 2007. It will replace a number of schemes, allowing eligible parents to claim the childcare element of working families' tax credits, including the Childcare Approval Scheme. The OCR covers two different types of carers:

- Compulsory OCR – for those who want to provide childcare for children for more than two hours in any one day who are not in the early years foundation stage (see EYR register below) but are aged

under eight **must** register with OCR before they can become childcare providers.
- Voluntary OCR – for those who care for children aged eight and over, home-based carers such as nannies and other providers such as those providing sports coaching who are exempt from compulsory registration can choose whether to join the **voluntary** part of the OCR.

For everyone who applies to register on the OCR, Ofsted will carry out a number of checks including checks with the Criminal Records Bureau. Nannies are not required to register on the OCR, but remember that if you want to claim the childcare element of WTCs or childcare vouchers, your nanny must be registered with Ofsted.

From September 2008 Ofsted will operate a new Early Years Register (EYR).

- EYR – registration will be compulsory for childcare providers (unless they are exempt) who care for children from birth to 31 August following their fifth birthday.

Childminders caring for children aged from birth to less than eight will have to join the EYR (for the 0–5s) and the compulsory OCR (for the 5–8s). Registration on the voluntary part of the OCR to look after children aged eight and over is entirely up to the childminder.

## Children's Information Service

The Children's Information Service (CIS) (branches of which are being renamed Family Information Services – FIS – going forward) is part of ChildcareLink, which is a national childcare information service. Each local CIS/FIS will help you with any childcare query either face to face or on the phone. You can call 0800 2346346 or, alternatively, visit www.childcarelink.gov.uk and put in your postcode or click on the map to find out about childcare options in your area. A comprehensive list of these services is available in Section 6.

## Visas and Work Permits

If you want to employ someone from abroad to look after your children in the UK you will need to know if it is legal for them to work and whether they will need a work permit or visa. Unless your childcarer is British, a citizen of one of the EEA countries (see appendix for EAA countries list) or a Swiss national, they may need a visa before they travel to the UK. To check if someone is from an EAA country you will need to see their passport, national identity card or Home Office Residence Permit. Watch out; it is your obligation to establish someone's right to work in the UK. If you employ someone illegally you can face stiff fines. To find out more call the employer's helpline on 0845 010 6677 or visit www.ukvisas.gov.uk.

If your childcarer is not from an EEA country or Switzerland they are likely to need a work permit to work in the UK. The person cannot apply for a work permit themselves; they will need you as the employer to do it for them. To find out more about applying for a work permit call 0114 207 4074 or visit www.bia.homeoffice.gov.uk/workingintheuk/workpermits. If you are planning to employ someone from abroad then you should:

- Try to use a nanny agency that specialises in recruiting from that particular country.
- Check references thoroughly and get someone who speaks the language to ask the questions!
- Remember that there is no point in doing a CRB check until they have been in the country at least six months. There is an overseas service that will provide information about overseas convictions; www.crb.gov.uk.

## Government Guidelines for Au Pairs

The goal of the UK's au pair scheme is to give young people from certain countries the chance to live with an English-speaking family for up to two years. The family must provide the au pair with her own room and weekly pocket money in exchange for some help in the home.

### What are the UK's au pair requirements?

To come to the UK under the official scheme au pairs must:

- Be single
- Have no dependants
- Be aged between 17 and 27
- Plan to stay in the UK as an au pair for no more than two years
- Not claim any state benefits
- Be a national of one of the following countries: Andorra; Bosnia-Herzegovina; Croatia; Faroe Islands; Greenland; Macedonia; Monaco; San Marino; Turkey

## TECHNICAL QUESTIONS

Nationals of European Economic Area countries and Swiss nationals are not included in the official au pair scheme but are free to come to the UK as au pairs.

The following countries are members of the EEA: Austria; Belgium; Bulgaria†; Cyprus; Czech Republic*; Denmark; Estonia*; Finland, France; Germany; Greece; Hungary*, Iceland, Ireland; Italy, Latvia*; Liechtenstein; Lithuania*; Luxembourg; Malta; Netherlands; Norway; Poland*; Portugal; Romania†; Slovakia*; Slovenia*; Spain; Sweden; UK.

Depending on which country they are from au pairs may need to apply for a visa before travelling to the UK and might also need to register with the police on arrival.

### How much can they work and what jobs they can do?

Au pairs are allowed to 'help in the home' for up to five hours a day, 25 hours a week, with two nights' additional babysitting. Government guidelines say that the work an au pair is expected to do will depend on the host family but suggests it is likely to include looking after the family's children; taking the children to and from school; light housework; cleaning; washing up and helping at meal times.

### Money and benefits

The au pair must be given her own bedroom as well as all meals in exchange for the 'help'. The family must also give the au pair pocket money of at least £60/week and at least two full days off per week. Two evenings babysitting per week are included. Au pairs are entitled to a minimum of two weeks paid holiday per year – one week for every six month stay. If the au pair is attending English lessons then the host family must make sure that the work is arranged to allow time to attend lessons.

### Moving on

Au pairs are allowed to move to another host family after arriving in the UK provided that the work, pay and conditions of the new placement meet the same

---

* Nationals of these countries who come to the UK to work need to register under the Worker Registration Scheme.

† Bulgarians and Romanians need to apply for an accession worker card before working.

requirements. Au pairs can only change host families if they have been in the country for less than two years. It is also possible for an au pair to extend her visa provided she still has a placement and it would not make the stay longer than two years.

## Au pair plus

An au pair plus can work up to 35 hours/week plus two night's babysitting. An au pair plus is not able to visit the UK under the official au pair scheme, but EEA citizens can be an au pair plus as there are no restrictions on working hours for them. Please note that if you pay your au pair over £105/week (for 2008/2009 tax year) then you will incur tax and NI.

# CRB Checks

## What is the CRB?

The Criminal Records Bureau, an executive agency of the Home Office, provides wider access to criminal record information through its Disclosure service. It checks police records and, in relevant cases, information held by the Department of Health and Department for Children, Schools and Families.

## What is a CRB check?

A CRB disclosure or check is a document containing information held on a person by police and government departments. It will show if someone has a criminal record. Many nanny agencies ask all their candidates to have a CRB check as a matter of course.

There are two types of CRB check:

- Standard Disclosure is mainly for anyone involved in working with children or vulnerable adults, as well as certain other jobs. It contains information on current and spent convictions, cautions, reprimands and warnings held on the Police National Computer. If the post involves working with children or vulnerable adults, the Protection of Children Act (POCA) List, the Protection of Vulnerable Adults (POVA) List and information held under Section 142 of the Education Act 2002 (formerly known as List 99) are checked.
- Enhanced Disclosure is the highest level of check available to anyone involved in regularly caring for, training, supervising or being

in sole charge of children or vulnerable adults. It contains the same information as the Standard Disclosure but with the addition of any relevant information held by the local police forces.

## How can I run a CRB check on someone?

Parents who employ a nanny, au pair or babysitter directly cannot apply for a CRB check under current legislation. If, however, a recruitment agency supplies the childcarer then the agency is permitted to carry out a CRB check. You can also, of course, ask your childcarer to provide her own CRB check.

To apply for a CRB disclosure, childcarers should visit www.crb.org.uk. General enquiries can be made on 0870 9090811. You could offer to pay for the disclosure – a standard disclosure costs approximately £31 in 2008/2009.

You can (with your nanny's permission) get a Basic Disclosure from Disclosure Scotland, which will show any unspent convictions. Call 0870 6096006 or visit www.disclosurescotland.co.uk. Alternatively, you can get a Subject Access Check from your local police force which will also show any unspent convictions.

If you are employing a foreign childcarer then a CRB check can only be done if she has been in the UK for at least six months. The check will not, however, show any overseas convictions, only those that have been recorded in the UK. There is however an overseas information service that shows you how to get this information; visit www.crb.gov.uk.

## How long is it valid for?

A CRB check is not valid for any specific timescale. The information on the disclosure is a 'snap shot' in time at the point the checks were done.

## Who needs a CRB check?

Everyone who works closely with children in a childcare setting needs a CRB check.

## What kind of document proves that one has been carried out?

A CRB Disclosure Certificate is the official document giving details of name, address, date of birth as well as details of who carried out the check.

## Au pairs

Au pair agencies who are members of the British Au Pair Agencies Association (BAPAA) insist on criminal records checks from the au pair's home country; see www.bapaa.org.uk.

## Qualifications

The sheer number of childcare qualifications available makes it extremely confusing for anyone employing a childcarer, so it is worth trying to keep up with the most up-to-date and recognised qualifications. The key thing to remember is that any person working 'unsupervised' with children (childminders, nursery nurses, nursery managers, playworkers) should have a level 3 qualification specific to the care and development of birth–8 years, in order to have a licence to practice. Childcarers working with children in a 'supervised' capacity must have a level 2 qualification, and should have completed some kind of practical training through a placement. Qualifications for nannies and mother's helps are not compulsory and many parents seek out experience before qualifications.

The Children's Workforce Development Council (CWDC) is currently revising its database of childcare qualifications in line with changes to the curriculum for learning, development and care for children from birth to five, due in September 2008. The Early Years Foundation Stage (EYFS) will replace the statutory Curriculum Guidance for the Foundation Stage and all early years' childcare providers of children up to 5 years (e.g. nurseries, pre-schools, childminders, etc.) will be required to use the EYFS. Early years qualifications are under review to comply with the EYFS and further information is due during 2008.

Here is a list of the most up-to-date qualifications for early years' childcare providers:

- **NVQ –** National Vocational Qualifications (NVQs) are nationally recognised competence-based qualifications. A number of awarding bodies such as CACHE and City and Guilds also offer NVQs or SVQs (Scottish Vocational Qualifications). The key childcare ones are:
  - Children's Care, Learning and Development – level 2–4
  - Playwork – level 2–4
  - Childcare and Education – level 2–3

Variations of these qualifications are available throughout the UK. The National Database of Accredited Qualifications (NDAQ) contains details of qualifications that are accredited by the government's regulatory organisations in England (QCA), Wales (DCELLS) and Northern Ireland (CCEA). Contact NDAQ on 020 7509 5556 or go to www.accreditedqualifications.org.uk. In Scotland, try the Scottish Qualifications Authority on 0845 279 1000, or go to www.sqa.org.uk.

Check the CWDC for childcare qualifications in England and Wales (www.cwdcouncil.org.uk). You can also contact the Care Council for Wales (www.ccwales.org.uk). For information on childcare qualifications in Scotland, contact the Scottish Social Services Council on 0845 6030891. Alternatively, visit www.sssc.uk.com.

- **CACHE** - (Council for Awards in Children's Care and Education)
  - Certificate in Early Years Foundation Stage Practice – level 3
  - Child Care and Education – level 2 or 3
  - Home-based Childcare – level 2 or 3
  - Early Years and Child Care for Playworkers – level 3
  - Playwork for Early Years and Childcare Workers – level 3
  - Playwork – level 2 or 3

- **City and Guilds**
  - Certificate in Early Years Foundation Stage Practice – level 3
  - Playwork – level 2–3
  - Safeguarding Children and Young People – level 3
  - Early Years and Child Care for Playworkers – level 3
  - Playwork for Early Years and Childcare Workers – level 3
  - Work with Children – level 3

- **Edexcel** – offer BTEC qualifications:
  - Children's Care Learning and Development level 2
  - Early Years level 3

- **Degree courses** – are run by a number of universities and are most likely to have been taken by someone in a managerial role within the childcare industry. The most popular course is the BA (Hons) in Early Childhood Studies.

- **Montessori** – training is principally for people wanting to work with nursery-aged children. Montessori runs a number of courses in the UK. The key course to look for is the 'International stage 3' qualification. Check www.cwdcouncil.org.uk for a list of recognised qualifications.

## What level of qualifications does each type of childcare need?

### After-school club staff

An after-school club (also before school and during the holidays) manager must have at least a level 3 qualification and a minimum of two years' experience of working in a day care setting. At least half of all staff must hold an appropriate level 2 qualification. Staff should be regularly trained in child protection, health and safety, behaviour management and food hygiene. The qualifications requirements are for England but are similar throughout the UK.

### Nannies

Nannies do not currently require any qualifications to practice and many parents find that experience is an important aspect when looking after very young children. The Association of Nanny Agencies encourages nannies to get qualifications and actively promotes further professional development and training. To be Ofsted-registered a nanny must confirm she is suitable to work with children, have an enhanced CRB check, have training in the common core and a current first aid certificate. For more information on the common core skills visit www.everychildmatters.gov.uk.

### Day nursery staff

Fifty percent of staff in a registered nursery must hold an official childcare qualification at level 2. Nursery managers must have at least a level 3 qualification appropriate to working in a nursery as well as two years' experience of working in a day care setting. Supervisors at nurseries must hold a level 3 qualification while nursery assistants who are supervised by someone else should have a level 2 childcare qualification. At least one member of staff on duty at all times should hold an up-to-date first-aid certificate.

The manager must ensure that all staff are trained on health and safety and child protection policies and procedures in their first week of employment. Once again, the qualifications requirements are for England but are similar throughout the UK.

### Childminders

As part of the national standards for childminding in England, all childminders must take two courses that are both recognised by Ofsted and their local authority:
- A pre-registration training course
- A paediatric first-aid training course

Ideally these should be done before the childminder's registration is completed, but they may be taken up to six months from the date on their registration certificate. From September 2008 all childminders registered in England who care for children under five must deliver the Early Years Foundation Stage and will be registered and inspected against it by Ofsted.

Prospective childminders living in Wales must complete the first unit of the Diploma in Home-based Childcare before registering. In Scotland, childminders do not need any formal qualification but must register with the Care Commission and show they have the necessary skills and knowledge. Likewise, in Northern Ireland childminders do not need any formal training but they must register with their local Health & Social Care Trust.

## First-aid training

Government guidelines for childcarers state that first-aid training must:

- Cater for practitioners caring for children in the absence of their parents
- Include a minimum of 12 hours training
- Cover what to keep in a first-aid kit for babies and children
- Demonstrate resuscitation techniques using models of babies and children, and give practitioners a chance to practise on models of each age group
- Include instruction on how to record accidents and incidents

Contact your local authority for information on first-aid courses. St John Ambulance (0870 010 4950) and British Red Cross (0870 170 9110) both run courses suitable for childminders and other home-based childcarers. Many qualifications are valid for three years but it is recommended that childcarers take them annually.

## How do you train for the qualifications?

Childcare qualifications are available in schools, colleges and local education authorities throughout the UK. Independent colleges such as Chiltern College and Norland also offer various CACHE and NVQ diplomas. Chiltern has its own certificate which requires extra practical training, course work and probationary six month periods in a child-related setting. Norland students get their diploma after completing a one-year probationary post.

For information on early years and playwork qualifications approved by Ofsted contact the CWDC (www.cwdcouncil.org.uk; tel. 0113 2446311).

## Professional development

Since late 2006, early years care and education professionals have been able to work towards Early Years Professional (EYP) Status. EYPs are seen as role models to other people working in the early years' workforce.

To become an EYP you need to gain EYP Status – which is at level 6 – by demonstrating you meet a series of national standards. Training and assessment is funded through the Transformation Fund. Visit www.everychildmatters.gov.uk/earlyyearsworkforce.

Further information on EYPs can be found on www.cwdcouncil.org.uk/projects/earlyyears.htm; individuals can also call 0845 0450048.

## Childcare hours

Domestic workers in private houses – nannies and mother's helps – are not covered by the Working Time Regulation, which states you should not have to work more than a 48-hour week.

Having said this, if you are employing a nanny it is important to clearly state in a contract what the hours are and how much you would pay for any extra hours for the sake of a happy working relationship.

Au pairs are treated differently and are restricted to 25 hours/week. An au pair plus can work 35 hours/week.

Day nurseries are not restricted to the number of hours they can operate for but they must have appropriate insurance to cover their opening hours.

## Childcare ratios

### What are the ratios for carers to children in nurseries?

The number of children that can be in a nursery is strictly controlled by government guidelines. There are ratios for adults to children of different ages:

1:3 for children under the age of two
1:4 for children of two years old
1:8 for children of three to five years*

The above ratios are for England but are similar throughout the rest of the UK.

---

*This can rise to 1:13 under new regulations being introduced in September 2008 if the individual is a qualified teacher, Early Years Professional or someone with a level 6 qualification who is working directly with children between 8am and 4pm.

TECHNICAL QUESTIONS

## What are the ratios for childminders?

Childminders are restricted by law to the number of children that they may look after at any one time. The maximum number of children who can be cared for may be less than shown here as numbers may be reduced on inspection due to the amount of space available. If a childminder either employs an assistant or works with another childminder then the following numbers apply to each of them.

- One childminder at home may look after six children under the age of eight.[†]
- Of these six, no more than three may be under five years of age. Where children aged four attend ten early education sessions a week they may be classed as age five for these ratios.[**]
- Of these three youngest children, normally no more than one child may be under the age of one unless the childminder can show she can meet the needs of all children she is caring for.[††]

These numbers must include the childminder's own children and any other children for whom she is responsible and who are in her home. Exceptions can be made, for example for multiple births, or for the younger siblings of children who are already being cared for provided that the total number of children under eight being cared for does not exceed six.

Children over the age of eight are treated separately – the childminder may care for over eights without them counting towards their ratio, provided it does not adversely affect the care provided for those children who are under eight.

These ratios are for England but are similar throughout the rest of the UK.

## What are the ratios for after-school clubs?

There must be one qualified staff member for every eight children under the age of eight. There must be enough other staff to ensure that the number of older children at the facility does not have a negative impact on the younger children.

These ratios are for England but are similar throughout the rest of the UK.

---

[†] In Scotland and Northern Ireland the ratio is six children under the age of twelve.

[**] When EYFS is introduced in England in September 2008 the rule changes slightly. Children aged four and five who only attend the childminder before and/or after a normal school day may be classed as age five for these ratios.

[††] In Wales, no more than two may be under 18 months of age.

# section SIX
# listings

- AGENCIES
- CHILDREN'S INFORMATION SERVICE
- USEFUL WEBSITES

# Agencies

## General Childcare Agencies: Regional Listings

Disclaimer: Although the following regional listings offer a guideline as to the areas in which a childcare agency operates, parents are strongly advised to check that the individual agencies are authorised to operate in their specific area. Please note that different registration laws may apply in Scotland and Northern Ireland.

The following list of agencies offer childcare services ranging from au pairs and nannies to mother's helps and babysitters. We have split this list according to the regions in which the agencies are based. Some agencies offer nationwide services. These are indicated with a * beside their names.

## London

### Abbeville Nannies
www.abbevillenannies.co.uk
**Tel:** 020 7627 3352
**Email:** info@abbevillenannies.co.uk
*Agency provides nannies, night nannies, nanny shares, maternity nurses, mother's helps and babysitters to families in London.*

### Absolute Childcare
www.absolutechildcare.co.uk
**Tel:** 020 8288 1807
**Email:** info@absolutechildcare.co.uk
*Places nannies, maternity nurses, night nannies, mother's helps and babysitters in London and Surrey.*

### * Absolutely Au Pairs
www.absolutelyaupairs.com
**Tel:** 020 8835 8594 (south), 0161 491 2758 (north)
**Email:** info@absolutelyaupairs.com
*With offices in London and the north of England, this agency places au pairs in homes across the UK.*

### Aegis Nannies
www.aegisnannies.co.uk
**Tel:** 020 8392 1658
**Email:** sarah@aegisnannies.co.uk
*This agency provides nannies, maternity nurses and mother's helps in London and across other parts of southern England.*

### * ABC Au Pairs
www.abc-aupairs.co.uk/
**Tel:** 020 8299 3052
**Email:** enquiries@abc-aupairs.co.uk
*BAPAA-member agency that provides au pairs and mother's helps all over UK.*

### * A-One Au Pairs & Nannies
www.aupairsetc.co.uk
**Tel:** 020 8905 3355/4400
**Email:** info@aupairsetc.co.uk
*Founder member of BAPAA, places au pairs, nannies and mother's helps all over the UK.*

### Applejack Nannies Ltd
www.applejacknanniesltd.co.uk
**Tel:** 020 8878 5778
**Email:** info@applejacksltd.co.uk
*Agency places nannies and mother's helps in London and the surrounding areas.*

### * The Au Pair Agency
www.aupairagency.com
**Tel:** 020 8958 1750
**Email:** elaine@aupairagency.com
*Places au pairs and mother's helps across the UK.*

## AGENCIES

**Agency Au Pairs**
www.agencyaupairs.co.uk
Tel: 020 8847 2910
Email: info@agencyaupairs.co.uk
*Places au pairs across London and other areas in the south of England.*

**\* Au Pair Professional**
www.aupairprofessional.com
Tel: 07723 378970
Email: info@aupairprofessional.com
*With its head office in London, this agency places au pairs, mother's helps and nannies in the UK.*

**Au Pairs 4 London**
www.aupairs4london.co.uk
Tel: 0845 430 94 83
Email: enquiries@aupair4london.co.uk
*Agency places au pairs across London.*

**\* Bellamy of Mayfair Recruitment**
www.bellamyofmayfair.com
Tel: 020 7569 6734
Email: kathy@bellamyofmayfair.com
(for general)
*Agency that provides nannies, maternity nurses and au pairs.*

**\* Au Pair Network International**
www.apni.co.uk
Tel: 020 7871 9533
Email: admin@apni.co.uk
*BAPAA-member agency that provides au pairs, nannies and mother's helps to families across the UK.*

**Bloomsbury Au Pairs**
www.bloomsburyaupairs.co.uk
Tel: 020 3122 0025
Email: bloomsbury@aol.com
*London-based agency that was established in the 1970s places au pairs in and around London and the Home Counties.*

**\* Burlington Nannies**
www.burlingtonnannies.com
Tel: 020 7821 9911
Email: enquiries@burlingtonnannies.com
*With an office in Kent and another in London, this agency places nannies in London and overseas*

**\* Busy Bee Nannies**
www.busybeenannies.co.uk
Tel: 020 7096 1059
Email: info@busybeenannies.co.uk
*Agency places nannies, mother's helps and maternity nurses across the UK.*

## LISTINGS

**Bibi & Becks**
www.bbchildcare.co.uk
Tel: 0870 236 80 66
Email: info@bbchildcare.co.uk
*Provides nannies, maternity nurses and babysitters to families in London.*

**Buttons Nanny Agency**
www.buttonsnannyagency.com
Tel: (Surrey) 020 8644 7001
Email: recruit@buttonsnannyagency.co.uk, 020 8998 6660 (London)
Email: patricia@buttonsnannyagency.co.uk
*Temporary and permanent nannies.*

**\* Childcare International**
www.childint.co.uk/
Tel: 020 8906 3116
Email: office@childint.co.uk
*BAPAA-member agency places au pairs, nannies and mother's helps throughout the UK.*

**Colourful Care Nannies**
www.colourfulcarenannies.com
Tel: 07877 894 241
Email: enquiries@colourfulcarenannies.com
*Agency provides nannies, mother's helps and maternity nurses throughout London and the surrounding areas.*

**Childhood Nannies**
www.childhoodnannies.com
Tel: 020 8874 3554
Email: nannies@childhoodnannies.com
*Agency provides nannies, night nannies, mother's helps and maternity nurses across London.*

**Czech It Out**
www.czechitout.co.uk
Tel: 020 8332 6745
Email: jara@czechitout.co.uk
*Agency places au pairs from the Czech and Slovak Republics across England.*

**The Childcare Recruitment Company**
www.childcarerecruitment.co.uk
Tel: 0845 450 25 50
Email: enquiries@childcarerecruitment.co.uk
*Nannies, mother's helps, maternity nurses and after-school care.*

**Eden Childcare**
www.eden-nannies.co.uk
Tel: 0845 128 42 79
Email: info@eden-nannies.co.uk
*Agency provides nannies, mother's helps and maternity nurses to families in England.*

## AGENCIES

**\* Cinderella Au Pairs**
www.cinderellaaupairs.co.uk
Tel: 020 8659 1689
Email: aupairs@cinderella.co.uk
*Agency places au pairs throughout UK.*

**\* Elite Nannies**
www.elitenannies.co.uk
Tel: 020 7723 6531
Email: info@elitenannies.co.uk
*Agency provides nannies, mother's helps and maternity nurses across the UK.*

**\* Euro Pair Agency**
www.euro-pair.co.uk
Tel: 020 8421 2100
Email: info@europair.net
*Agency places mainly French au pairs across the UK.*

**\* Gwendolen House Nannies**
www.gwendolennannies.com
Tel: 020 8785 2147
Email: enquiries@gwendolennannies.com
*Agency place nannies, maternity nurses and mother's helps all over the UK and worldwide.*

**\* Exclusively Nannies**
www.exclusivelynannies.com
Tel: 020 7938 2222
Email: info@exclusivelynannies.com
*Agency provides nannies and mother's helps (as well as governesses) to families across the UK.*

**Hampstead Au Pair Agency**
www.hampsteadaupairs.com
Tel: 020 7435 0200
Email: info@hampsteadaupairs.com
*Agency place au pairs mainly in London and the surrounding areas.*

**Gina's Nannies**
www.ginasnannies.com
Tel: 020 8542 7503
Email: info@ginasnannies.com
*Provides nannies and mother's helps to families in Wimbledon and Chelsea.*

**Happy Home Childcare**
www.happyhomechildcare.com
Tel: 07811 196864
Email: info@happyhomechildcare.co.uk
*Agency place nannies and mother's helps in central London.*

## LISTINGS

### * Grey Coat Nannies
www.greycoatplacements.co.uk
**Tel:** 020 7233 9950
**Email:** info@greycoatplacements.co.uk
*Specialist provider of nannies, maternity nurses and other household staff in London and most other parts of the UK.*

### * Hungarian Au Pair Agency
www.hungarianaupairagency.com
**Tel:** 020 8399 8663
**Email:** agnes@hungarianaupair agency.com
*Place mainly Hungarian au pairs (though not exclusively) in homes throughout the UK.*

### * Ideal Nannies
www.idealnannies.com
**Tel:** (Chiswick) 020 899 45888/ (Leeds) 0113 3466099
**Email:** contact through website
*This agency offers nannies, mother's helps and maternity nurses across most parts of the UK.*

### * Imperial Nannies
www.imperialstaff.com
**Tel:** 020 7795 6220
**Email for nannies:** nannies@imperialstaff.com
**Email for maternity nurses:** maternally@imperialstaff.com
*Agency provides nannies, mother's helps, au pairs and maternity nurses.*

### Hullabaloo
www.hullabaloo-kids.co.uk
**Tel:** 020 8785 0415
**Email:** info@hullabaloo-kids.co.uk
*Place nannies in central and southwest London.*

### * Kensington Nannies
www.kensington-nannies.com
**Tel:** 020 7937 2333 or 020 7937 3299
**Email:** nannies@easynet.co.uk
*BAPAA-member places nannies across most parts of the UK.*

### Kiwioz Nannies
www.kiwioznannies.co.uk
**Tel:** 020 7602 5070
**Email:** contact@kiwioznannies.co.uk
*Agency specialises in placing Australasian nannies, mother's helps and babysitters in London.*

### * Les Papillotes
www.lespapillotes.com
**Tel:** 020 7589 8755
**Email:** parents@lespapillotes.com
*Specialises in the recruitment of French nannies, maternity nurses, mother's helps and au pairs.*

## AGENCIES

**\* Just Au Pair's**
www.justaupairs.co.uk
**Tel:** 020 8905 3355/4400
**Email:** info@justaupairs.co.uk
*BAPAA-member agency provides families with au pairs, mother's helps and nannies throughout the UK.*

**\* Little Ones**
www.littleoneslondon.co.uk
**Tel:** 020 7323 9364
**Email:** nannies@littleoneslondon.co.uk
*Specialises in bilingual nannies. Makes placements across most parts of the UK.*

**The London Au Pair and Nanny Agency**
www.londonaupair.co.uk/
**Tel:** 020 7435 3891
**Email:** londonaupair.nannyagency@virgin.net
*BAPAA-member agency that places au pairs and nannies in London.*

**\* M Kelly Au Pair Agency**
www.mkellyaupair.co.uk
**Tel:** 020 8575 3336
**Email:** info@mkellyaupair.co.uk
*Agency places au pairs and mother's helps across the UK.*

**The London Nanny Company**
www.londonnannycompany.co.uk
**Tel:** 020 7361 0011
**Email:** info@londonnannycompany.co.uk
*Acquired by its sister company Family Match in 2006, agency provides nannies, mother's helps and maternity nurses across London.*

**Montrose Agency International**
www.montroseagency.co.uk
**Tel:** 020 8958 9209
**Email:** montroseagency@montroseagency.co.uk
*Agency places au pairs, nannies and mother's helps with families in south-east England.*

**The Manny Service**
www.mannyservice.co.uk
**Tel:** 020 8141 5224
**Email:** info@mannyservice.co.uk
*Founded by a former male nanny, this agency provides 'mannies' and male au pairs to families in London and south-east England.*

**My Big Buddy**
www.mybigbuddy.com
**Tel:** 07912 885766/ 07809 777884
**Email:** mybigbuddyinfo@yahoo.com
*This male nanny agency provides full and part-time 'mannies' on a permanent or casual basis across London.*

## LISTINGS

### * Massey's Agency
www.masseysagency.co.uk
**Tel:** 020 3033 0000
**Email:** mail@masseysagency.co.uk
*Live-in services are available throughout the UK and live-out are only available in London.*

### Nannies in London
www.nanniesinlondon.com
**Tel:** 020 8785 5755
**Email:** through site
*Provides nannies, mother's helps and maternity nurses to families living in London.*

### Nannies Incorporated
www.nanniesinc.com
**Tel:** 020 7038 3757
**Email:** nanniesinc@aol.com
*Based in London with an office in Paris, this agency places live-in/daily nannies and maternity nurses in London and overseas.*

### The Nanny Service
www.nannyservice.co.uk
**Tel:** 020 7935 3515
**Email:** through webpage
*Agency that provides live-in and live-out nannies, maternity nurses and mother's helps in London and the Home Counties.*

### Nannies Unlimited
www.nanniesunlimited.co.uk
**Tel:** 020 8788 9640
**Email:** enquiries@nanniesunlimited.co.uk
*Places nannies, mother's helps and maternity nurses in London and the Home Counties.*

### * Nannyworld Ltd
www.nannyworld.co.uk
**Tel:** 020 7225 1555
*Agency has three distinct parts – Occassional & Permanent Nannies, Domestic Solutions and Maternity Solutions) that have grown from Occassional and Permanent Nannies. Agency places nannies and mother's helps across most parts of the UK.*

### Nanny Avenue
www.nannyavenue.co.uk
**Tel:** 020 8704 4894
**Email:** admin@nannyavenue.co.uk
*Provides nannies in and around London.*

### North London Nannies
www.northlondonnannies.co.uk
**Tel:** 020 8444 4911
**Email:** enquiries@northlondonnannies.co.uk
*Agency places nannies, au pairs, mother's helps, babysitters and maternity nurses in London.*

## AGENCIES

**Nanny Search**
www.nanny-search.co.uk
Tel: 020 8348 4111
Email: info@nanny-search.co.uk
*Places nannies, maternity nurses and babysitters in London.*

**The Park Nanny Agency**
www.parknannies.co.uk
Tel: 020 7604 4000
Email: info@parknannies.co.uk
*Company providing nannies and mother's helps in London.*

**\* Peek a Boo Childcare**
www.peekaboochildcare.com
Tel: 020 7600 9880
Email: info@peekaboochildcare.com
*BAPAA-member agency that places au pairs, nannies, mother's helps, maternity nurses and babysitters in the UK.*

**Simply Angelic**
www.simplyangelic.co.uk
Tel: 020 7681 6490
Email: aupairs@simplyangelic.uk
nannies@simplyangelic.co.uk
*With offices in London and Cambridge, this agency places au pairs and mother's helps with families across the UK, and nannies predominantly in London and the surrounding areas.*

**\* Quickhelp Agency Ltd**
www.quickhelp.co.uk
Tel: 020 7794 8666
Email: mailbox@quickhelp.freeserve.co.uk
*BAPAA-member agency that places au pairs, nannies and mother's helps across the UK.*

**St James and Temporary Nannies**
www.stjamesandtempnannies.com
Tel: 020 7348 6100
Email: nanniesstjames@aol.com/
temporarynannies@aol.com
*Provides nannies, mother's helps and maternity nurses in England and Wales.*

**\* Regency Nannies**
www.regencynannies.com
Tel: 0207 225 1055 or
020 8420 4401
Email: regencynannies@aol.com
*The agency provides nannies and maternity nurses across the UK and overseas.*

**\* Sunflower Au Pair Agency**
www.sunfloweragency.co.uk
Tel: 020 8245 4789
Email: info@sunfloweragency.co.uk
*Places au pairs and mother's helps across the UK.*

## LISTINGS

### Riverside Nannies
www.riversidechildcare.net
Tel: 020 7374 6364
Email: info@riversidechildcare.net
Agency supplies nannies, mother's helps, maternity nurses and babysitters across London.

### Swansons Nanny Agency
www.swansonnannies.co.uk
Tel: 020 8994 5275
Email: anne@swansonsnannies.co.uk
With two London offices, agency places nannies and mother's helps across London.

### *Tinies
www.tinies.co.uk
Tel: 020 7384 0322
Email: info@tinies.com
Provides maternity nurses, mother's helps and nannies to families across the UK.

### *Top Notch Nannies
www.topnotchnannies.com/
Tel: 020 7259 2626
Email: theteam@topnotchnannies.com
Offers services including maternity nurses, babysitters and nannies to families in most parts of the UK.

### * Sunshine Au Pair Agency
www.sunshineaupairs.co.uk
Tel: 0845 006 62 45
Email: info@sunshineaupairs.co.uk
With offices in Derby and London, agency places au pairs all over the UK.

### * UK & Overseas Domestic Agency
www.nannys.co.uk
Tel: 020 7993 2937
Email: through webpage
Agency places nannies, maternity nurses and mother's helps (as well as other domestic staff) in the UK and overseas.

### Wimbledon Nannies
www.wimbledonnannies.co.uk
Tel: 020 8947 4666
Email: info@wimbledonnannies.co.uk
Nanny and maternity nurse agency that offers services in London, Kent and Dorset as well as Manchester and the north-west.

## South-East England

### * A1 Kidscare UK
www.a1kidscare.com
**Tel:** 01843 220992/01843 571716
**Email:** info@a1kidscare.co.uk
*Kent-based agency that places au pairs across the UK.*

### * Abacus Au Pairs
www.abacusaupairagency.co.uk
**Tel:** 01273 203803
**Email:** info@abacusaupairagency.co.uk
*Based in Hove, agency places au pairs and mother's helps throughout the UK.*

### * Adria Recruitment
www.adriarecruitment.com
**Tel:** 023 80 254 287
**Email:** info@adriatrecruitment.com
*Southampton-based recruitment agency that specialises in childcare; placing au pairs, mother's helps and nannies across the UK.*

### * The Au Pair Company
www.theaupaircompany.com
**Email:** felix@theaupaircompany.com
*Kent-based agency that places au pairs across the UK.*

### * All Counties Nannies
www.allcountiesnannies.co.uk
**Tel:** 01235 524462
**Email:** lynda@allcountiesnannies.co.uk
*Based in Oxfordshire, agency provides nannies and mother's helps to families in the UK.*

### Baby Rock Childcare Agency
www.babyrockchildcare.co.uk
**Tel:** 01273 729297
**Email:** babyrockchildcare@yahoo.co.uk
*Brighton-based agency that provides nannies, mother's helps and babysitters in south-east England.*

### * Angel Au Pairs
www.angelaupairs.com
**Tel:** 01252 321802/321812
**Email:** mail@angelaupairs.com
*BAPAA-member agency based in Surrey which places au pairs throughout the UK.*

### Bright Eyes Nanny Agency
www.brighteyesnannyagency.co.uk
**Tel:** 01483 506150
**Email:** brighteyesnannys@aol.com
*The agency covers Surrey and the surrounding areas, providing nannies and mother's helps as well as childcare for those with special needs.*

## LISTINGS

**\* Au Pairs 4 U Agency**
www.aupairs4uagency.co.uk
Tel: 01753 537437
Email: aupairs4uagency@aol.com
*Based in Berkshire, agency places au pairs all over UK.*

**\* Burlington Nannies**
www.burlingtonnannies.com
Tel: 020 7821 9911
Email: enquiries@burlingtonnannies.com
*Agency places nannies in London and overseas, and maternity nurses across the UK.*

**Buttons Nanny Agency**
www.buttonsnannyagency.com
Tel: (surrey) 020 8644 7001
Email: recruit@buttonsnannyagency.co.uk, (west london) 020 8998 6660,
Email: patricia@buttonsnannyagency.co.uk
*With offices in Surrey and west London, agency specialises in the placement of temporary and permenant nannies throughout Surrey and west London.*

**Chalfont Nannies**
www.chalfontnannies.co.uk
Tel: 01494 816660
Email: mail@chalfontnannies.co.uk
*Agency provides nannies, nanny/housekeepers, mother's helps, maternity nurses and babysitters to families in Buckinghamshire, Berkshire, Hertfordshire, Middlesex and north-west London.*

**Bunnies of Brighton**
www.bunniesofbrightonnannyagency.co.uk
Tel: 01273 505001
*Brighton-based agency that provides nannies, maternity nurses and au pairs to families in Brighton and surrounding areas of Sussex.*

**\* Childcare Unlimited**
www.childcareunlimited.uk.com
Tel: 020 8466 7658
Email: adele@childcareunlimited.uk.com
*Based in Kent, provides nannies, au pairs and maternity nurses to families in most parts of the UK.*

**Choices in Childcare**
www.choiceschildcare.co.uk
Tel: 01737 850 212
Email: choiceschildcare@btinternet.com
*Surrey-based agency that was a founder member of the ANA. Provides nannies, maternity nurses, night nannies, mother's helps and babysitters in south London and Surrey.*

**\* County Nannies**
www.countynannies.co.uk
Tel: 01795 520 060 (maternity nurses and nannies) 01795 522 544 (au pairs)
Email: info@countynannies.co.uk
*Offers nannies, maternity nurses and au pairs across the UK, focusing on London and the Home Counties.*

AGENCIES

**\*The Childcare Company**
www.thechildcarecompany.co.uk
**Tel:** 01732 451997 (Kent and Surrey office) 01234 352688 (East & West Midlands office),
**Email:** mary_elder@thechildcare company.co.uk/
hannahsurridge@thechildcarecompany.co.uk/
BAPAA-member agency with offices in Kent and the East Midlands. Provides au pairs, nannies, mother's helps, babysitters and maternity nurses to families in areas across the UK.

**Delaney International**
www.delaney-nannies.com
**Tel:** 01483 894300
**Email:** info@delaney-nannies.com
Surrey-based employment agency that places nannies, mother's helps and au pairs across the UK.

**Dreamcatcher Agency Ltd**
www.dreamcatcheragency.co.uk
**Tel:** 01344 621116
**Email:** dreamcatcheragency@yahoo.co.uk
Based in Berkshire, agency places nannies with families in Berskshire, Surrey and Hampshire.

**Family Match**
www.familymatch.com
**Tel:** 01962 855799
**Email:** info@familymatch.com
Agency covers Hampshire, Berkshire, Wiltshire, Dorset, Surrey and West Sussex areas and provides nannies, mother's helps and maternity nurses.

**The Countrywide Au Pair Agency**
www.countrywideaupairs.co.uk
**Tel:** 01869 369722
**Email:** enquiries@countrywideaupairs.com
Specialises in au pairs from the Czech Republic. Places au pairs with families in south-east England.

**\*The Good Nanny Company**
www.goodnannycompany.co.uk
**Tel:** 01730 829179
**Email:** info@goodnannycompany.co.uk
Agency places nannies, including school holiday nannies, mother's helps and maternity nurses across most parts of the UK.

**Happy Kids Au Pair Agency**
www.happykidsaupairs.co.uk
**Tel:** 01273 494773
**Email:** info@happykidsaupairagency.co.uk
Based in Brighton, agency provides au pairs to families in the local area.

**Harmony at Home**
www.harmonyathome.co.uk
**Tel:** 0870 442 32 37
**Email:** info@harmonyathome.co.uk
Provides nannies, maternity nurses, mother's helps and babysitters with families in south-east England.

## LISTINGS

### Freedom Childcare
www.freedomchildcare.com
**Tel:** 0845 330 04 03
**Email:** info@freedomchildcare.com
*Based in Hampshire, agency places au pairs, nannies and babysitters in Hampshire, West Sussex and the Isle of Wight.*

### * Holliday Au Pairs
www.holliday-aupairs.com
**Tel:** 01483 563447
**Email:** jill@holliday-aupairs.com
*Based in Surrey, agency provides au pairs across the UK.*

### * Hyde Park International Ltd
www.hydeparkint.co.uk
**Tel:** 01962 733 466
**Email:** enquiries@hyde-park-int.co.uk
*Based in Hampshire, agency provides nannies and maternity nurses (as well as other forms of domestic staff) throughout the UK.*

### Ideal Au Pairs
www.idealaupairs.com
**Tel:** 01372 374176
**Email:** info@idealaupairs.com
*Surrey-based agency that places au pairs and mother's helps in London and the south-east.*

### Hattie's Nannies
www.hattiesnannies.co.uk
**Tel:** 01483 415 406
**Email:** info@hattiesnannies.co.uk
*Provides families with nannies, maternity nurses and mother's helps in Surrey, Hampshire, West Sussex and Berkshire.*

### Lemonjelly Nanny Solutions
www.lemonjellynannysolutions.com
**Tel:** 07847 922483
**Email:** enquiries@lemonjellynannysolutions.com
*Agency places nannies, mother's helps and babysitters in Oxfordshire and Buckinghamshire.*

### * Lienka Au Pair Agency
www.lienkaaupair.com
**Tel:** 07766 822299
**Email:** lienka_aupair@hotmail.com
*Surrey-based agency that places au pairs across UK.*

### Little Laura's Nanny Agency
www.littlelauras.co.uk
**Tel:** 01730 814757
**Email:** laura.keates@littlelauras.co.uk
*West Sussex agency providing local nannies and babysitters to families in the West Sussex area.*

## AGENCIES

### Larah Au Pairs
www.larahaupairs.freewebspace.com
**Tel:** 01932 341704
**Email:** larahaupairs@ntlworld.com
*Based in Surrey, this agency places au pairs in Surrey and south London.*

### Little Masters and Misses
www.littlemastersandmisses.com
**Tel:** 020 8650 3232
**Email:** through website
*Based in Kent, agency places nannies and babysitters in Kent and Surrey.*

### Lollipop Childcare
www.lollipopchildcare.co.uk
**Tel:** 01753 832124
**Email:** through website
*Based in Berkshire, agency provides nannies, night nannies, maternity nurses and mother's helps in the area.*

### * Nanny Select
www.nannyselect.co.uk
**Email:** webmaster@nannyselect.co.uk
*Kent-based agency that provides families across the UK with nannies and mother's helps.*

### * Millennium Au Pairs
www.millenniumaupairs.co.uk
**Tel:** 020 8241 9752
**Email:** info@millenniumaupairs.co.uk
*BAPAA-member agency places au pairs, mother's helps and nannies across the UK but especially in London, the south-east and the Home Counties.*

### Nannykins
www.nannykins.net
**Tel:** 020 8641 1811
**Email:** mail@nannykins.net
*Surrey-based agency which places nannies in Surrey and the surrounding areas.*

### Minitots Nanny Agency
www.mini-tots.co.uk
**Tel:** 07810 771940
**Email:** info@mini-tots.co.uk
*Surrey-based agency that provides nannies, mother's helps and babysitters to families in Middlesex and Surrey.*

### Newbury Nannies
www.newburynannies.co.uk
**Tel:** 01635 203399
**Email:** info@newburynannies.co.uk
*Placing nannies, mother's helps, maternity nurses, nannies/housekeepers and babysitters in Berkshire and the surrounding area.*

## LISTINGS

### The Nanny Agency
www.the-nannyagency.co.uk
Tel: 01428 714410
Email: info@the-nannyagency.co.uk
Surrey-based agency placing nannies in south-west Surrey and north Hampshire.

### Paramount Nanny Agency
www.paramountnannyagency.co.uk
Tel: 01293 400491
Email: info@paramountnannyagency.co.uk
Places nannies, maternity nurses, mother's helps and babysitters.

### * Peter Pan Au Pairs
www.peterpanaupairs.co.uk
Tel: 0800 980 9696/ 01795 886475
Email: nicky@peterpan-aupairs.com
BAPAA-member agency based in Kent agency that places au pairs throughout the UK.

### * Smart Au Pairs
www.smartaupairs.com
Tel: 01233 712500
Email: info@smartaupairs.com
BAPAA-member agency based in Kent that places au pairs and mother's helps across the UK.

### Playtime Nanny Agency
www.playtimenannies.co.uk
Tel: 01483 488511
Email: info@playtimenannies.co.uk
Surrey-based agency that places nannies and mother's helps in homes in Surrey and the surrounding areas.

### Smileys Childcare Agency
www.smileys-childcare.co.uk
Tel: 0845 201 16 30
Email: enquiries@smileys-childcare.co.uk
Agency places nannies, mother's helps, maternity nurses and babysitters throughout Berkshire, Buckinghamshire, Surrey and Oxfordshire.

### Rockinghorse Nannies
www.rockinghorsenannies.com
Tel: 01993 810 126
Email: parentinfo@rockinghorsenannies.com
Based in Oxford, agency provides nannies, maternity help and babysitters to families in Oxfordshire and the Home Counties. Also offers event childcare cover.

### Sunny Smiles Au Pair Agency
www.sunnysmiles.co.uk
Tel: 01732 452282
Email: info@sunnysmiles.co.uk
Based in Kent, agency places au pairs across England.

## AGENCIES

### Select Nannies
www.select-nannies.co.uk
Tel: 01932 402146
Email: selectnannies@hotmail.com
*Based in Surrey, agency offers nannies in the local area.*

### Sussex Nanny Register
www.sussexnannyregister.com
Tel: 01273 585811
Email: info@sussexnannyregister.com
*Based in Brighton, agency covers East and West Sussex and places nannies, mother's helps, maternity nurses and night nannies.*

### Tigerlily Childcare
www.tigerlilychildcare.co.uk
contact through website
Email: london@tigerlilychildcare.co.uk
*With its head office in Brighton, agency has other offices across south-east England and offers families in those areas nannies, mother's helps and maternity nurses.*

### Toybox Agency
www.toyboxagency.co.uk
Tel: 0845 230 01 91
Email: headoffice@toyboxagency.co.uk
*Supplies nannies, babysitters and a small number of special needs carers.*

### TLC Nannies
www.tlcnannies.co.uk
Tel: 020 8763 6848/ 01737 850 212
Email: admin@tlcnannies.co.uk
*Surrey-based agency that places nannies, maternity nurses and mother's helps in London and Surrey.*

## South-West England

### 1st Choice Childcare
www.1stchoicechildcare.com
Tel: 01202 434394
Email: admin@1stchoicechildcare.com
*Dorset-based agency that provides nannies, maternity nurses, mother's helps and babysitters to families in the south of England, particularly around Dorset.*

### Ace Au Pairs
www.aceaupairs.co.uk
Tel: 01793 430091
Email: info@aceaupairs.co.uk
*Wiltshire-based agency that places au pairs across England.*

## LISTINGS

**\* A2Z Au Pairs**
www.a2zaupairs.com
**Tel:** 01984 632422
**Email:** through website
*Somerset-based BAPAA-member agency that places au pairs throughout the UK.*

**Alphabet Childcare**
www.alphabet-childcare.co.uk
**Tel:** 0117 959 1161
**Email:** enquiries@alphabet-childcare.co.uk
*Agency provides nannies, mother's helps, maternity nurses and babysitters in the south-west.*

**\* Antoinette's Nanny & Au Pair Agency**
www.childcare-agency.co.uk
**Tel:** 01326 572660
**Email:** antoinettes_mgr@btinternet.com
*Agency places au pairs, nannies, babysitters, maternity nurses, and nursery nurses in homes across UK.*

**\* Bohemia King**
www.bohemiaking.co.uk
**Tel:** 01202 828886
**Email:** info@bohemiaking.co.uk
*Based in Dorset, the agency places mostly Eastern European au pairs, nannies and mother's helps (as well as domestic staff) across the UK.*

**Aegis Nannies**
www.aegisnannies.co.uk
**Tel:** 020 8392 1658
**Email:** sarah@aegisnannies.co.uk
*Agency provides nannies, maternity nurses and mother's helps primarily in London and other parts of southern England.*

**\* Genevieve Brown Ltd (Au Pairs)**
www.genevievebrown.co.uk
**Tel:** 01249 812551
**Email:** ask@genevievebrowne.co.uk
*Agency places au pairs with families mainly in the south of England although also in other areas across the UK.*

**The Parent & Child Nanny Agency**
www.parentandchildnannies.co.uk
**Tel:** 01392 428035
**Email:** info@parentandchildnannies.co.uk
*Nannies and nanny shares, mother's helps, babysitters and maternity nurses throughout Devon and the south-west of England.*

**\* Poppins Nannies and Domestic Staff**
www.abcpoppins.com
**Tel:** 01793 815313
**Email:** poppins@mac.com
*Agency places nannies, mother's helps and maternity nurses.*

## AGENCIES

**First Steps Childcare Agency**
www.myearlyyears.co.uk
Tel: 0844 800 84 34
Email: enquiries@firststepschildcare
agency.co.uk
*Provides nannies, maternity nurses and babysitters for families in Wiltshire and the surrounding areas.*

**Sunshine Nannies**
www.sunshinenannies.co.uk/
Tel: 0800 073 96 99
Email: mail@sunshinenannies.co.uk
*Based in Wiltshire, agency places nannies, mother's helps and maternity nurses across the south of England.*

**\* Toto's Au Pair Agency**
www.totosaupairagency.co.uk
Tel: 01666 841225
Email: info@totosaupairagency.co.uk
*Based in Wiltshire, agency places au pairs and mother's helps all over the UK.*

### East of England

**\* Au Pair Search Ltd**
www.aupairsearch.co.uk
Tel: 01787 463318
Email: info@aupairsearch.co.uk
*With its headquarters in Essex, agency provides au pairs to families across the UK.*

**Bluebell Nanny Agency**
www.bluebellnannyagency.co.uk
Tel: 01277 658135
Email: info@bluebellnannyagency.co.uk
*Essex-based agency places nannies, mother's helps and babysitters in south-east England.*

**\* Au Pairs by Pebbles**
www.aupairsbypebbles.com
Tel: 0870 066 47 43
Email: info@aupairsbypebbles.co.uk
*With its head office in Bedfordshire but offices in London and France, agency specialises in placing French au pairs across the UK.*

**Bumble Bee Childcare Recruitment**
www.bumblebeechildcare
recruitment.co.uk
Tel: 0845 638 0711
Email: info@bumblebeechildcare
recruitment.co.uk
*Nannies, mother's helps and maternity nurses in the south of England.*

## LISTINGS

### * Bilingual Nanny
www.bilingualnanny.co.uk/
**Tel:** 01582 517061
**Email:** info@bilingualnanny.co.uk
*International agency based in Bedfordshire, places multi-lingual nannies, au pairs and mother's helps across the UK.*

### Cambridge Connection Au Pair Agency
www.aupairagency.co.uk
**Tel:** 01954 206489
**Email:** caroline@cambridge connection.co.uk
*European au pairs in Cambridge and outer London.*

### Capable Nannies
www.capablenannies.co.uk
**Tel:** 01223 464808
**Email:** enquiries@capablenannies.co.uk
*Nannies, nanny/housekeepers, nursery nurses, maternity nurses, mother's helps, babysitters and other childcare staff across East Anglia.*

### Central Nannies
WWW.centralnannies.net
**Tel:** 01992 470196
**Email:** lynne.centralnannies@ntlworld.com
*Agency places nannies, maternity nurses and mother's helps in Hertfordshire and around the Essex borders.*

### * Busy Bee Au Pairs
www.busybeeaupairs.co.uk
**Tel:** 01245 401238
**Email:** through website
*Essex-based BAPAA-member agency that places au pairs (including summer au pairs) across the UK.*

### Cosy Toes Nanny Agency
www.cosytoesnannyagency.co.uk
**Tel:** 01621 892080
**Email:** admin@cosytoesnannyagency.co.uk
*Founder member of ANA, provides nannies and babysitters in Essex and the surrounding areas.*

### Cribs Nanny Agency
www.cribs-nannyagency.co.uk
**Tel:** 01245 360690
**Email:** cribsnannyagency@tiscali.co.uk
*Essex-based agency that provides nannies, maternity nurses and babysitters to families in Essex.*

### Early Birds Nanny Agency
WWW.earlybirdsnannyagency.co.uk
**Tel:** 01992 448 349
**Email:** earybirds@btconnect.com
*Based in Hertfordshire, agency offers nannies and mother's helps to families in Hertfordshire, Essex, North London and the A1 & A10 corridor.*

## AGENCIES

*** Cosmopolitan Au Pairs**
www.cosmopolitanaupairs.com
Tel: 01438 798727
Email: caro@cosmopolitanaupairs.com
*Based in Hertfordshire, agency places au pairs across most parts of the UK.*

**Hilary's Agency**
www.hilarysagency.co.uk
Tel: 020 8559 1110
Email: hilarysagency@tiscali.co.uk
*Provides au pairs, nannies, maternity nurses and mother's helps. Au pairs can be placed across England while nannies can only be placed in the local area.*

**Norma Lewis Au pair Agency**
www.normalewisaupairs.co.uk
Tel: 020 8950 8611
Email: norma_lewis1@hotmail.com
*Based in Hertfordshire, agency places au pairs, nannies, mother's helps and after-school childcare in parts of Hertfordshire, Middlesex and London.*

**Simply Angelic**
www.simplyangelic.co.uk
Tel: 020 7681 6490
Email: aupairs@simplyangelic.uk/
nannies@simplyangelic.co.uk
*Based in London with an office in Cambridge, agency places au pairs and mother's helps with families across the UK, and nannies predominantly in London and the surrounding areas.*

**\* Quick Au Pair and Nanny Agency**
www.quickaupair.co.uk
Tel: 01603 503434
Email: info@quickaupair.co.uk
*Based in Norwich, BAPAA-member agency provides au pairs, nannies and mother's helps throughout UK.*

**Sweet Dreams Nanny Agency**
www.sweetdreamsnannies.co.uk
Tel: 01923 221884
Email: info@sweetdreamsnannies.co.uk
*Agency provides nannies, mother's helps and babysitters in Hertfordshire, Buckinghamshire and Middlesex.*

**Safe & Sound Childcare Agency**
www.safeandsoundnannyagency.com
Tel: 01621 772703
Email: sandsnanny@btconnect.com
*Essex-based agency placing nannies, mother's helps and babysitters in Essex and east London.*

LISTINGS

## The Midlands and North England

### 100s Au Pairs
www.100s-aupairs.co.uk
contact through website
*An umbrella organisation that comprises of a number of agencies offering various services including placement of au pairs, nannies and mother's helps with families in certain areas of the UK. One branch is based in Sollihull and places nannies in the West Midlands.*

### * 1st Choice Au pairs
www.1stchoiceaupairs.co.uk
Tel: 0845 4300 230
Email: info@1stchoiceaupairs.co.uk
*Based in Northamptonshire, agency with links to Romania and Slovakia places au pairs across the UK.*

### * About Aupairs
www.aboutaupairs.com
Tel: 01904 789050/ 01904 625758
Email: anja@aboutaupairs.com/ katrin@aboutaupairs.com
*Small York-based agency that provides au pairs throughout UK.*

### * Au Pairs Direct
www.aupairsdirect.co.uk
Tel: 0161 941 5356
Email: enquiries@aupairsdirect.co.uk
*Based in Cheshire, BAPAA-member agency places au pairs across the UK.*

### * Absolutely Au Pairs
www.absolutelyaupairs.com
Tel: 0161 491 2758 (north) 020 8835 8594 (south)
Email: info@absolutelyaupairs.com
*With offices in London and the north of England, agency places au pairs in homes across the UK.*

### * Avon Au Pair Agency
www.avonaupairs.co.uk
Tel: 07800 552181
Email: contact@avonaupairs.co.uk
*Based in Warwickshire, agency places au pairs across mainland UK, although focuses on central England.*

### * Amber Au Pairs
www.amberaupairs.co.uk
Tel: 01746 783822
Email: through webpage
*Based in the Midlands, agency provides mainly Eastern European au pairs for families throughout the UK.*

### Brick Au Pair Agency
www.brickaupairs.co.uk
Tel: 0114 276 0564
Email: recruit@brickaupairs.co.uk
*Sheffield-based agency placing Hungarian au pairs in the north of England.*

## AGENCIES

**\* Applewood Au Pair Agency**
www.applewoodaupair.co.uk
**Tel:** 01889 808426
**Email:** info@applewoodaupair.co.uk
*Based in Staffordshire, agency places au pairs throughout the UK.*

**\* Bunbury Care Agency**
www.bunburyagency.com
**Tel:** 01829 773260
**Email:** info@bunburyagency.com
*Based in Cheshire, agency provides nannies, mother's helps and maternity nurses to families across most parts of the UK.*

**\* Bunters Au Pair Agency**
www.aupairsnannies.com
**Tel:** 01327 831144
**Email:** office@aupairsnannies.co.uk
*Based in Northamptonshire, BAPAA-member agency places au pairs throughout UK.*

**Ebor Nannies**
www.ebornannies.co.uk
**Tel:** 01904 767777 email through website
*York-based agency offering au pairs, nannies, mother's helps, maternity nurses and babysitters accross England and Wales.*

**Caroline Lee Nanny Agency**
www.caroline-lee.co.uk
**Tel:** 01904 629865
**Email:** caroline@caroline-lee.co.uk
*Based in York, agency provides nannies, maternity nurses and babysitters to families in York.*

**Family Connections**
www.familyconnections.co.uk
**Tel:** 0870 888 30 92
**Email:** kate@familyconnections.co.uk
*With the head office in Birmingham, agency places au pairs, nannies, mother's helps and babysitters with families in Warwickshire, Staffordshire, Worcestershire, Herefordshire, Gloucestershire and the West Midlands.*

**\* Chatsworth Nannies**
www.chatsworthnannies.co.uk
**Tel:** 0113 269 0010
**Email:** hilary@chatsworthnannies.co.uk
*Leeds-based agency that provides mother's helps and nannies to families mainly in the Yorkshire area, although the agency also makes placements in other parts of the UK.*

**\* First Class Nannies and Helpers**
www.firstclassnannies.co.uk
**Tel:** 01347 822207
**Email:** firstclassnanny@btconnect.com
*York-based agency that provides nannies, maternity nurses, mother's helps and babysitters to families throughout UK.*

# LISTINGS

**East Midlands Nannies & Au Pairs**
www.eastmidlandsnanniesand
aupairs.co.uk
Tel: 01636 830898
Email: info@eastmidlandsnannies
andaupairs.co.uk
*Based in the East Midlands, the agency provides au pairs, nannies, mother's helps and maternity nurses to families in most of the major towns and cities in the East Midlands.*

**Gems**
www.gemsservices.co.uk
Tel: 0191 286 7210
Email: gems@btconnect.com
*Based in Newcastle, agency provides nannies, mother's helps and babysitters to families in the north-east of England.*

**Holly's House**
www.hollyshouse.net
Tel: 01527 880746
Email: info@hollyshouse.net
*Based in Worcestershire, agency provides nannies, mother's helps, maternity nurses and babysitters to families in the Midlands.*

**\* Matchmaker Au Pairs**
www.matchmakeraupairs.co.uk
Tel: 01565 651703
Email: mmaupair@aol.com
*Based in Cheshire, BAPAA-member agency places au pairs across the UK.*

**\* Ideal Nannies**
www.idealnannies.com
contact through website
*With its head office in London and another office in Leeds, agency offers nannies, mother's helps and maternity nurses across most parts of the UK.*

**Midland Nannies**
www.midlandnannies.co.uk
Tel: 01676 535097
Email: claire.jervis@midlandnannies.co.uk

**Kids Matter**
www.kidsmatter.uk.com
Tel: 0845 331 3507
Email: info@kidsmatter.uk.com
*With its main branch based in Leicestershire, agency provides nannies, mother's helps and maternity nurses across England.*

**\* Mum's Army Ltd**
www.mumsarmy.u-net.com
Tel: 01527 402266
Email: marion@mumsarmy.u-net.com
*Based in Worcestershire, agency places au pairs across most parts of the UK.*

### Lauvic Babysitters & Nanny Service
www.lauvic.com
**Tel:** 0870 443 08 70
**Email:** info@lauvic.com
*Agency provides nannies, mother's helps, maternity nurses and babysitters around the areas where their offices are based; Worcester, Oxford, Cheltenham and Cardiff.*

### Nanny Plus
www.nannyplus.co.uk
**Tel:** 01925 768188
**Email:** support@nannyplus.co.uk
*Placing nannies, maternity nurses, mother's helps and babysitters in Cheshire, Lancashire, Merseyside, Wirral and Greater Manchester.*

### Nanny UK
www.nannyuk.com
**Tel:** 0151 2808247
**Email:** hello@nannyuk.com
*Based in Merseyside, agency places nannies in north-west England, including in Cheshire and Merseyside.*

### * Premier Au pair Agency
www.premieraupair.co.uk
**Tel:** 01299 828383
**Email:** aupairs@premieraupair.co.uk
*With its main office in Worcestershire, agency places European au pairs and nannies with families across the UK.*

### Network 0 to 5
www.network0to5.co.uk
**Tel:** 0161 928 0225
**Email:** alison0to5@hotmail.com
*Based in Sale, agency places nannies (including nanny shares), maternity nurses and mother's helps in north-west England.*

### * Richmond & Twickenham Au Pairs and Nannies
www.aupairsnationwide.co.uk
**Tel:** 01283 538921
**Email:** info@aupairsnationwide.co.uk
*This BAPAA-member agency places au pairs across the UK and nannies and mother's helps mainly in the local areas.*

### * Northern Au Pair Agency
www.northernaupairagency.co.uk
**Tel:** 0161 740 1828
**Email:** napag@btinternet.com
*Manchester-based agency that places au pairs across the UK.*

### * Sunshine Au Pair Agency
www.sunshineaupairs.co.uk
**Tel:** 0845 006 62 45
**Email:** info@sunshineaupairs.co.uk
*With offices in Derby and London, agency places au pairs all over the UK.*

## LISTINGS

**Nottinghamshire Nannies & Au Pairs**
www.nottsnannies.co.uk
Tel: 01636 830898
Email: info@nottsnannies.co.uk
*Agency provides au pairs, nannies, night nannies, mother's helps and maternity nurses in Nottinghamshire, Derbyshire, Leicestershire, Rutland, Lincolnshire, South Yorkshire, Northamptonshire and the surrounding counties.*

**\* The Childcare Company**
www.thechildcarecompany.co.uk
Tel: 01732 451997 (Kent and Surrey office) 01234 352688 (East & West Midlands office),
*With offices in Kent and the East Midlands, BAPAA-member agency provides au pairs, nannies, mother's helps, babysitters and maternity nurses to families in areas across the UK.*

**The Childcare Recruitment Company**
www.childcarerecruitment.co.uk
Tel: 0845 450 25 50
Email: enquiries@childcarerecruitment.co.uk

**\* The Janet White Agency**
www.janetwhite.com
Tel: 0113 266 6507
Email: info@janetwhite.com
*Based in Leeds, BAPAA-member agency places au pairs, nannies and maternity nurses all over the UK and overseas.*

## Wales

**\* Lloyds Agency**
www.lloydsagency.co.uk
Tel: 01633 841230
Email: gaynor@lloydsagency.co.uk
*Based in Newport, agency places nannies, mother's helps, au pairs and babysitters (as well as domestic help) across the UK.*

**\* Nags 'N' Nannies**
www.nagsandnannies.com
Tel: 01248 602814
Email: info@nagsandnannies.co.uk
*Based in Bangor, agency offers nannies and mother's helps to families across the UK.*

## Scotland

### A & H Childcare Consultancy Ltd
www.aandhchildcare.co.uk
**Tel:** 0141 248 6444
**Email:** info@aandhchildcare.co.uk
*Glasgow-based consultancy company that places nannies, mother's helps, maternity nurses and babysitters across Scotland.*

### Au Pair Ecosse
www.aupairecosse.com
**Tel:** 01786 474573
**Email:** aupairecosse@fsmail.net
*Based in Stirling, agency places French and Spanish au pairs with families in Scotland.*

### Butterfly Personnel
www.nanny-agency.net
**Tel:** 0131 659 5065
**Email:** enquiries@nanny-agency.net
*Based in Edinburgh, agency places nannies, maternity nurses and babysitters in Edinburgh.*

### Select Au Pairs
www.select-aupairs.com
**Tel:** 0141 884 8361
**Email:** selectaupairs@aol.com
*Based in Renfrewshire, agency places au pairs in Scotland and the north of England.*

### Care Solutions (Scotland)
www.caresolutionsscotland.com
**Tel:** 01592 646607
**Email:** enquiries@caresolutionsscotland.com
*Based in Fife, agency supplies families all over Scotland with au pairs from Eastern European countries.*

### Thank Evans
www.thank-evans.co.uk
**Tel:** 01467 632396
**Email:** enquiries@thank-evans.co.uk
*Based in Aberdeenshire, agency provides nannies to families in the local area.*

### Family Circle Care
www.familycircles.org
**Tel:** 0131 554 9500
**Email:** jbeaton@familycircles.org
*Based in Edinburgh, agency provides nannies, maternity nurses and babysitters in the Edinburgh area.*

### The West of Scotland Nanny Agency
www.thewestofscotlandnannyagency.com
**Tel:** 0800 634 86 81
**Email:** westscotnanny@aol.com
*Provides nannnies, mother's helps, maternity nurses and babysitters to families in the west of Scotland.*

### Panda's Nanny Agency
www.pandasnannyagency.co.uk
**Tel:** 0131 663 3967
**Email:** pandasnannies@ukonline.co.uk
*Nannies, mother's helps and babysitters to families in Edinburgh, Lothians, Fife and Perth.*

## Northern Ireland

### * Nannies from Ireland
www.nanniesfromireland.co.uk
**Tel:** 0289 269 2754
**Email:** andrea@nanniesfromireland.com
*Nannies, night nannies, babysitters and au pairs in Northern Ireland and most other parts of the UK.*

## Specialised Childcare Agencies

Whilst a number of the other agencies listed above offer some of these services, the following agencies offer a specialised service which is tailored towards one of these specific types of childcare:

### Maternity Nurses and Night Nannies

### Happy Babies Maternity
www.happybabiesmaternity.co.uk
**Tel:** 0560 1851728
**Email:** catrina.thomson@btinternet.com
*Maternity nurses and night nannies in Essex, some areas of London and the Home Counties.*

### * Maternally Yours
www.maternallyyours.co.uk
**Tel:** 020 7795 6299
**Email:** maternally@imperialstaff.co.uk
*Part of Imperial Recruitment, London-based agency provides maternity nurses and night nannies across most parts of the UK.*

## AGENCIES

**\* Maternal Response**
WWW.maternalresponse.co.uk
**Tel:** 0845 838 28 85
**Email:** info@maternalresponse.co.uk
*Surrey-based agency that provides maternity nurses to families in the UK.*

**\* Mayfair Maternity**
WWW.mayfairmaternity.com
**Tel:** 0870 442 32 62
**Email:** office@mayfairmaternity.com
*Based in London, agency provides families throughout the UK with maternity nurses.*

**Newborn Nannies**
www.newbornnannies.co.uk
**Tel:** 0161 785 8811 (Manchester, north-west and Dorset), 01689 898 484 (London and Kent).
**Email:** nb.nannies@ntlworld.com
*Agency places night nannies and maternity nurses (as well as nannies) in London, Kent, Dorset, Manchester and the north-west.*

**Sleeptight Nannies**
www.sleeptightnannies.co.uk
**Tel:** 020 8292 2618/ 01992 628643
*London-based agency that provides night nannies and maternity nurses, as well as babysitters in London and Hertfordshire.*

**Night Nannies**
www.night-nannies.com
**Tel:** see website for regional numbers
**Email:** enquiries@nightnannies.com
*With offices across England, agency provides night nannies in mainly the south of England with some coverage in the north-west.*

**\* The Maternity Nurse Company**
www.maternitynurse.co.uk
**Tel:** 0845 257 84 00
**Email:** ruth@maternitynurse.co.uk
*Based in London, agency provides maternity nurses across UK.*

**\* Sleeping Babies**
www.sleepingbabies.co.uk
**Tel:** 020 8420 7117
**Email:** through website
*Based in Harrow, agency places maternity nurses and night nannies across the UK.*

LISTINGS

## After-school and Holiday Nannies

### After-school Nannies
WWW.afterschoolnannies.com
Tel: 020 8871 2211
Email: info@afterschoolnannies.com
Based in Greater London, agency provides after-school/ part-time nannies to families in the Greater London area.

### * Holiday Nanny
WWW.holidaynanny.org
Tel: 01494 772400
Email: holiday.nanny@btconnect.com
Based in Buckinghamshire, agency offers families across the UK nannies to accompany them on holiday.

## Babysitters

### Allbairns Babysitters
www.allbairns.com
Tel: 01494 793889
Email: enquiries@albairns.com
Small agency with 150 babysitters registered. Provides service in south Buckinghamshire, the Chilterns, some parts of south-west Hertfordshire.

### * Miss Molly
www.missmolly.co.uk
Email: through website
A babysitting directory that offers parents membership enabling them access to the details of more than 1,200 babysitters across the UK.

### * Babysit Club
www.babysitclub.co.uk
Tel: 07971 293149
Website for parents and babysitters with free search tool (parents pay to contact babysitters). Operates across the UK.

### * Safehands Babysitters
www.safehandsbabysitters.com
Tel: 0870 844 66 88
Email: through website
Based in Lancashire, babysitting agency also offers nannies and out of school holiday provision to families across the UK.

### * Find A Babysitter.com
www.findababysitter.com
Website enables parents to view profiles and availability of babysitters (and nannies) in areas across the UK, although profiles are weighted in favour of those in the south of England.

### * Sitters
www.sitters.co.uk
Tel: 0800 38 900 38
Email: enquiries@sitters.co.uk
An evening childcare provider that comprises of a nationwide network of babysitters across mainland UK.

## AGENCIES

**\* Find A Sitter**
www.findasitter.co.uk
Email: info@findasitter.co.uk
*A 'matching' site set up by a parent that acts as a web-based directory of babysitters. Operates across the UK.*

**Sunset Babysitting Agency**
www.sunsetbabysittingagency.com
Tel: 01202 267768/07815 887425
Email: carly.painter@sunsetbaby sittingagency.com
*Provides babysitters to families in Dorset, Hampshire and Wiltshire. Also has an attached nanny agency covering the same area.*

## Nanny Shares

**\* Nannyshare.co.uk**
www.nannyshare.co.uk
Email: theteam@nannychare.co.uk
*A resource for nannies and parents alike. Website includes a job postings board where parents can advertise for their dream nanny.*

**\* The Nanny Sharers**
www.thenannysharers.co.uk
Tel: 020 8789 9556
Email: hello@thenannysharers.co.uk
*Central database for parents across the UK who are looking for a nanny share. Also includes links to agencies with discounted rates.*

## Special Needs Childcare

**Bright Eyes Nanny Agency**
www.brighteyesnannyagency.co.uk
Tel: 01483 506150
Email: brighteyesnannys@aol.com
*Agency covers Surrey and the surrounding areas, providing nannies and mother's helps as well as childcare for those with special needs.*

**\* SNAP Childcare**
www.snapchildcare.co.uk
Tel: 020 7729 2200
Email: info@snapchildcare.co.uk
*London-based special needs agency that provides nannies, mother's helps and carers across most parts of the UK.*

**Everyday Angels**
www.everydayangels.co.uk
Tel: 020 8785 5600
Email: info@everydayangels.co.uk
*London-based agency that provides special needs care in the form of nannies, after-school and weekend respite and care workers for families*

**Toybox Agency**
www.toyboxagency.co.uk
Tel: 0845 230 01 91
Email: HeadOffice@ToyboxAgency.co.uk
*Supplies nannies, babysitters and a small number of special needs carers.*

# Children's Information Service

The organisations commonly referred to as either the CIS or FIS in England, and the Early Year's Teams in Northern Ireland, are your port of call for information relating to local childcare in your area. A phone call to your local CIS or Early Years Team will allow you to obtain information relating to nurseries, childminders and after-school care that are in your local area, and may also provide you with other information on related childcare services.

## England

### London

| | |
|---|---|
| Bromley CIS | 0208 464 0276 |
| Croydon CIS | 0845 111 1100 |
| Harrow CIS | 0208 861 5609 |
| Newham CIS | 0800 074 1017 |
| Barking and Dagenham CIS | 0208 215 3004 |
| Barnet CIS | 0800 389 8312 |
| Bexley CIS | 0208 856 5398 |

## LISTINGS

| | |
|---|---|
| Brent CIS | 0208 937 3001 |
| Camden CIS | 0207 974 1679 |
| Corporation of London CIS | 0207 332 1002 |
| Ealing CIS | 0208 825 5588 |
| Enfield CIS | 0208 482 1066 |
| Greenwich CIS | 0208 921 6921 |
| Hackney CIS | 0208 820 7590 |
| Hammersmith & Fulham CIS | 0208 735 5868 |
| Haringey CIS | 0208 489 1546 |
| Havering CIS | 0800 678 1991 |
| Hillingdon CIS | 0800 073 4800 |
| Hounslow CIS | 0800 783 1696 |
| Islington CIS | 0207 527 5959 |
| Kensington & Chelsea CIS | 0207 361 3302 |
| Kingston CIS | 0208 547 6582 |
| Lambeth CIS | 0845 601 5317 |
| Lewisham CIS | 0800 085 0606 |
| Merton CIS | 0208 545 3800 |
| Redbridge CIS | 0800 587 7500 |
| Richmond CIS | 0208 831 6298 |
| Southwark CIS | 0800 013 0639 |
| Sutton CIS | 0208 770 6000 |
| Tower Hamlets CIS | 0207 364 6495 |
| Waltham Forest CIS | 0208 496 3566 |
| Wandsworth CIS | 0208 871 7899 |
| Westminster CIS | 0207 641 7929 |

## South-East England

| | |
|---|---|
| Berkshire CIS | 0800 328 9148 |
| Brighton & Hove CIS | 0127 329 3545 |
| Buckinghamshire CIS | 0800 328 3317 |
| East Sussex FIS | 0845 601 0777 |
| Hampshire CIS | 0845 602 1125 |
| Isle of Wight FIS (Family Information Zone) | 0198 382 1999 |
| Kent CIS | 0800 032 3230 |
| Medway CIS | 0163 433 5566 |

| | |
|---|---|
| Milton Keynes FIS | 0800 035 0335 |
| Oxfordshire CIS | 0845 226 2636 |
| Portsmouth CIS (CHAT) | 0239 269 5000 |
| Slough CIS | 0162 866 0098 |
| Southampton CIS | 0800 169 8833 |
| Surrey CIS | 0845 601 1777 |
| West Sussex CIS | 0124 377 7807 |
| Windsor and Maidenhead CIS | 0162 878 1430 |
| Wokingham Borough FIS | 0118 935 2255 |

## South-West England

| | |
|---|---|
| Bath & North-East Somerset FIS | 0800 073 1214 |
| Bournemouth CIS | 0120 245 6222 |
| Bristol CIS | 0845 129 7217 |
| Cornwall FIS | 0800 587 8191 |
| Devon (and Torbay) CIS | 0800 056 3666 |
| Dorset CIS | 0845 355 2099 |
| Gloucestershire CIS | 0800 542 0202 |
| Isles of Scilly CIS | 0172 042 3680 |
| North Somerset CIS | 0127 588 8778 |
| Plymouth FIS | 0800 783 4259 |
| Poole CIS | 0120 226 1999 |
| Somerset CIS | 0845 345 9122 |
| South Gloucestershire CIS | 0145 486 8008 |
| Swindon CIS | 0179 354 1786 |
| Wiltshire CIS | 0845 758 5072 |

## East of England

| | |
|---|---|
| Bedfordshire FIS (INFORM 0-19) | 0800 023 2057 |
| Cambridgeshire CIS | 0845 045 4014 |
| Essex CIS | 0124 544 0400 |
| Hertfordshire CIS | 0143 873 7502 |
| Luton CIS | 01582 54 8888 |
| Norfolk CIS | 0160 362 2292 |
| Peterborough CIS | 0800 298 9121 |

| | |
|---|---|
| Southend on Sea CIS | 0170 239 2468 |
| Thurrock CIS | 0137 565 2801 |

## The Midlands and North England

| | |
|---|---|
| Barnsley CIS | 0800 034 5340 |
| Birmingham CIS (Childcare Information Bureau) | 0121 303 3521 |
| Blackburn with Darwen CIS | 0125 466 7877 |
| Blackpool CIS | 0800 092 2332 |
| Bolton CIS | 0120 438 6030 |
| Bradford CIS | 01274 43 7503 |
| Bury CIS | 0800 731 4611 |
| Calderdale CIS | 0142 225 3053 |
| Cheshire CIS | 0800 085 2863 |
| City of Stoke-on-Trent CIS | 0800 015 1120 |
| Coventry CIS | 0247 683 4373 |
| Cumbria CIS | 0845 712 5737 |
| Darlington CIS | 0800 917 2121 |
| Derby City CIS | 0133 271 6381 |
| Derbyshire CIS | 01629 585 585 |
| Doncaster CIS | 0800 138 4568 |
| Dudley CIS | 0138 481 4398 |
| Durham County Council CIS | 0800 917 2917 |
| East Riding of Yorkshire FIS | 0148 239 6469 |
| Gateshead CIS | 0191 433 8515 |
| Halton CIS | 0192 870 4306 |
| Hartlepool CIS | 0142 928 4284 |
| Herefordshire CIS | 0143 226 1681 |
| Kingston-Upon-Hull CIS | 0148 231 8318 |
| Kirklees CIS | 0148 422 3041 |
| Knowsley CIS | 0800 085 2022 |
| Lancashire CIS | 0800 195 0137 |
| Leeds CIS | 0113 247 4386 |
| Leicester City CIS | 0116 225 4890 |
| Leicestershire CIS | 0116 265 6545 |
| Lincolnshire CIS | 0800 195 1635 |
| Liverpool CIS | 0800 085 2022 |

| | |
|---|---|
| Manchester CIS | 0800 083 7921 |
| Middlesborough CIS | 0164 235 4200 |
| Newcastle CIS | 0191 277 4133 |
| North East Lincolnshire FIS | 0800 183 0317 |
| North Lincolnshire CIS (Kidslincs) | 0172 429 6629 |
| North Tyneside CIS | 0191 200 1417 |
| North Yorkshire CIS | 0845 601 1630 |
| Northamptonshire CIS | 0160 423 7935 |
| Northumberland CIS | 0800 023 4440 |
| Nottingham City FIS | 0800 458 4114 |
| Nottinghamshire CIS | 0800 781 2168 |
| Oldham FIS | 0800 731 1518 |
| Redcar and Cleveland CIS | 0164 277 1173 |
| Rochdale FIS | 0170 671 9900 |
| Rotheram CIS | 0800 073 0230 |
| Rutland CIS | 0157 275 8495 |
| Salford CIS | 0800 195 5565 |
| Sandwell CIS | 0121 569 4914 |
| Sefton CIS | 0800 085 2022 |
| Sheffield CIS | 0114 275 6699 |
| Shropshire CIS | 01743 25 4400 |
| Solihull CIS | 0800 389 8667 |
| South Tyneside CIS | 0800 783 4645 |
| St Helens CIS | 0800 073 0526 |
| Staffordshire CIS | 0845 650 9876 |
| Stockport FIS | 0808 800 0606 |
| Stockton CIS | 0164 252 7225 |
| Sunderland CIS | 0191 520 5505 |
| Tameside | 0161 342 5434 |
| Telford and Wrekin CIS | 0195 238 5385 |
| Trafford | 0161 912 1053 |
| Wakefield District CIS | 0800 587 8042 |
| Walsall CIS | 0192 265 3383 |
| Warrington CIS | 0192 544 3131 |
| Warwickshire CIS | 0845 090 8044 |
| Wigan CIS | 0194 248 6960 |
| Wirral CIS | 0800 085 8743 |

| | |
|---|---|
| Wolverhampton CIS | 0800 294 9939 |
| Worcestershire FIS | 0190 579 0560 |
| York CIS | 0190 455 4628 |

## Wales

| | |
|---|---|
| Anglesey CIS | 0124 875 2699 |
| Blaenau GIS | 0800 032 3339 |
| Bridgend CIS | 0800 180 4320 |
| Caerphilly CIS | 0144 386 3232 |
| Cardiff CIS | 0292 052 0100 |
| Carmathenshire CIS | 0126 722 4224 |
| Ceredigion CIS | 0154 557 4187 |
| Conwy CIS | 0149 287 6260 |
| Denbighshire CIS | 0182 470 8220 |
| Flintshire CIS | 0124 454 7017 |
| Gwynedd CIS | 0128 667 5570 |
| Merthr Tydfil CIS | 0168 572 7400 |
| Monmouthshire CIS | 0163 364 4527 |
| Neath Port Talbot CIS | 0179 286 5914 |
| Newport CIS | 0800 328 8483 |
| Pembrokeshire CIS | 0143 776 3344 |
| Powys CIS | 0845 130 3637 |
| Rhondda Cynon Taf CIS | 0800 180 4151 |
| Swansea CIS | 0179 251 7222 |
| Torfaen CIS | 0800 019 6330 |
| Vale of Glamorgan CIS | 0144 670 4704 |
| Wrexham CIS | 0197 829 2094 |

## Scotland

| | |
|---|---|
| Aberdeen City CIS | 0122 444 3344 |
| Aberdeenshire CIS | 0800 298 3330 |
| Angus CIS | 0845 277 7778 |
| Argyll and Bute CIS | 0136 9708 504 |
| Ayrshire CIS | 0845 351 3000 |
| Clackmannanshire CIS | 0125 945 2440 |

| | |
|---|---|
| Dumfries and Galloway CIS | 0845 601 0191 |
| Dundee City CIS | 01382 433900 or 01382 433651 |
| East Dunbartonshire CIS | 0141 570 0091 |
| East Lothian CIS | 0800 028 8629 |
| East Renfrewshire CIS | 0141 577 3990 |
| Edinburgh City CIS | 0800 032 0323 |
| Falkirk CIS | 0132 450 6632 |
| Fife CIS | 0159 277 6406 |
| Glasgow City CIS | 0141 287 5223 |
| Highland CIS | 0845 601 1345 |
| Inverclyde CIS | 0800 052 9126 |
| Midlothian CIS | 0131 271 3754 |
| Moray CIS | 0134 354 5368 |
| North Lanarkshire CIS | 0123 681 2281 |
| Orkney Islands CIS | 0185 687 3535 |
| Perth and Kinross CIS | 0845 601 4477 |
| Renfrewshire CIS | 0141 840 3853 |
| Scottish Borders CIS | 0189 675 8186 |
| Shetland Islands CIS | 0159 569 7460 |
| South Lanarkshire CIS | 0169 872 7939 |
| Stirling CIS | 0178 644 2626 |
| West Dunbartonshire CIS | 0800 980 4683 |
| West Lothian CIS | 0150 677 6660 |
| Western Isles CIS | 0185 182 2282 |

## Northern Ireland

| | |
|---|---|
| Armagh & Dungannon Trust | 0283 752 2262 |
| Ballymena Homefirst Trust | 0282 564 1207 |
| Carrickfergus Homefirst Trust | 0289 331 5112 |
| Co. Fermanagh Sperrin Lakeland Trust | 0286 638 4000 |
| Co. Tyrone Sperrin Lakeland Trust | 0288 283 5020 |
| Coleraine Causeway Trust | 0287 035 8158 |
| Craigavon & Banbridge Trust | 0283 833 3747 |
| Downpatrick Down and Lisburn Trust | 0284 461 3311 |
| Foyle Trust | 0287 132 0950 |
| Lisburn Down and Lisburn Trust | 0289 250 1266 |

| | |
|---|---|
| Magherafelt Homefirsy Trust | 0287 930 1700 |
| Newry & Mourne Trust | 0283 082 5000 |
| North and West Belfast Trust | 0289 030 3907 |
| South and East Belfast Trust | 0289 056 4977 |
| Ulster Community and Hospitals Trust | 0289 127 0672 |

# Useful websites

There are also a number of online resources which offer parents advice and information – or even just a place to chat and share experiences. We have included a selection of the best information and do-it-yourself sites below.

In this section you will find details for relevant associations and organising bodies.

## Associations

**Association of Nanny Agencies**
www.anauk.org
**Email:** admin@anauk.org.
*Central organisation which aims to promote measurable standards of practise for nanny agencies. Website lists agencies registered with ANA.*

**British Au Pair Agencies Association**
www.bapaa.org.uk/
**Tel:** 07946 149 916
**Email:** info@bapaa.org.uk
*The union of au pair agencies within the UK, setting standards for the industry and informing families about quality agencies. Operates on a purely non-commercial basis.*

## LISTINGS

### National Association of Children's Information Services
www.nacis.org.uk
**Tel:** 020 7515 9000
**Email:** through website
*This association supports, links and promotes the Children's Information Service, which is the reference point for parents wanting information on what registered childcare there is in their area.*

### NCMA (National Childminding Association of England and Wales)
www.ncma.org.uk
**Tel:** 0845 880 0044
**Email:** info@ncma.org.uk
*A professional association and charity founded by childminders, parents and local authorities. Works with parents, childminders and nannies.*

### National Day Nurseries Association
www.ndna.org.uk
**Tel:** 0870 774 4244
*Association is a charity that aims to promote, support and enhance childcare for young children. Operates a useful FAQ resource for parents and has a 'Choosing Childcare' section with lists of NDNA member nurseries.*

### The Grandparents' Association
www.grandparents-association.org.uk
**Tel:** 0845 4349585
**Email:** info@grandparentsassociation.org.uk
*Organisation whose primary aim is to improve the lives of grandparents who have either lost or are losing contact with their grandchildren; are caring for their grandchildren on a full-time basis; or are interested in the educational and welfare needs of their grandchildren.*

## Government Websites

### Care Standards Inspectorate for Wales (CSIW)
www.csiw.wales.gov.uk
**Tel:** (Cardiff) 02920478600. See website for telephone numbers for regional offices.
*Parents in Wales wanting to obtain information on how the law relates to issues of childcare, or those wanting to make a complaint, should consult this site.*

### Children's Workforce Development Council
www.cwdcouncil.org.uk
**Tel:** 0113 244 6311
**Email:** info@cwdcouncil.org.uk
*The Council aims to improve the lives of children, young people, their families and carers by ensuring that all people working with them - including nannies and nursery staff - have the best possible training, qualifications, support and advice.*

## USEFUL WEBSITES

**ChildcareLink**
www.childcarelink.gov.uk
Email: childcarelink@opp-links.org.uk
*Allows parents to search care facilities by region. Includes listings for nurseries and childminders.*

**Department of Trade and Industry**
www.dti.gov.uk
Tel: 020 7215 5000
Email: enquiries@berr.gsi.gov.uk
*Government department that has an 'Employment Matters' section which provides information concerning employment and maternity/paternity rights.*

**Directgov**
www.directgov.uk
*Government resource with links to information on all public services including childcare services.*

**Scottish Commission for the Regulation of Care**
www.carecommission.com/
Tel: (Headquarters) 01382 207100.
See website for telephone contacts for regional offices
*Website of the regulating body for residents of Scotland. Parents wanting to obtain information on how the law relates to issues of childcare, or those wanting to make a complaint should consult this site.*

**Department for children, schools and families**
http://www.dfes.gov.uk
Tel: 0870 000 2288
Email: info@dcsf.gsi.gov.uk
*Set up by the Prime Minister in June 2007, this department aims to improve outcomes for children in areas including finance and health.*

**Sure Start**
www.surestart.gov.uk
Tel: 0870 000 2288
Email: info@dcsf.gsi.gov.uk
*Government childcare programme that aims to support parents and improve availability of childcare. Downloadable booklet includes information on childcare costs, advice on seeking childcare and information on legal entitlements. Also runs Childcare Approval Scheme.*

**Tax Credit Helpline**
www.hmrc.gov.uk
Tel: 0845 3003900
Email: see website for individual departments
*Provides information on tax issues relating to childcare, including details on eligibility for Child Benefit.*

335

LISTINGS

## Advice and Information-Sharing Websites

### Best Bear Childcare
www.bestbear.co.uk
**Tel:** 08707 201 277
**Email:** feedback@bestbear.co.uk
*Advertises itself as guide to childcare agencies across UK. Includes links to sites and opportunities for parents to post adverts.*

### Mother @ Work
www.motheratwork.co.uk
**Tel:** 01273 670 003
*Monthly webzine dedicated to working mothers. Includes listings of helpful organisations and an 'ask the experts' section.*

### My Baby Sense
www.mybabysense.co.uk
**Email:** antoinette@babysense.com
*Information and advice on all things baby-related, including helpful Q&A section.*

### UK Parents
www.ukparents.co.uk
**Tel:** 07932 065767
**Email:** through webpage
*A discussion forum for parents wanting to discuss anything and everything parenting related. Website also includes articles and features on everything from the car-seat law to new childcare products and has a section dedicated to up-to-date news for parents.*

### Nanny Nanny
www.nanny-nanny.co.uk
*Free advice for parents, nannies and nanny agencies. Includes links to regional nanny agencies across the UK.*

### Working Families
www.workingfamilies.org.uk
**Tel:** 0207 253 7243
**Email:** office@workingfamilies.org.uk
*UK's leading work-life balance organisation. Provides information and advice for working families.*

### Parentscentre
www.parentscentre.gov.uk
*No contact details available; web resource only*
*A forum where parents can discuss all things relating to parenting with other parents, as well as experts.*

USEFUL WEBSITES

## Charities

### Contact A Family
www.cafamily.org.uk
Tel: 0808 808 3555
Email: info@cafamily.org.uk
*UK-wide charity that provides support, advice and information for families with disabled children.*

### Daycare Trust
www.daycaretrust.org.uk
Tel: 020 7840 3350
Email: info@daycaretrust.org.uk
*National childcare charity that provides parents with information on childcare, including costs. Offers a consultancy service and information for parents in specific circumstances such as those with children with special needs and young or working parents.*

### Employers for Childcare
www.employersforchildcare.org
Tel: 028 9261 0661
Email: info@employersforchildcare.org
*Charity based in Northern Ireland that offers parents childcare advice. Includes an online childcare search facility.*

### One Parent Families/ Gingerbread
www.oneparentfamilies.org.uk
Tel: 0800 018 5026
Email: info@oneparentfamilies.org.uk
*Charity that offers information and advice for lone parents.*

### Home-Start
http://www.home-start.org.uk/
Tel: 0800 068 63 68
Email: support@home-start.org.uk
*A leading family support charity that offers free, confidential support for parents who may want advice or practical help.*

### Parentline Plus
www.parentlineplus.org.uk
Tel: 020 7284 5500
Email: through webpage
*National charity that works for and with, parents. Includes list of contact offices across England, information materials and forum.*

LISTINGS

**INA (International Nanny Association)**
www.nanny.org
**Tel:** (Toll Free) 001 888 8781477
**Email:** through website
*Based in the USA, INA is an international resource. The association acts as a non-profit, educational association for nannies and those who educate, place, employ, and support professional in-home child care. Membership open to all involved with in-home childcare, including families who employ such childcare.*

**The National Society for the Prevention of Cruelty to Children (NSPCC)**
www.nspcc.org.uk
**Tel:** 0808 8005000
**Email:** help@nspcc.org.uk
*Well-established UK charity that works to protect children from abuse.*

**National Childbirth Trust (NCT)**
www.nct.org.uk
**Tel:** 0870 4440709
**Email:** through website
*A leading UK charity that offers support through the experience of pregnancy, birth and early parenting. Website includes information and e-groups where parents can discuss issues, as well as a tool which enables parents to search for local NCT branches and antenatal classes.*

## Family directories

**All 4 Kids UK**
www.all4kidsuk.com
**Tel:** 01707 659383
**Email:** information@all4kidsuk.com
*Family directory service with easy to use category/location search keys.*

**Kids Guide**
www.kidsguide.co.uk
**Email:** contact@kidsguide.co.uk
*Serves families in north-west England. Site includes a noticeboard where families may advertise services or seek advice as well as lists of places of interest and extracurricular activities.*

USEFUL WEBSITES

## Fill a Post/Find a Job

### Greatcare.co.uk
www.greatcare.co.uk
**Tel:** 020 7978 7744
*Childcare jobs website which also has a good list of childcare recruitment agencies.*

### Simply Childcare
www.simplychildcare.com
**Tel:** 020 7701 6111
**Email:** info@simplychildcare.com
*Website alongside childcare listings magazine which matches families with childcare professionals.*

### Gumtree
www.gumtree.com
N/A
*Popular classified ads and community site where families and childcarers advertise. Nationwide service though particularly prominent in London.*

### The Nanny PA Company
www.nannypacompany.com
**Tel:** 0845 241 0477
**Email:** info@nannypacompany.co.uk
*Independent company which searches across agencies, sourcing suitable childcare candidates. Company acts in a PA capacity working for families on their behalf.*

### Nannyjob
www.nannyjob.co.uk
**Email:** info@nannyjob.co.uk
*Extensive resource for childcare that includes agency listings for au pairs and nannies.*

## Ofsted and Tax

www.ofsted.gov.uk
**Tel:** 08456 404040 (8am - 8pm, Monday to Friday)
**Email:** enquiries@ofsted.gov.uk

# Index

## A

Accidents, 160, 171, 278
Accommodation for live-in help, 53, 220
Advertising
 in print, 143–144
 online, 140–142
 by word of mouth, 129–131
After-school babysitters, 26–28, 198, 212–214
After-school clubs, 22–26, 144–147, 179–182 , 21–212
After-school nannies, 26–28, 212–214
Age, 106–110
Agencies, 132–138, 293–320
Au pairs, 49–56, 237–232, 270–271 , 281–283

## B

Babysitting agencies, 148–149, 322–323
Babysitting circles, 149
Bad experiences, 253
Bank holidays, 10, 275
Birth to Three Matters, 9
Boys and girls, differences between, 110–113

## C

CACHE qualifications, 165, 285–286, 288
Check-ups, 202
Child benefit, 266
Childcare combination, 74–75
Children's Centres, 12
Childcare hours, 289
Childcare ratios, 289
Childcare vouchers, 260–264
Childminders, 13–20, 152–161
Children's Information Service, 325–332
Child Tax Credit, 266–267
Communication, importance of, 159–160, 172
Complaints procedures, 207, 212
Confidentiality, 270
Contracts, 272
Crunch times of the day, 119

## D

Discipline, 159, 181

## E

Early Years Foundation, 278, 285–286
Effect of childcare on children, 75–76
Emergencies, 247

## F

Facilities, 180
Family activities, 80–81
Family Information Service, 280
First-aid training, 288
Foundation stage, 9, 285
Full Service Extended Schools, 24–25

## G

Government Guidelines for Au Pairs, 281–283
Grandparents, 57–62 , 233–238

## H

Health and Safety issues, 278–279

# INDEX

Hidden costs
  of au pairs, 53–54
  of nannies, 32–33
  of nanny shares, 39
Host family responsibilities, 227, 232
House rules, xix, 273–275
Housework, 50

## I

Insurance, 277
  liability, 276, 277
  household, 276
Interviews, 127, 157–158, 183–199

## J

Job combining, 36
Job descriptions, 189

## K

Key workers, 6, 167–168, 181

## L

Late collection, 171
Learning, 253
Legal requirements (childcarers), 161–162
Letters of Employment, 268

## M

Male nannies, 29–30
Mannies (see male nannies)
Maternity leave, 275
Maternity nurses, 63–68, 94–96, 149–150, 238–241, 320–321
Messy play, 82–83
Montessori, 6, 286

## N

Nannies, 29–36, 73–74, 214–222
Nanny shares, 37–41, 222–223
National Childminding Association, 15–16, 272, 334
National Insurance, 264
Night nurses, 68, 320–321
Notice period, 272, 276
Nurseries, 5–11, 144–147, 161–179, 205–208, 272–273
NVQs, 285

## O

Ofsted, 144, 151–152, 279–280, 339
Outgrowing care, 249–250

## P

Pension arrangements, 269
Personal habits of nannies, 220–222
Pets, 81–82
Principles, 190–191
Professional development, 289

## Q

Qualifications, 165–166, 184–185, 285–288

## R

Record keeping, 173
References, 161, 174, 196
Routines, 169

## S

Security, 172, 182, 278
Shared care (see also nanny shares}, 29–30
SMOGs (Smug Mothers of Girls), 112

Social Services, 208
Sole-charge care, 29–30, 203
Special needs children, 101–104, 323
Staff ratios, 11, 165
Statutory maternity pay, 275–276
Statutory sick pay, 269

## T
Tax, 264–268
Termination of agreement, 272
Tidiness, 220
Time off, 10, 17, 27, 33, 40, 45, 54, 66
Trust, 66, 202

## U

## V
Verbal agreements, 268
Visas, 28–281

## W
Welcome letters, 51, 271
Word-of-mouth recommendations, 129–131
Work permits, 280–281
Working full time, 87–89
Working part time, 89–90
Working tax credit, 261–262, 267–268

## X

## Y

## Z

www.crimsonpublishing.co.uk